PRESERVING POTTING & PICKLING

Food from the Storecupboards of Europe

ELISABETH LUARD

GRUB STREET • LONDON

Acknowledgements

I owe a great debt of gratitude to those who, on my travels throughout Europe, were generous enough to share the contents of their storecupboards. Thanks are also due to Priscilla White, who valiantly tested the recipes in my kitchen, to Venetia Parkes who performed the same service in her own, and to my family for tolerance and constructive criticism of the results (particularly as applied to cakes and biscuits). For the original edition of the book published in 1987 as *The Barricaded Larder*, companion volume to *European Peasant Cookery*, thanks are due to editor Kate Parkin at Transworld, the late Abner Stein and, for support and enthusiasm for this newly illustrated edition, to publisher Anne Dolamore and designer Lucy Thorne.

For my children, Caspar, Francesca, Poppy, and Honey, without whom there would have been no book.

Published in 2020 by
Grub Street
4 Rainham Close
London
SW11 6SS

Email: food@grubstreet.co.uk
Web: www.grubstreet.co.uk
Twitter: @grub_street
Facebook: Grub Street Publishing

Text and illustrations © Elisabeth Luard 2020
Design by Lucy Thorne © Grub Street 2020
Copyright this edition © Grub Street 2020
First published by Bantam Press in 1988

A CIP catalogue record for this book is available from the British Library.

ISBN 978-1-911621-38-6

Printed and bound by Hussar Books, Poland

Contents

Introduction

'A well-stocked larder was my mother's most precious possession,' a Hungarian friend explained to me when I was organizing a research trip to Eastern Europe for this book and its predecessor, *European Peasant Cookery*. 'She never locked her street doors, front or back. There was no need for such precautions in a small isolated community where everyone knew everyone else's business. Her money was kept under her mattress in a little kid-skin purse embroidered with bright flowers. The blankets and shawls were kept in a painted wooden chest which stood on one side of the fireplace. We children perched on it to huddle close to the warmth and the cooking-pot in winter. The chest had a little box fitted inside one corner where my mother kept her precious spices – I remember pepper and cloves and cinnamon.

'The only door which had a padlock was the door to the larder. In normal times, that was not locked either. It was only in times of war, when the soldiers came – any soldiers, Magyars, Czechs, Turks, Russians, Germans, our own even – then the door was barred with a great iron bolt and the padlock was fixed. Then that larder was barricaded and defended to the death. That is exactly what it meant to my family, that barricaded larder, it held the difference between life and death.'

Europe's peasantry has long been dependent for a healthy diet on a well-stocked store-cupboard. In these luxurious days of supermarkets and freezers it is easy to forget that until recently the prime duty of the careful housewife was to spend half the year laying in stores for the remaining half.

My Scottish grandmother lifted her potatoes in the autumn and carefully stored them in barrels against the light which would cause them to green and sprout. Carrots and turnips were buried in sand-filled boxes, and retrieving them was, to the child I was then, as exciting as a lucky-dip at the local fair. Every autumn she filled the slatted shelves in her loft with perfect rosy apples from her own orchard. It was my job, when I visited her during the school holidays, to climb into the dark warm rafters and check each apple one by one for the soft brown bruises which could turn all the apples bad. Towards the end of the winter, the quiet air was filled with their wine-scented breath.

Bunches of pink and blue delphiniums, orange-globed Chinese lanterns and whiskered brown teazle-brushes hung head-down from the rafters. Best of all, a pair of barn owls took up residence each spring under the owl-hole by the chimney breast. Their pellets could be soaked and bleached to yield a treasure trove of tiny vole's ribs, minute leg bones and perfect fragile mouse skulls. I could spend hours up in the roof, munching apples and sorting through the trunk of old clothes – ostrich and osprey-feather head-dresses, long soft crêpe de chine tea gowns, their colours glowing dark and rich as my eyes accustomed themselves to the dusk – until I could resist no longer the scent of baking gingerbread or fruit cake which drifted up through the open trapdoor.

Today Western Europe still preserves, pots, pickles and bakes for its larder, but now it is from choice rather than necessity. The WI markets confirm that Britain's housewives still like to put up their own jams, marmalades and chutneys; the French rural farmer's wife will often salt her own hams and sausages rather than buying them in the charcuterie; untreated olives are still on sale in the markets of Spain for the local ladies to brine their own. The housewives of rural Eastern Europe still have more urgent reasons for the provisioning of their larders: they have to stock up against the shortages that the quota and collective systems impose.

A peasant family would share one cooked meal a day. In summer and at harvest time this might well come fresh from the kitchen garden and barnyard. In winter it was a different story: store grains – wheat, barley, oats and rye – and dried vegetables such as beans, peas and lentils would supply the bulk needed in the cold. Larder stores provided fats and preserved meat and fish, and would make the difference between good and indifferent fare – a bit of home-cured bacon or sausage for flavour, dried mushrooms to enrich the soup broth, herbs and a head of garlic to perfume the stew. This main meal was usually served around sundown when the workers came home from the fields – whether it be a 'meat-tea' in Britain, bean or pasta-based meal in Italy, France's wonderful soup-stews such as the *pot-au-feu* and the *garbure*, or the German soup-and-dumpling supper. The rest of the day's meals would be more or less self-catering, with each member of the household selecting his or her own preferred snack as they felt hungry. As long as the larder to be raided contained good homemade stores, with nuts and seeds and dried fruit to nibble, our diet remained healthy.

This grazing habit is quite proper to those whose ancestors were gatherers as well as hunters. It is our attempt to satisfy this natural appetite from our modern larderful of sugary biscuits, chocolate-coated snacks and packets of artificially flavoured novelty foods which causes nutritional problems. Travelling through northern Norway last year to the spring cod fishing on the Lofoten Islands I shared a table on the ferry with a tall young blond-moustached Norwegian sailor. On his way to visit his girlfriend in Svolvaer, the islands' little capital, he was chomping between strong white teeth a piece of the dried cod which is the Lofotens' speciality. He could, he said, recommend the snack very highly. It had, after all, fuelled the Vikings, his ancestors, who had certainly got the better of my ancestors. He had his supplies from his girlfriend's uncle, whose little boat was part of the inshore fleet. The fish, *klipfisk*, is prepared every year after the spring cod migration – in a single day a single fisherman can catch, gut and hang his seaharvest on the forest of poles which surrounds all the Lofotens' harbours.

Charlotte Gower Chapman was one of a handful of young American sociologists funded by the US government in the 1920s to acquire background knowledge on the

European communities from whom the New World's immigrants were drawn. In 1928 Miss Chapman spent a year in Sicily, whose immigrants to her home territory had been giving more than the usual trouble to the government of the time. Eating habits were one of her fields of study:

> Pasta is served at only one meal a day, usually in the evening when the man of the house is back from the fields. During the day each member of the family satisfies his hunger when it makes itself felt, by taking a piece of bread and fruit, nuts, some cheese, salted sardines, or possibly an egg, with or without a swallow of wine. The untranslatable word *campanaggio* refers to any of these things which are eaten with the bread. The man in the fields may cut himself a raw artichoke or a bunch of grapes for his *campanaggio*, or his employer may provide something in the way of cheese, onions, or boiled greens.[1]

Outdoor workers throughout Europe would take pocket-food for the midday meal, and this still varies from region to region, or even household to household, as much as the cooked meal. The modern businessman with his lunchtime sandwiches is following an ancient custom which owes little to the eponymous Earl. The storecupboard provides the heart of the meal: cheese is the great peasant staple protein-source, as are dried or preserved meats and fish. With a slice of onion or a pickle or a clove of garlic for flavour and vitamins, a piece of fruit and, in good times, something from the cake or biscuit tin, the countryman had all he required to break his midday fast. Homemade beer, wine, milk – fresh, buttermilk or soured – quenched his thirst and provided a valuable additional food-source. If the ingredients are honest and homemade by the careful housewife, it is a healthy diet which never palls.

The common denominator is some form of bread, that most portable and durable foodstuff. There is no substitute for bread, as I found when travelling in Eastern Europe in the autumn of 1985 to research this book and its predecessor, *European Peasant Cookery*. Bread in both Bulgaria and Romania was rationed. The markets had sheep's cheese and smoked sausage, pickled vegetables and ripe tomatoes, beautiful honey both liquid and in the comb, but bread was only available with coupons, not supplied to non-residents. After a few days of frustration and short commons, I took to sneaking the rationed breakfast rolls from the tourist-hotel dining-room. After that we picnicked well enough, with a supply of new storecupboard treats every day.

On a three-month trek with my husband Nicholas across the Kalahari desert in central Africa, my midday meal was always the same: bread (baked in an earth-oven once a week – good solid provender), a slice of raw onion and a piece of cheese, sometimes replaced with a bit of dried meat, with an orange to suck later in the shade of a thorn tree. I do

---

1. Charlotte Gower Chapman *Milocca: A Sicilian Village* Allen and Unwin, London, 1973.

remember being very particular about the onions we took – the large sweet purple ones are best for eating raw. The French field-worker would appreciate my Kalahari diet – although he might add a trickle of olive oil and rub of garlic to spice his bread. A sweet-sour pickle and a piece of cheese suited the English ploughman; a sausage and a trickle of mild mustard on his bread still satisfies the German labourer; slow-cooked caramelized whey cheese and salt-dried lamb, with a handful of wild berries from the hill, cheers the Scandinavian harvester gathering his hay.

Children, a valuable commodity in a labour-intensive farming community where healthy offspring were the chief treasure, were encouraged to raid the storecupboard and appleloft, abundance permitting, and eat when they were hungry. When I lived in a rural peasant community in southern Spain, my children were always greeted with food whenever they went visiting. This might have been a cup of coffee laced with spoonfuls of condensed milk (considered much more of a treat than milk fresh from the cow), a handful of roasted sunflower or pumpkin seeds, an orange or a little bunch of sweet grapes from the arbour which shaded the patio. Around the Christmas season there would be dried figs and walnuts, a square of homemade quince paste, or the delicious almond-and-honey nougat which is a legacy of the Moors. Maria, who acted *in loco parentis* to my family, kept a stock of little round shortbreads so crumbly they had to be stored wrapped up in twists of tissue paper, to be saved for visiting children from one feastday to the next. The same attitude was evident when we all moved to France, and the neighbouring farmer's wife would often lean out of the half-door of her kitchen with a piece of *pain d'epice* or an almond and sugar macaroon for the children trudging home from school in the winter snow of the Languedoc.

All of Europe has its treasure trove of these little treats. Today their manufacture has often been taken over by the local bakery. France has many regional recipes for sweetmeats such as the various nougats and marzipans of Provence. Denmark has a taste for short crumbly biscuits. The Scots, with their tablet (this becomes fudge south of the Border), treacle toffee and acid drops, have the sweetest tooth of all.

Throughout Europe, homemade syrups and cordials come out on special occasions for adults, and for children more or less on request. Sometimes these preparations were allowed to ferment into alcohol – the human race has always appreciated intoxicating liquor, a taste not confined to us alone. Baboons and elephants will travel great distances to gorge themselves on fermenting baobab fruit. Even the insect kingdom is not averse to a little tipple: a Northamptonshire apple orchard of which I once had care always attracted a cloud of red admiral butterflies round the cider-scented windfalls each autumn. Within a few minutes, the insects were as dizzy as champagne-sipping debutantes.

Regional larders vary. In England, bottled sauces and jams are seen as a part of the diet and used to enliven plain food. Sweet jams are kept in the cupboards of Eastern Europe for greeting. Germany, northern France, Austria, Switzerland and the Balkans have a taste for salted soured cabbage and vinegar pickles. Greece and Italy have a range of lightly pickled storecupboard treats, often put up in oil and herbs.

North and south often have different ideas of what makes a healthy snack. Frederik Poulsen, a Dane travelling through Eastern Europe just before the Great War, had a hard time provisioning himself. In his book, *Travels and Sketches,* published in 1923, Poulsen describes the local gastronomic preferences in a small village in north-eastern Greece.

> As early as 7 am the lady of the house brought me with a curtsy a plate of sweetmeats, of which etiquette forbade me to take more than a spoonful… Breakfast at 12 o'clock was mutton or goats-flesh, on fast days two stuffed tomatoes and rice, followed by cheese and pears. Two hours afterwards I was well-nigh wild with hunger; and then began calls in the company of the school-master: we visited the house of every single well-to-do citizen of Portoria, but the entertainment was everywhere the same, a spoonful of sweetmeats. For the most part the men were on commercial journeys in Egypt and Turkey; the few who were left we met in the café at 4 pm. Here one could get coffee and sweet 'loukoumi', but one day when I asked for bread and cheese I embarrassed both hosts and guests: it was an unheard-of requirement. While my stomach cried out, and my brain drew pictures of salmon or prawns with buttered rolls, I had to debate the high politics of the East, discuss the murder of the King of Serbia or describe Denmark.

Food was also used as a first aid, sometimes for hangovers, some times for colds and winter's ills. Apart from strengthening soups and broths, remedies range from egg-and-alcohol pick-me-ups to Hungarian paprika tea. The French remain keen herbalists, and natural preparations and infusions such as lime-blossom and camomile are still the first resort of those who have care of a family.

The philosopher Jean Jacques Rousseau (who gave the French Revolution its slogan, 'Liberté, Egalité, Fraternité') shared his countrymen's enthusiasms for dietary solutions to human problems. Rousseau believed, perhaps optimistically, that members of his own species were naturally simple, peaceful ruminants, and it was only civilization which corrupted them and turned them into aggressive meat-eaters. In his novel *Emile* he explored the problems of nurturing and bringing up children:

> To tempt a child's appetite you need not stimulate it, you need only satisfy it; and the commonest things will do this if you do not attempt to refine children's taste. Their perpetual hunger, the result of their need for growth, will be the best sauce. Fruit, milk and a piece of cake just a little better than ordinary bread, and above all the art of dispensing these things prudently, by these means you may lead a host of children to the world's end, without on the one hand giving them a taste for strong flavours, nor on the other hand letting them get tired of their food.
>
> In conclusion, whatever food you give your children, provided you accustom

them to nothing but plain and simple dishes, let them eat and run and play as much as they want; you may be sure they will never eat too much and will never have indigestion; but if you keep them hungry half their time, when they do contrive to evade your vigilance, they will take advantage of it as far as they can; they will eat till they are sick, they will gorge themselves until they can eat no more...I return to my usual illustration: among peasants the cupboard and the apple-loft are always left open, and indigestion is unknown alike to children and grown-up people.

On my travels I learned there was a great deal more than recipes involved in the preparation of food; and that the heart of the matter lay not so much in the ingredients, utensils and methods which differed from nation to nation, as in a far more important *shared* culinary vocabulary which united rather than divided a small-farming household, say, in Norway, with a peasant family on an Andalusian hillside.

One man's caviar is another man's potato. Peasant cooking is limited by that which can be grown, herded, gathered or hunted locally, plus those imported goods – salt and a few spices, followed later by sugar, tea and coffee – which could easily be purchased or exchanged on market day. Culinary habits which included pepper and spices needed to have ready access through exchange and barter – the Scandinavian dried cod trade supplied northerners not only with necessities such as salt for the fisherman and wool for his wife, but also satisfied more surprising tastes: nutmeg, cinnamon and cloves for biscuits and to spice stews and sausages. In exchange the peasantry of the Mediterranean has a wide repertoire of salt-cod dishes, where there is no cod to be fished in their own home seas.

Bourgeois cookery – the cookery of those who live in towns – has other limitations. Price and perishability were important factors when food had to be transported slowly overland before refrigeration eased the problem. The rich would eat dishes prepared with the prime cuts of beef or the choicest of fish – taking their pick according to their pocket. The poor would make dishes with the tripe and the cheaper cuts, the less dainty supplies. *Tripe à la mode de Caen* and kiwifruit cheesecake is inevitably bourgeois cookery. Where anything and everything is available at a price, ingredients are sometimes new and strange and not much understood. Recipes have to be invented to accommodate them – so bourgeois cookery is in a constant state of change.

The third tradition of the European kitchen, *haute cuisine* – offspring of the medieval banquet and grandchild of the extravagant cooks of Rome – is essentially a palace-kitchen/restaurant tradition. Its requirements are different from those of home cooking, whether peasant or bourgeois. Having spent a full working day in the kitchens of a *maître-chef* who owes his allegiance directly to Escoffier, the father of *haute cuisine*, I can confirm this with fervour. A reduction of half a bullock, bones and all, does not normally go into the preparation of my family's beef broth, nor essence of truffle and asparagus mousse to sauce my poached egg.

A peasant diet is naturally self-limiting – which also means it has to be self-balancing. The peasant housewife needs to keep her family in good health, or they will not be able to work and the group will suffer.

Ten years spent with my growing family of four children in the deep rural isolation of Andalusia in southern Spain and the remote country side of France's Languedoc taught me a great many things which an English catering college had not even touched on. Beans did not come ready prepared in a tin, but were sown and harvested, podded and dried and stored for winter. Chickens might be bought from the baker's wife, but would be handed over still fully feathered and usually live and squawking too. Since I had a fairly large household, it was suggested by my neighbours that I was honour-bound to keep a pig so that the vegetable peelings and food which might otherwise be thrown away would go to a good home. The neighbours, in any event, always helped out at everyone else's pig-killing, so I, woefully ignorant and untutored in such basic skills, would have no shortage of helpers to show me what to do with the end product. Indeed I had helpers, and I certainly learned more in that single day than the Eastbourne School of Domestic Economy managed to din into me in a year.

That day also I learned that the preparation of food by simple people, people who live close to the earth and are dependent on it for their survival, is in itself a celebration of success. Pride is taken in the plumpness of the pig, the snowy whiteness of the scrubbed tripe for making the evening pig-killing meal to which all the valley were welcome, the fragrance of the home-grown herbs used in seasoning the meat to make sausages for *chorizo*, the purity of the salt for which I had to make a special trip to the nearby salt-flats at Cadiz.

In Spain and France I had the great benefit of having my young children in local schools (a Mediterranean nation will open all doors to children – I can thoroughly recommend them as a research aid). But when, later, I was travelling without them, I found that my most useful asset was my sketchbook and paintbox. An artist can sketch anywhere without upsetting the models – stallholders, children, housewives will all come up and start chatting – for it is a friendly medium, unlike photography. The camera can sometimes seem as threatening, particularly in Eastern Europe, as a gun. Artists are like troubadours – they're good entertainment. Drawing has the added advantage that it is a splendid aid to communication. A quick sketch of ingredients for a recipe will bring delighted confirmation or correction, even in rural Bulgaria where all communication is conducted in an impenetrable Slav dialect.

Maria my neighbour in the Andalusian valley stocked up her storecupboard every autumn with home-grown beans and chickpeas, dried red peppers, garlic, onions and a good selection of dried pork sausages, bacon and hams and spiced lard – which was spread on bread instead of butter. This storecupboard, supplemented by vegetables from her garden and fresh greens from the wild – most European country people still crop the wild for mushrooms, berries, leaves and herbs – gave her the basis for a variety of what my children called beans-and-bones dishes. These are one-pot stews, cooked over a top heat which is all most country people had, which are my family's favourite of all peasant dishes. Variations on the theme are found all round the Mediterranean – cassoulet in France, Italy's minestrone, the Balkan bean stews all belong to the same family. Seasonal fruit – oranges, grapes, melons – cheese from the valley's herd of goats, rough red wine, olives and olive oil, eggs and the odd young cockerel or old boiling fowl completed her family's menu. Almonds, sunflower seeds, pine kernels and honey were the treats. The diet included practically no dairy products, no butter and very little sugar. My family thrived on it.

It is this balance in the diet, this understanding of the composition of a healthy meal worked out in trial and error over the centuries, which is more important than the nutritionist's facts and figures. And the climate does not have to be Mediterranean for the system to work.

In northern Norway, 200 miles inside the Arctic Circle near Mo i Rana, I visited Elisabeth Andreasson, a young mother of three, married to a farmer with a smallholding. Although as a teacher in a local school, with her husband working part-time for the state as an engineer, the Andreassons had a cash income certainly ten times greater than that of Maria's family, the Norwegian family still stocked their storecupboard largely from the fruits of their own labours.

The storehouses are an essential part of the farm's equipment. All the barns are built with ventilation slats between the planks to protect against rain and snow. The drying, preserving wind is allowed free access. Hams, sausages and fish are all wind-dried and will keep from one year to the next. Inside on a summer day a big barn is like the interior of a cathedral. The light pours through the gaps and makes stained-glass-window patterns in the darkness. The cattle barn also had a part to play in the making of aquavit, Scandinavia's favourite tipple. In the old days, when sugar and yeast were expensive and hard to come by, aquavit was distilled from potato liquor. The potatoes broke down more quickly after they had been frozen in the ground, and fermentation was speeded up by burying the urn under the cowshed so that the warmth of manuring cows could keep the temperature warm and even. Such a hiding place did not encourage excisemen's inspection either, should any official interest be taken in the products of the farm.

For a long time after I finished my research in continental Europe, I reluctantly accepted the traditional wisdom that the peasantry of Britain had been squeezed out by the land enclosures, which began with the Restoration in 1660 and continued with the Highland clearances. Recently, however, I have visited some of the remoter corners of my own country to look for some of our traditional baking recipes. I have now begun to revise my opinion about whether we still have a home-grown peasantry.

Certainly the crofters and small farmers still left on the Celtic fringe of our islands – in Scotland, Wales and Ireland – earn their living outside their garden plots and spend their wages on manufactured goods, including food such as butter and cheese which in the old days would have been produced in-house. But the potatoes (everyone has a tattie patch – sometimes high on the hill and grown in earthed-up lazy-beds), the mutton, occasionally even the pig, the raspberries and fruit for jam, the vegetables, the milk, the eggs, the chickens, are still all home-grown or exchanged for similar goods with the neighbours. Peat is still cut and firewood gathered from the shore. There is much in the storecupboard which has never been near a shop – very little bread is bought in, oatcakes and scones take its place on the family dinner table.

The Scots take pride in their baking – the Welsh and the Irish too. The making of wheat- and grain-based dishes has always been a skill valued above all others in peasant households. Grain was the most reliable storecupboard item of all. It was not the sauce or the stew which showed the cook's real strength – what was admired most was skill in the kneading of bread, the mixing of a featherlight dumpling, the smooth rolling of noodles and pasta. The secret of the moist crumb in a perfect scone, the cool fingers for the making of light crisp pastry – those were the treasures proudly passed on from one generation to the next.

My neighbour Betsy on the island of Mull, my husband's family home-hillside, learned much of her cooking from her grandmother, who used to bake on an open range. Betsy still uses the girdle her grandmother left her to make her own girdle scones – a skill at which she has no rival on the island. The egg included in the girdle scone mix gives a smooth golden brown crust under a dusty veil of pale flour. In the old days all the baking was done without chemical raising agents – although now a little baking powder goes into the mix. The key to such cooking lies in a light hand and good ingredients – above all the beautiful eggs, from the household's own chickens, which go into the baking. Baking has a natural rhythm which many a rural housewife uses therapeutically, rather as busy office workers go to yoga classes.

Apart from the basic need for fuel-food, good cookery is a major item in our limited vocabulary for expressing affection – be the recipient lover or spouse, child, parent or friend. We have available to us, after all, three basic methods of communication: speech, touch and the sharing of food.

Of the three, cooking is the easiest of expression, the most naturally offered. This feeling of *giving* to those you love came over so strongly during my travels round Europe – whether it be a fisherman's wife in the Hebrides, the priest's housekeeper in the little village in Haute Provence, a farming family in Italy, a goatherd's wife in Andalusia – that I can only conclude it must be an underlying motivating force in us all. It is no accident that our secular celebrations, whether national holiday or a private birthday, are so often marked with a feast. Or that our religious ceremonies also employ the powerful imagery of bread and wine.

A well-stocked larder – consisting of ingredients which have undergone preserving, potting, and pickling – makes available a vocabulary of love, available at our fingertips every day, so valuable it is no surprise that it was the one room in the house which needed to be barricaded.

1. Storecupboard Snacks

Stock an accessible shelf with a few jars of homemade snacks which need no more effort than that required to open a bag of crisps.

The modern pattern of one main meal a day, supplemented by snacks, is not new. Primitive man cracked seeds and nuts to fortify him on his hunting forays. Until modern farming methods and petrol fumes made such activities difficult, country children on the way to school could scour the hedgerows for little delicacies: wild strawberries and raspberries, beechnuts and filberts, the various flowers, stalks and tiny leaves which could be sucked for their nectar or nibbled for their tender sharpness.

These days a vast industry prepares and markets their own versions of these snacks. Such commercially prepared products are often spiked with more additives, sugar and salt than is good for their buyers. Take advantage of a rainy day to stock up the storecupboard with some home-prepared goodies.

Roasted Peanuts

Peanuts or groundnuts belong to the same family, the *Leguminosae*, as peas and beans. A native of Peru, the leafy little shrub bears yellow flowers which, once pollinated, elongate their stems to plunge the young seedpod into the ground. Once mature, the woody capsules have to be harvested like potatoes – along with potatoes, they were a valuable Inca crop.

QUANTITY
1 lb/500g nuts

TIME
Preparation: 10 minutes
Cooking: 30-40 minutes

1 lb/500g raw peanuts
   salt

UTENSILS
A baking tray

Shell the peanuts. Put them to roast gently in a low oven, 250°F/130°C/ Gas 1, for 30-40 minutes, until they are toasted golden. Rub them to free the papery skins, and blow the fragments aside.

Lightly salt the nuts and let them cool. Stored in an airtight jar or tin, they keep for months.

PEANUT BUTTER_____Make a private supply: simply put the peanuts in the food processor and liquidize them (not too fiercely) until they are as smooth as you like your peanut butter. If you have no suitable machinery, crush them in a mortar. That's all: easy and delicious and very nutritious, particularly in the American classic, peanut-butter-and-jelly (clear jam) sandwich.

AMERICAN PEANUT BUTTER COOKIES_____For 4 dozen cookies, you will need 4 oz/100g butter, 4 level tablespoons sugar, 1 egg, 5 heaped tablespoons self-raising flour, ¼ teaspoon salt, 4 oz/100g rough-textured peanut butter. Cream the sugar and butter. Beat in the egg. Fold in the flour and salt. Stir in the peanut butter. Drop teaspoons of the mixture onto a baking sheet (no need to butter it). Bake at 375°F/190°C/ Gas 5 for 10-15 minutes, until the cookies are golden and well-risen.

INDONESIAN PEANUT SAUCE_____For kebabs (*satay*). Peel and chop 1 small onion and 1 clove garlic, and put them to fry until golden and soft in a tablespoon of oil. Stir in ½ teaspoon chilli powder, 1 tablespoon lemon juice or vinegar, 1 teaspoon brown sugar, ½ pint/300ml water and 4 tablespoons peanut butter. Allow to bubble up. Serve with grilled meat.

Devilled Almonds

Almonds have stocked the Mediterranean larder since pre-historic times. The almond tree's beautiful white blossom is the first delight of spring.

Probably native to Asia Minor, almonds receive favourable mention in Genesis, feature in the inventories of the Palace of Knossos in Crete, were nibbled at the banquets of Babylon and appreciated by the court of Charlemagne. The Moors, declaring the fragrant snow-watered gardens of conquered Granada to be the anteroom to Paradise, planted almonds from the Jordan valley in its shaded alleys. The sweet-loving Easterners taught the native Spaniards how to make *halvas* and marchpanes with the imported almonds (see pages 282-283).

The English, as becomes a non-conformist nation, like their almonds devilled.

QUANTITY
1 lb/500g nuts

TIME
Preparation: 15 minutes
Cooking: 30-40 minutes

1 lb/500g almonds
1 teaspoon paprika
1 tablespoon nut *or*
  vegetable oil
1 teaspoon chilli
1 teaspoon ground
  coriander
1 teaspoon salt
1 teaspoon ground cumin
  or celery seeds

UTENSILS
A baking tray

Blanch the almonds by pouring boiling water over them in a bowl. As the skins loosen, slip out the sweet white kernels. Dry them in a clean cloth.

Warm the oil in a baking tray and put in the blanched almonds. Roast the nuts gently at 250°F/130°C/Gas 1 for 30-40 minutes until they are well toasted and squeaky when you bite into them. Stir in the ground coriander and let its aroma develop for a moment before adding the cumin (or celery seeds), paprika, chilli and salt.

Let them cool and store them in airtight jars or a tin. Cashew nuts, pecans, peanuts and roasted chickpeas are also good prepared this way.

SUGGESTIONS

Roughly chop the nuts and sprinkle them on a soup. Particularly delicious with a cold *gazpacho* or a hot vegetable soup.

Serve devilled almonds after dinner instead of chocolates, to clear the palate and aid digestion.

Dress new potatoes with chopped devilled almonds. They are good on brussels sprouts and carrots too.

Roasted Chickpeas

The poor man's salted almond, roasted chickpeas remain a popular treat at Mediterranean village fairs where they are sold, hot from the brazier, by itinerant peddlers. Crisp, nutty and conveniently home-grown, these little snacks have long been appreciated by Mediterranean children. There is evidence they were the favourite nibble in pre-Neolithic Sicily. The Ancient Egyptians cultivated acres of them. Chickpea plants trailed their delicate leaves over Nebuchadnezzar's hanging gardens of Babylon.

In *feria* time, my local village baker in southern Spain would put a tray of chickpeas to roast in his cooling bread oven as a special treat for the children who went to the little school.

. . . .

QUANTITY
1 lb/500g chickpeas

TIME
Start 2 hours before
Cooking: 1½ hours

1 lb/500g chickpeas
1 tablespoon oil
1 pint/600ml water

UTENSILS
A bowl and a baking tray
  or frying pan

Soak the chickpeas for 2 hours in cold fresh water. Drain them thoroughly. Put them on a tray, lubricated with a little oil, to roast in a low oven, 250°F/130°C/Gas 1, until dry, crisp and golden – about 1½ hours. Or dry-fry them in a lightly oiled pan over a low heat on the top of the stove – be careful, they have a tendency to jump like popcorn.

Delicious eaten warm. To store, transfer them when cool to a tin or glass jar with a well-fitting lid. They will keep for months.

SUGGESTIONS

Crush a handful of roasted chickpeas and sprinkle them on a tomato salad.

Serve a small bowl of roasted chickpeas, a sliced tomato dressed with chopped onion, a tin of salted anchovies and a bowl of olives as a quick and easy starter to a meal.

Serve as an appetizer when you have made a bean or chickpea stew. It sharpens the taste buds for what is to come.

Toasted Seeds

Sunflower, pumpkin, melon and marrow seeds can all be harvested when perfectly ripe and, in the case of the last three, separated from the pulp and left in a warm place – a very low oven or an airing cupboard – to dry out.

QUANTITY
1 lb/500g seeds

TIME
Preparation: 5 minutes
Cooking: 30 minutes

1 lb/500g sunflower
   seeds
salt

UTENSILS
A baking tray

Sprinkle the seeds on a baking tray with a little salt, and toast gently in a low oven, 250°F/130°C/Gas 1, for 30 minutes until the kernels are crisp and golden (the husk will not change colour much).

Let them cool and store in a dry, airtight tin. They will keep almost indefinitely. With practice, you can become as adept as a Mediterranean urchin at cracking the shells between your teeth and rejecting all but the sweet little nut inside. The Greeks call these seeds *passu tempo* – pastimes – which exactly captures the atmosphere.

Potato Crisps

Potato crisps are everyone's favourite snack. The difference in flavour if you make your own is quite remarkable. I find Wilja and Pentland Dell the best potato varieties for crisps – you need mature rather than new.

QUANTITY

Makes about 1 lb/500g crisps

TIME

Preparation: 15 minutes
Cooking: 20 minutes

1 lb/500g old potatoes
salt
2 pints/1.2 litres oil for frying

UTENSILS

A food processor *or* manual slicer, and a deep-frying pan

Wash and peel the potatoes (you can leave the skins on of course – they are better food-value – but the skins are a little tough when deep-fried).

Slice the potatoes into very fine discs. Various gadgets can replace hard work with a sharp knife. Food processors have a special arrangement for fine slicing; there is also an instrument, widely available in kitchen shops, called a *mandoline*, which is a pair of sharp steel blades set into a wooden or steel frame like a miniature washboard; or there are usually two thin sharp lips on a grater which serve the purpose.

Rinse excess starch off the sliced potatoes. Drain and dry them thoroughly in a clean cloth.

Heat the oil in a deep-frying pan. Watch for a faint blue haze to mist the surface. Scatter in the potato slices – only a handful at a time or the temperature of the oil will drop too abruptly. Stir and turn them as they fritter to a golden brown. Remove and drain thoroughly on kitchen paper. Continue until all are done.

Crisps keep well, unsalted, in a tightly lidded tin or in well-sealed plastic bags. If they go soggy, they can be crisped up again in a warm oven.

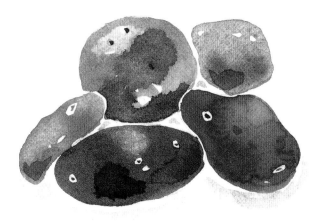

Dried Fruit

Dried fruit remains an important winter store throughout Europe. In medieval times northerners would put their stores of apples and pears, cherries and plums in the oven to dry after the bread was baked. Southerners still take advantage of the autumn sunshine to dry raisins, figs, peaches and apricots. All of Europe features dried fruit in its Christmas celebrations. The English have their puddings, mince pies and rich fruit cakes. The Germans bake raisin-stuffed *stollen*. The Danes stuff their Christmas goose with apples and prunes.

Mediterranean countries, accustomed to serving fresh fruit at the conclusion of summer meals, often put out a selection of dried fruit to complete the Christmas feast. The Provençaux include dried fruits and nuts in their traditional thirteen desserts which commemorate Jesus and his twelve disciples. The array of nougats, oranges, dates and other goodies are displayed on the festive table for the Christmas Eve *Gros Soupa*. Dried fruits gently satirize the four mendicant orders of monks, any of whom was likely, in the old days, to beg a place at the family celebration: wrinkled brown walnuts stand for the Augustinians, dried figs for the Franciscans, pale almonds for the Carmelites, and plump raisins for the Dominicans.

QUANTITY

Makes about 2 lb/1kg
dried fruit

TIME

Preparation: 10 minutes
Drying: 6-48 hours

4 lb/2kg fruit – apples,
pears, peaches,
apricots, figs, cherries,
plums, grapes

UTENSILS

Drying racks, kilner
jars and a bain marie
(*optional*)

Prepare the fruit: apples should be peeled, cored and sliced into rings; pears are halved and cored; peaches and apricots are halved and stoned; figs, cherries, plums and grapes are left whole.

Put the prepared fruit on racks in a single layer – whole fruit should have their stalks in the air. There are special wooden frames with mesh bottoms sold for the purpose in markets which cater to the farmwives of Europe, but ordinary baking racks will do. Put the fruit to dry either in the airing cupboard, when it will take a day or two, or in a very low oven with the door open, 250°F/130°C/Gas 1, for 4-5 hours. Leave the dried fruit to breathe for at least 3 hours before storing.

To keep the fruit succulent for a long time, do not let it dry completely, but transfer it while still a little moist to sterilized kilner-type jars. Seal and sterilize: immerse the jars in cold water in a bain marie. Bring the water to the boil and remove the jars immediately. They will keep for double the time.

MARINATED WINTER FRUITS___Leave a handful of dried fruit to swell for a few hours in enough orange juice to cover. Have the compote with yoghurt and a sprinkle of toasted almonds, or with *pain perdu* as a light supper.

WINTER FRUIT IN BRANDY___Any dried fruit is delicious macerated and bottled in alcohol (plain *eau-de-vie* is excellent). Raisins are good in an anis-flavoured liquor (Kummel or Anisette). Prunes or dried apricots take well to brandy. Soak 1 lb/500g dried fruit in a syrup made with ½ pint/300ml water and 8 oz/250g sugar. Leave overnight. The next day bottle the fruit and cover with 1 bottle of the chosen alcohol. It will be ready in a month. Serve the fruit in small helpings accompanied by a nut biscuit, as a very special winter dessert. Include the pleasure of a tiny glass of the soaking liquor.

WINTER FRUIT COMPOTE___Put 1 lb/500g dried fruit to soak overnight in hot, well-perfumed tea (Lapsang Suchong gives good results). The drier the fruit the more the liquid needed. The next day simmer the fruit gently for 20-30 minutes in its soaking liquid with a stick of cinnamon and a few cloves. Serve the compote warm, with cream or a custard. Or use it in a winter fruit tart.

Quince Paste

The beautiful downy-yellow quince was until recently widely cultivated all over Europe. Quince trees are still to be found fruiting alongside the silkworm's mulberry trees in old gardens. Although our modern sugar-hungry palate finds quince too sour to eat raw, the fruit loses its harshness when cooked and turns a soft and pretty pink. In Mediterranean countries it is mostly used to make a popular preserve. Orleans specializes in *cotignac*, an industrially prepared quince paste. In Spain it is widely known as *dulce de membrillo*, and in Portugal, where the word for quince is *marmelo*, the same preparation was the ancestor of that British breakfast staple, marmalade. It appears on market stalls which specialize in nougat and nuts and other winter treats around Christmas and the New Year – in Spain it is a speciality of the Day of the Kings, 6 January, when all good children, in company with the new-born Holy Infant himself, receive their presents.

QUANTITY
Makes about 4 lb/2kg
   paste

TIME
Preparation: 40 minutes
Maturing: 5-6 days

5 lb/2-3kg ripe quinces

1 short piece vanilla pod
   or 1 tablespoon water
   vanilla sugar
about 4 lb/2kg sugar

UTENSILS
A large bowl, a piece
of muslin, a roomy
saucepan, sieve and cloth,
and enamel plates *or*
baking tray

Peel, quarter and core the quinces and drop the cut fruit into a bowl of cold water so that it does not go brown – a cut quince is even faster to brown than an apple. Tie the peelings and cores into a clean piece of muslin.

Put the prepared fruit, the bag of peelings and cores, and the piece of vanilla (if you are using vanilla sugar, it goes in later) into a roomy saucepan or preserving pan and pour in enough cold water to cover. Bring to the boil, turn down the heat, and simmer gently for 20-30 minutes until the fruit is soft.

Line a large sieve with a clean cloth, or pin a clean cloth to the legs of an upturned stool, with a bowl beneath to catch the liquid. Pour the fruit and its juice into the cloth and allow the fruit to drain without pressing it. Save the clear juice to make jelly – quince jelly is particularly beautiful and fragrant.

Weigh the fruit solids (without the bag of peelings), and match it with the same weight of sugar. Return the fruit and sugar to the preserving pan and stir all well together over a gentle heat to dissolve the sugar. Beat over a low heat until you have a thick smooth paste – the pulp should not be overheated and boiled, or the flavour will change.

Pour the mixture either into deep enamel plates or a baking tray – the layer should be no more than a finger's width thick. Leave the paste in a warm place – on a shelf above the cooker or in the airing cupboard – for 5-6 days to dry out. Cut it into strips and store in an airtight tin.

Olives

The Provençal country people say the olive is immortal. A tree grown from a cutting can expect a lifespan of 300 years, yielding its first fruit after six to twelve years: a century to grow, a century to live, a century to die, the olive-men say. But the wild olive will always sprout again, however many times the original trunk is destroyed by frost or lightning, drought or flood. A tree which appears slender and young might be grafted on root stock a thousand years old: it will grow fast on the huge old roots. There may even be a few which reach back to the original plantings of the Greeks twenty-five centuries ago. Such trees were already old when the Romans built their amphitheatre and elegant houses at Vaison-la-Romaine – Hannibal's elephants might well have snatched a mouthful of the grey-green leaves from their branches as his soldiers dozed in the shade.

Harvesting olives remains as labour-intensive as it has always been. Until recently it has proved impossible to invent a machine which will pick the fruit without stripping the olive's leaves and jeopardizing the tree. The olives were always gathered by being shaken from the branches onto cloths on the ground below. In some areas the harvesters still climb the trees, scarves tied round their heads and shoulders to protect them from the dark juice, and pick by hand straight into baskets slung from their necks.

Mile Louise Morell, octogenarian daughter of the Baronnies of Haute Provence, told me in 1984 that when she was a young girl it was the women of the family who would harvest the olives. When the fruit was ready for picking in December, as soon as the sun was up, she and her mother and two sisters would join the rest of the family groups to climb the hills. They took their baskets and shawls, with bread, an onion and a piece of cheese for the midday meal. All day long they would stay up in the trees, leaving just one of their number as a modesty look-out in case some young swain or peeping Tom should catch them unaware, their petticoats hitched high as they straddled the branches.

Whole unpitted olives can be bought loose by weight, or ready-pickled in brine, or dry-preserved in a jar. They will be green, purple or black, depending on the stage of ripeness at which they are picked, and have undergone preliminary leaching to remove the fruit's natural bitterness. Olives can be cured in brine, in oil, in frequently changed salted water with lye such as wood ash, or in a combination of the five processes. These simply prepared olives are excellent raw material for your own marinades. It is worth looking out for a specially designed perforated wooden ladle which is used to fish the olives out of their brine.

Ready-stuffed olives are a speciality of the Spanish olive industry. Spain has perfected sophisticated machinery for punching out the olive pits and replacing them with almonds, chopped pepper, anchovies or pickled onions. These stuffed olives have already received all the attention they need. Once opened, pour off some of the brine, put a slice of lemon over the top layer, and keep them in the fridge. Here are three suggestions for mixtures. Experiment with your own combinations.

Oil-pickled black olives

An oil pickle is wonderful for black olives, making them plump and sweet.

QUANTITY
1 lb/500g olives

TIME
Preparation: 10 minutes
Resting: 1 week

1 lb/500g drained,
   prepared black olives
1 tablespoon dried
   tarragon
1 tablespoon dried
   oregano *or* marjoram
2 bayleaves, crumbled
1 tablespoon dried thyme
approximately 2 pints/1.2
   litres olive oil

UTENSILS
A large glass jar with a
   lid

Transfer the olives to the jar. Put in the herbs, lid and shake the jar to distribute the flavourings thoroughly. Pour in enough oil to cover the olives – they will sink below the surface. Seal and leave to infuse.

Ready in a week, these prepared olives keep well in a cool larder. The oil is marvellously piquant on salads or sprinkled over pizza.

Brine-pickled green olives

QUANTITY
1 lb/500g olives

TIME
Preparation: 15 minutes
Resting: 1 week

1 lb/500g drained,
   prepared green olives
1 teaspoon crushed
   coriander seeds
1 lemon
2 bayleaves, crumbled
2-3 peeled, quartered
   cloves garlic
2 oz/50g salt dissolved in
   2 pints/1.2 litres water
1 tablespoon dried fennel
   stalks *or* 1 teaspoon
   aniseeds

UTENSILS
A large glass jar with a
   lid

Mix the olives with the lemon (chopped roughly, but with one good slice held back) and the herbs in a large glass jar. Pour in enough salt-and-water brine to submerge the olives. Top with the slice of lemon to keep the olives under the brine. Refrigerate. Ready in a week, these olives are best within a month.

SUGGESTIONS

OLIVE PASTE____Pit a handful of olives and put them with a trickle of olive oil in the liquidizer (or pound by hand with a pestle and mortar) to make a delicious spread for toast. This primitive tapenade works as well with green olives as with purple or black.

Chilli-pickled purple olives

QUANTITY
1 lb/500g olives

TIME
Preparation: 15 minutes
Resting: 1 week

1 lb/500g drained,
  prepared purple olives
¼ pint/150ml wine
  vinegar
4-5 little dried chillies
1 oz/25g salt dissolved in
  2 pints/1.2 litres water
2 bayleaves, crumbled
2 peeled, quartered
  cloves garlic
2 tablespoons olive oil

UTENSILS
A large glass jar with a
  lid

Put the olives in a glass jar, layering in the chillies, bayleaves and garlic as you go. Pour in the wine vinegar, then enough brine to cover the olives. Float the olive oil on the surface to keep the olives submerged. Cover and store in a cool larder or the fridge. Ready in a week.

SUGGESTIONS

OLIVE-STUFFED EGGS___ Ideal as a light lunch for 2 people. Cut 4 hard-boiled eggs in half, take out the yolks and pound with 2 tablespoons of olive paste. Serve with quartered lettuce hearts (no dressing), fresh bread and a homemade mayonnaise.

ELIES ME KOLIANDRON___ To make this Cypriot speciality, pound 1 lb/500g green olives with 2 cloves garlic, 1 tablespoon coriander seeds, 6 tablespoons olive oil, 6 tablespoons vinegar. Pot and keep in a cool place. It will keep for 3-4 weeks in the refrigerator. Serve with fresh bread or hot toast as a snack or first course. Stir a teaspoon into your usual oil-and-vinegar salad dressing – it will give a deliciously piquant flavour.

2. Secret Ingredients

No storecupboard is complete without its secret ingredients – little preparations used in small quantities which, with the minimum of effort, give a lift to your favourite dishes. These secret stores vary throughout Europe, reflecting the raw materials available and the historical influences on the native population. The English repertoire is largely aimed at helping with the favourite meat dishes – for example gravy brownings and meat concentrates, of which Bovril is the modern descendant. The Mediterranean bottles its sunshine – tomatoes and peppers are dried or preserved in oil for stirring into the stews and soups of colder days. Flavoured sugars and *vin cuit* sweeten the long dark European winter.

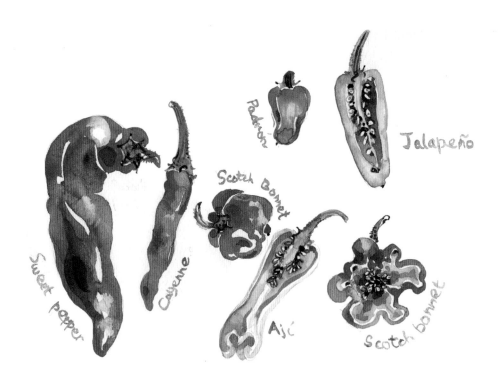

Red Pepper Paste
Massa de pimentão

The capsicums, both fiery chilli and mild salad peppers, are important seasonings in European kitchens. Many country housewives grow a small round variety of pepper for drying, and hang strings of the ox-blood red beads by the stove for use in winter seasonings and stews. The Catalans prefer their own special variety, the *ñora*, and the gardeners of Hungary have an even wider choice.

Red pepper paste, *massa de pimentão*, is a speciality of Portugal. It is made with the large juicy red peppers which are normally eaten fresh (and which are easily available in our shops). In home territory, the peppers would be merely sprinkled with the salt and left to pickle for a few days in the warmth of the Mediterranean kitchen, before being pounded up in a mortar with the oil and garlic. Portuguese cooks use the paste as a marinade for meat stir-fried Oriental-style, culinary habits picked up by the adventurous Portuguese sailors through their sixteenth- and seventeenth-century trading activities with the Far East.

. . . .

QUANTITY
Makes approximately
1½ lb/750g

TIME
Start the day before
Preparation: 20 minutes
Cooking: 1 hour

2 lb/1kg ripe red peppers
¼ pint/150ml olive oil
2 tablespoons coarse salt
2 large cloves garlic

UTENSILS
A shallow dish, a wide
saucepan, a food
processor and a
sterilized storage jar

Hull, pip and cut the peppers into strips lengthwise. Layer them in a shallow dish with the salt. Leave overnight. Pour off the salty juices. Heat the oil gently in a saucepan and put in the peppers. Leave barely to simmer, uncovered, for an hour in the oil. By the end most of the juices should have evaporated and the peppers will have a gently roasted flavour.

Peel and roughly chop the garlic. Put the peppers, the oil in which they cooked, and the garlic into the food processor and blend to a paste.

Bottle, seal and keep in a cool larder or in the fridge.

Stir a little into a stew to add flavour and richness. A spoonful will transform baked beans.

ROUILLE__You can quickly make this to serve with a main-meal soup. The Marseillais accompany their famous fish soup, *Bouillabaise*, with this fiery little sauce – but it is just as good with a *pot au feu*, or vegetable soup. To make the sauce: Put 2 tablespoons of the paste into a bowl and beat in 1 tablespoon fresh breadcrumbs soaked in water, 1 tablespoon wine vinegar and 4 tablespoons olive oil. Add a teaspoon of chilli to give it extra punch.

Use as a marinade to rub on chicken joints or meat for frying or barbecuing. It's particularly good rubbed all over a whole pork fillet. Slice the fillet into medallions, grill them and serve with bread and quartered lemons.

Gravy Browning

This is the English up to their tricks: the French struggle with reductions to sauce roast meats, Italians leave the natural juices to speak for themselves, but Britain's traditional cooks like a gravy darkened with gravy-browning – caramelized-sugar water – to sauce the Sunday roast. Strained cold tea will perform the same function and give a delicate herby taste to a gravy.

Barbecue Marinade
Chimichurri

This is the sauce used to baste a barbecue by the *gauchos*, the cowboys of the Argentine. It really has no business in a book of European food, but I lived in South America as a young girl, and this particular secret ingredient is my earliest culinary memory. My elder brother and I used to spend our school holidays at an *estancia*, a cattle ranch where we were mounted on small, bad-tempered ponies to ride out with the *gauchos*. My pony's favourite activity was to duck under a fig tree and scrape me out of my large comfortable saddle. The *gauchos* found the whole business very entertaining, and allowed us to stay for their wonderfully barbaric barbecues – whole sides of young bullock slowly grilled over charcoal, basted from a mysteriously-produced wine bottle filled with a magic essence, *Chimichurri*.

QUANTITY
About 1 pint/600ml

TIME
Preparation: 10 minutes

1 large onion
1 bunch parsley
6 cloves garlic
juice of 2 lemons
1 bunch thyme (best if
   fresh)
¾ pint/450ml olive oil

UTENSILS
1 empty wine bottle and
   a cork

Peel and chop the onion and garlic. Chop the herbs – you will need about 3 tablespoons. Put all these ingredients with the lemons and the oil into an empty wine bottle. Shake them all up and leave them to infuse in the fridge for a couple of weeks.

SUGGESTIONS

The mixture makes an excellent salad dressing – try it on new potatoes.

Use *chimichurri* as a marinade for a pot-roasted chicken. It does wonders for a battery bird.

Use the sauce to baste the meat when you have a barbecue, and you will capture the robust flavours of an Argentinian *asado* (roast).

Potherbs

The great potherbs throughout Europe are onion, garlic, celery and carrot. Early British potherbs were the Roman-planted alexander (an umbellifer *Smyrnium olustratum* called the black potherb from the colour of the seeds, which smells of aniseed when raw), of which the stem and sometimes the roots were chopped and added to stews; and cornsalad, *Valerianelle locusta*, called the white potherb and mostly used in salads.

Our modern homegrown potherbs are carrot, turnip, onion, leek, celery, parsnip, and parsley. Carrots used to be stored in sand (the French still do this), which keeps them sweet and well-flavoured. Turnips stored outside (clamping) were layered and roofed with plenty of straw and well covered with packed earth. Onions are best dried in the sun for a week or two, then bunched or plaited and hung up. Leeks, celery and parsnips can be left in the frosty ground and dug when needed. Parsley is a law unto itself.

Include at least three of these potherbs (one should be leek or onion) when you make winter soups or stews. Make a Northumberland *few broth* with a few of all these vegetables, a handful of barley or oatmeal, and a ham or lamb bone (it used to be a sheep's head).

Flavouring herbs
Bouquet garni

The classic French *bouquet garni* for perfuming a broth is a bunch of three fresh herbs – parsley, thyme and bay leaf – tied together by the stalk for easy removal when the stew is cooked.

Make up your own bouquets with dried herbs, using the lists below as a rough guide. Tie up your chosen aromatics in little squares of clean white cloth and store them in well-marked jars for use in stews and soups. Herbs and spices allow the cook to put an individual signature on a dish. Don't be limited by my suggestions – use them to develop your own special mixtures.

FOR PORK

Parsley, thyme, bay leaf, juniper, coriander, marjoram, rosemary, sage, savory.

FOR GAME BIRDS

Parsley, thyme, bay leaf, rosemary, savory, juniper, oregano, cloves, cummin (for pigeons and partridge).

FOR LAMB

Parsley, thyme, bay leaf, marjoram, oregano, savory, coriander, cumin, cinnamon.

FOR POULTRY

Parsley, thyme, bay leaf, tarragon, chives, rosemary, sage (for goose).

FOR BEEF AND VENISON

Parsley, thyme, bay leaf, rosemary, cloves, dried orange peel, juniper berries, horseradish, mustard, fennel.

FOR FISH

Parsley, thyme, bay leaf, chervil, chives, tarragon, fennel, dill, white pepper, horseradish (for smoked fish), savory (in France, particularly for trout), mustard (with oily fish such as mackerel and herring), dried lemon peel.

FOR VEGETABLES Parsley, thyme, bay leaf, basil, tarragon, marjoram, oregano, savory (particularly for broad beans and pulse vegetables), sage, mint, rosemary (especially aubergines).

Truffle Brandy

A black truffle marinated in a bottle of brandy is a wonderful aromatic.

The truffle hunters of Morella in the province of Valencia in Spain sell most of their wares to the dealers from the canning factories of Barcelona and France. The town council auctions the rights to the truffle grounds among its own citizenry for 3- or 4-year periods and the season runs from November through to March.

Business, in the best tradition of a peasant community, is conducted with all the finesse and discretion of a poker game. The hunters gather on a Friday in the appointed bar and arrive at the week's price by, as far as the outsider can judge, osmosis – or perhaps by counting the wine-rings on the bar, or the olive pips under each others' feet.

A ripe truffle, in which the rich meaty perfume is fully developed, will be dark all the way through with a minimum of pale veining. Although the commercialization of the wild crop dates back only to 1970, a few of the peasant farmers have always dug them – alerted in the first instance by the enthusiasm of the family pig (a free-range pig has a most discriminating palate) for the tubers. On a warm day the keen hunter leaves his pig and his dog at home, and watches out for little swarms of reddish flies betraying an unusual interest in a patch of troubled ground under a scrub oak. These flies lay their eggs in the truffles, so their presence will indicate a fine ripe haul. Truffles will remain good buried in sand for a month.

Local housewives put a scrubbed truffle in a bottle of brandy, keep it on the shelf and use it to add flavour to meat and bean dishes. The truffle itself remains good and can be used as if fresh (although not raw – the alcohol flavour is too strong). The truffle meat marinates to a uniform dark red-brown. However, once you have used up the truffle, it will not be able to add its perfume to the brandy.

QUANTITY
Makes 2 pints/1.2 litres

TIME
Preparation: 10 minutes

1½-pint/1-litre bottle
   ordinary brandy
1 black truffle

UTENSILS
wide-mouthed
   litre-bottle

Scrub the truffle. You will need to wet it if it has been rolled in mud (this can happen, perish the thought, after it has been dug from its earthy bed – the mud adds a few grams to the weight). Put the cleaned truffle in the bottle of brandy. Cork tightly. Leave for a fortnight and use as required.

Pour a tablespoonful of the brandy over a grilled steak or chop. Flame it. Finish with a knob of butter and a sprinkle of chopped parsley. You will dine like Lucullus.

Add a tablespoonful to the gravy of ordinary everyday dishes like shepherd's pie or steak-and-kidney or oxtail stew.

Use the brandy to deglaze the pan juices of a roast joint. You will find it adds a wonderful richness to the gravy.

Portable Soup

The forerunner of the ubiquitous stock cube (a modern ingredient which renders a uniform nastiness to all it touches) is the traveller's joy: portable soup. Marion McNeil mentions that the Scots made a similar preparation with stag's antlers in her book *The Scots Kitchen*.

The late Lillian Hellman's co-author, Peter Feibleman, wrote of a fifteenth-century version in *Eating Together* (published in 1984, in the US by Little Brown). Feibleman was researching his book *The Columbus Tree*, in Seville's venerable library.

> One day I found an early-fifteenth-century letter from a female cousin, a countess of the Medina Sidonia family, saying she had taken a five-day carriage ride from Sanliicar to Seville … which was uncomfortable and unrewarding except for a great new recipe her cook had come up with. The letter was dated in December and the weather was unusually cold. Her cook, it seems, had a friend who had taught him to boil meat with nothing but a bay leaf, salt and two ram's horns for hours until nothing was left of the meat but a thick dark sticky substance. The cook put the substance outside till it was cold and hard, then cut it into cubes with a knife. During her trip to Seville, the countess said, she was forced to stop at several inns, and in one of them her cook went to work with the cubes he had made. All he asked for was a cup of boiling water. …

Here I have adapted Dorothy Hartley's recipe from *Food in England* (1954). However, I suspect that old leather shoes would probably do well enough in times of hardship – and it would be a great deal more palatable than the preparation which has replaced it.

Enough to make 10-12
  pints/6-7 litres broth

Preparation: 20 minutes
Cooking: 6 hours

2 gallons water (16
  pints/9 litres)
6 lb/2.75 kg beef bones
2 calf's feet
2 lb/1 kg chicken feet
  and necks

1 cauldron

Wash and split the calf's feet. Splinter the bones. Scrub the chicken's feet. Put all the ingredients in a huge boiling pan, bring to the boil, skim, turn down the heat and leave to simmer for 6 hours, loosely covered. If a little liquor sets when you pour it into a saucer, take it off the heat and strain the broth from the bones – if it doesn't set, stew it until it does. Leave it to cool. The next day, skim off the fat and reboil the stock until it is reduced to a glue-like consistency. Pour out into tartlet tins, and when set turn out onto a clean cloth and put them in a very low oven with the door open. Let them dry quite hard. Store in an airtight jar or tin. Use to make broth as required. Don't forget to add salt and pepper.

Scented Sugars

Use these sugars to flavour biscuits, cakes and sweet dishes. Strongly aromatic, they can be used to transform ready-made desserts as well as cutting down on preparation time for the home cook.

SUGGESTIONS

CINNAMON SUGAR——Bury a short stick of cinnamon (real cinnamon, which is a cedarwood-red parchment-like roll, not the cheaper cassia bark) in a jar with 1 lb/500g caster sugar. Lid tightly and leave to take the flavour. Ready in a week, it will keep for a year. Sprinkle on hot buttered toast or buns, or *pain perdu*. Good for flavouring biscuits.

CLOVE SUGAR——For 1 lb/500g sugar, dry 12 cloves in a low oven for 10 minutes. Crush the cloves in a mortar with 2 oz/50g sugar. Mix in the rest of the sugar. Transfer to a clean dry jar, seal and store. Ready in a week, it will keep all year. Delicious with cooked apples – particularly in a pie – or when mixed with dried fruit and used to stuff baked apples. Stir in a spoonful to perfume a winter fruit compote (see page 20).

LAVENDER SUGAR——To perfume 1 lb/500g sugar, dry 6 whole lavender flower heads in a very low oven. Crumble the heads into the sugar. Put in a jar, seal and store. Ready in a week, it keeps all year. Use it to sweeten a custard for a lavender ice, or to sprinkle on a custard or junket.

cinnamon

ORANGE SUGAR____To perfume 1 lb/500g sugar, pare the peel of 2 oranges very finely. Cut the peel into fine strips. Dry it in a very low oven. Bury the peel in the sugar. Pot, seal and store. It will be ready in 2 weeks. It is delicious with chocolate in any form, or used to make butter icing for a sponge cake – or any other way you would like the flavour of orange. Make LEMON SUGAR in the same way.

ROSE GERANIUM SUGAR____Bury 2-3 rose geranium leaves in 1 lb/500g sugar in a jar, lid and seal tightly. It will be ready in 2 weeks. Rose geranium has a subtle sweet fragrance – use it to scent an apple jelly (see pages 137-138), to flavour a sponge cake, and to bring the sweet fragrance of a rose garden to a summer fruit salad.

VANILLA SUGAR____To scent 1 lb/500g sugar bury a finger's length of vanilla pod in the sugar. Pot, lid and seal. It will be ready in 2 weeks. Stir a spoonful into a cup of hot chocolate. I find it delightful that the heady scent comes from the seed pod of a tree-climbing orchid. Just for the pleasure of it, scrape a few of the tiny black grains into the custard or icecream that you perfume with the vanilla sugar.

Fruit Essence
Vin cuit

Vin cuit, the unfermented essence of well-ripened grapes, is prepared for the storecupboard throughout rural Europe wherever vines are planted. Grape syrup was very popular before commercially prepared sugar became widely available and cheap. Northerners prepared the same syrups with apple or pear juice, or sometimes a mixture of the two. It was used for sweetening and flavouring, and in any recipes where honey is an ingredient. It has been prepared round the Mediterranean since classical times at least. The Romans imported unfermented sweet grape-must to add necessary sweetness to the sour dry wines which their English vineyards produced.

The Swiss use the preparation as an important ingredient in several traditional dishes – including *Moutarde de Benichon* (see page 45). These syrups are today more often commercially prepared: Liège in Belgium makes a particular speciality of the manufacture, both home and factory. Pressed apple or pear juice provides the raw material, and the pulp is fed to the pigs. 10 lb/4-5kg very sweet little grapes (red or white) will reduce to about 3 pints/2 litres syrup. Clean ash from a wood fire was sometimes used to clarify the liquid, which is otherwise cloudy.

QUANTITY
Yields 3-6 pints/1.75-3.5
  litres fruit essence

TIME
Cooking: 1-2 hours

10 pints/6 litres grape *or*
  apple *or* pear juice

UTENSILS
A large shallow
  preserving pan, storage
  bottles, and a bain
  marie

Tip the juice into a large preserving pan. For sweet grape juice, bring to the boil, turn down the heat and simmer uncovered until the juice is reduced by one third. Apple or pear will need a second cooking and reduction – be careful towards the end as it becomes a thick syrup and will need to be stirred.

Bottle in sterilized containers and seal. Sterilize by bringing the bottles to the boil in a bain marie (start in cold water). Store and use as needed.

Dilute in water for a refreshing drink. Most welcome for wine-drinkers in Lent.

Cut the *vin cuit* with an equal volume of *marc* for the traditional Christmas Eve drink of Provence, taken to accompany the *panade*. (See page 141).

WINE PIE____Use the *vin cuit* for a Swiss tart: make a shortcrust pastry by rubbing 3 oz/75g butter into 4 heaped tablespoons plain flour and 1 teaspoon sugar. Form it into a soft dough with 2-3 tablespoons cold water.

Roll the pastry out on a well-floured board into a circle large enough to fit an 8-in/20-cm pie dish. Lay in the pastry, easing it in gently – if you pull it the pastry will shrink back in the cooking and the filling will flow out. Trim and crimp the edges with a fork. Put the pastry case aside to rest while you prepare the filling.

You will need 1 wineglass of *vin cuit* or sweet wine reduced by boiling, 1 oz/25g butter, 1 tablespoon flour, ¼ pint/150ml milk, 2-3 tablespoons sugar, ½ teaspoon salt. Melt the butter in a saucepan, stir in the flour, let it fry for a moment until it is pale and sandy, then gradually beat in the milk until you have a smooth thick cream. Stir in the *vin cuit* (or reduced wine), sugar and salt. Fill the pie with this cream.

Bake at 400°F/200°C/Gas 6 for 30 minutes – keep an eye on it in case the filling overflows as it expands.

3. Mustards, Flavoured Vinegars, Aromatic Oils and Spiced Salts

Mustard

Mustard is one of the most ancient of Europe's native-grown aromatics. Its virtues as a *digestif* and appetite stimulant were appreciated by the Greeks and Romans, who would chew the whole seeds between courses to clear the palate. Apicius, whose first-century a.d. *De Re Coquinaria* provides our best authority on Roman culinary habits, includes mustard seeds as a preservative in pickled vegetables.

There are two species of mustard native to Europe: white/yellow (*Senapis alba* – a Greek-derived name) and black/brown (*Brassica nigra*). There is a third (*Brassica juncea*) which is native to the Himalayas and is much used in modern mixtures. Mustard seed is only pungent when it is broken and wetted, and the strength lies in the volatile oil which is released by this process.

White mustard can be sprouted on a damp cloth in a warm dark corner – the twin-leaved green shoots are delicious in salads or mustard-and-cress sandwiches. Nineteenth-century English lady travellers to the colonies would take seeds to sow in the privacy of their cabins, so that they had a little greenstuff on the long sea voyage.

English Mustard

English mustard is hot and smooth, made from very finely milled mustard powder, well sifted to extract the husks. A certain Mrs Clements of Durham, an early eighteenth-century entrepreneur, is responsible for the modern English taste. Until 1729, the seeds were pounded and boiled in must – unfermented grape juice. Mrs Clements milled and commercialized her own blend of strong English mustard, a brew which George I, perhaps nostalgic for the strong Hanoverian flavours of home, heartily endorsed. The old lady travelled the market towns of England selling her mixture. Messrs Keens of London purchased her secret recipe and manufactured it ('keen as mustard') until the firm in its turn was taken over by East Anglia-based Jeremiah Colman in 1814.

Experiment with your own mixtures. Add turmeric if you like a brilliant yellow tint. Try mixing in a little powdered ginger, ground white pepper, cayenne pepper, or grated horseradish. English mustard should be very strong, and needs robust flavourings if they are not to be overwhelmed. Save the delicate herbs for the milder French or German mixes. The fun of it is to invent your own special recipe.

Use it to add sparkle to a Welsh Rarebit, to a white sauce for a *fricassée*, and in anything devilled – from kidneys to chicken legs.

. . . .

QUANTITY
Enough for 1 meal for 6

TIME
Preparation: 5 minutes

3 heaped tablespoons
   fine-ground English
   mustard (mostly the
   white mustard)
3 tablespoons cold water
   or beer or milk
½ teaspoon salt

UTENSILS
A small bowl

Blend the powder with enough of your chosen liquid to give a smooth mix which will drop gently from a spoon.

Beer gives a stronger flavour, milk (or cream) gives a milder mustard. Add a pinch of salt for every tablespoon of mustard and the mixture will not dry out so quickly.

The best sauce for roast beef is a cup of stiffly whipped cream into which is folded a tablespoon of made mustard and a tablespoon of freshly grated horseradish.

French Mustard

A milder mustard, this is probably the closest to the Roman mix. Dijon uses sour grape juice to mix the powder – and this gives the mustard its particular flavour. Herbs such as tarragon, thyme, or green peppercorns can all be included.

. . . .

QUANTITY

Makes ¼ pint/150ml
 mustard

TIME

Preparation: 5 minutes

4 oz/100g fine-ground
 and sifted mild
 mustard powder (a
 blend of black and a
 little white mustard)
¼ pint/150ml sour grape
 juice *or* wine vinegar
2 tablespoons honey
1 teaspoon powdered
 cinnamon

UTENSILS

A bowl and 1-2 small
 pots

Mix the powdered mustard and the spice with juice or vinegar and the honey. Pot, seal and store.

Wholegrain Mustard
Moutarde de Meaux

This is wholegrain mustard which has its origins in Meaux in northern France. The mix is of black and white mustard seeds in the proportion roughly 3:5 of black to white. Here are Dumas' instructions, from his *Grand Dictionnaire de Cuisine* of 1873.

QUANTITY
Makes ½ pint/300ml
   mustard

TIME
Start the night before
Preparation: 10 minutes

8 oz/250g mustard seed
2 tablespoons honey
½ pint/300ml wine
   vinegar
2 tablespoons cinnamon

UTENSILS
A bowl, pestle and
   mortar, 1-2 storage jars

Steep the mustard seed in half the vinegar overnight. Next day, pound it up in a mortar with the honey and cinnamon. Mix it to a stiff paste with more vinegar. Pot, cover and seal.

Cremona Mustard
Mostarda di fruta

This Italian mustard, *mostarda di fruta*, is made with crystallized fruit. It is a preparation with a most venerable pedigree, which has survived the modern division of sweet from salt. Such flavours must have been familiar to the blind poet Homer himself. Fruit mustard is most usually served, as in Lombardy, with cold boiled meats – beef or ham. I can recommend it as an accompaniment to cold roast poultry or game (turkey and pheasant in particular) or smoked eel. Fortunate Italians can buy it by the ladleful from the barrel.

QUANTITY
Makes 3 pints/2 litres
    mustard

TIME
Start the day before
Preparation: 20 minutes

2 oz/50g mustard powder
2 oz/50g honey
1 pint/600ml *vin santo*,
    Marsala *or* Malaga
    sweet wine
1 teaspoon powdered
    cinnamon
½ teaspoon powdered
    nutmeg
8 oz/250g mixed
    crystallized fruits
½ teaspoon powdered
    cloves
1 tablespoon cornflour
½ teaspoon powdered
    ginger
1 pint/600ml water

Mix the mustard with the wine and leave it to soak overnight. Roughly chop the fruit. Mix the flour with a little cold water in a saucepan, stir in the rest of the water, the honey and the spices. Bring all gently to the boil, turn down the heat and simmer for 5 minutes, until the mixture thickens. Stir in the fruit and the wine and mustard. Bring back to the boil. Simmer until thick. Pot and store.

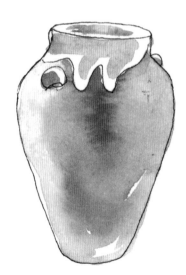

UTENSILS

A bowl, a large saucepan, and storage jars

Moutarde de Benichon

This mustard-flavoured sauce is a preparation popular in Switzerland. There are some similarities with the Italian fruit mustard in the preceding recipe, although the Swiss use it more as a jam than a condiment. It is served with a brioche bread, the *cuchaule*. But its most entertaining use is to celebrate the return of the dairy herds from their summer pastures high in the mountains. Then it is served as an accompaniment to *beignets de be-nichons*, deep-fried fritters. The mix for these is 1 lb/500g flour mixed to a soft dough with 3 eggs, 3 oz/75g sugar, 2 oz/50g melted butter, 3 tablespoons double cream, and 1 tablespoon kirsch or brandy. Roll out egg-sized nuggets of the dough into thin pancakes. Deep fry them until golden, turning once. Serve with the mustard, to celebrate anything at all. Lovely for a child's birthday party.

QUANTITY
Makes 2 pints/1.2 litres
    mustard

TIME
Start the night before
Cooking: 1 hour

1 oz/25g mustard powder
4 tablespoons granulated
    sugar
¼ pint/150ml white wine
4 tablespoons brown
    sugar
3 oz/75g flour
2 tablespoons honey
1 pint/600ml water
1 teaspoon powdered
    cinnamon
½ pint/300ml *vin cuit*
    (see page 37) *or* runny
    apple sauce
½ teaspoon powdered
    cloves
1 teaspoon powdered
    aniseed

Put the mustard to soak in the white wine the night before. Mix the flour with a little of the water in a saucepan. Stir in the rest of the water, the *vin cuit*, the sugar, honey and spices. Bring all to the boil, beating to keep the mixture smooth. Stir in the mustard and wine and bring back to the boil. Turn down the heat and simmer the mixture until it is as thick as runny apple purée.

Pot and seal down while still warm. It is ready to use, and will keep well in a cool larder.

UTENSILS

A bowl, a saucepan, and storage jars

Flavoured Vinegars

Vinegar is an excellent medium for preserving delicate flavours. These infusions are very useful for dressing salads – either to replace or reinforce the flavour of the fresh herbs. Stir a spoonful of herb vinegar into vegetable or potato soup just before serving. Splash a little raspberry vinegar into a gravy for roast pheasant, partridge or any feathered game. Use the vinegars in marinades for meat, fish or poultry.

Thyme, rosemary, dill, mint, garlic – any aromatic – can replace tarragon in the recipe which follows.

. . . .

Tarragon Vinegar

Use tarragon vinegar to make black butter sauce for skate, sweetbreads or brains. Or to flavour a bearnaise sauce. It is excellent on a potato salad, or with fennel or celery – or on any green salad, particularly tender spring leaves such as dandelion and rocket. Use it also to mix mustard.

QUANTITY
Makes 2 pints/1.2 litres
    vinegar

TIME
Start a week before
Preparation: 15 minutes

2 lb/1kg raspberries
2 pints/1.2 litres white
    wine vinegar

UTENSILS
A deep bowl, a cloth, and
    storage bottles

Wash the tarragon and dry it carefully. Put the sprigs of herb and the cloves into a bottle or bottles and pour in the vinegar. Cover tightly and leave on a sunny windowsill or in a warm cupboard to infuse. In 2 weeks it will be ready to transform your salads.

Raspberry Vinegar

This vinegar is at its best in a vinaigrette for avocados and artichokes. Try it too on cold braised endives, in a mayonnaise for cold chicken, and when dressing a salad which includes fruit. Use it to dress hot grated beetroot, one of the best accompaniments to game. Stir a spoonful into a pumpkin or tomato soup to give it an extra piquancy – much more interesting than cream. Raspberry vinegar has recently become fashionable as a seasoning for rare-cooked breast of duck.

QUANTITY
Makes 2 pints/1.2 litres
   vinegar

TIME
Preparation: 10 minutes

4 fresh healthy sprigs
   tarragon
2 pints/1.2 litres white
   wine vinegar
2 cloves

UTENSILS
Storage bottles

Pick over and rinse the raspberries. Put the fruit in a deep bowl and crush the berries. Pour in the vinegar, stir until well mixed, and cover the bowl with a cloth.

Leave to infuse for a week, stirring daily. Strain the beautiful scarlet liquid through a cloth. Bottle, lid tightly and store so that your winter salads will have the scent of summer.

Aromatic Oils

Make up your own aromatic oils to suit your culinary preferences. Keep them in a cool dark larder and label them carefully. While preparing them, make up a bottle or two without the garlic and pepper, to use as massage rubs or to scent the bath. Close your eyes and think of Provençal hills starred with butterflies and clothed in sage brush, wild thyme and rosemary.

Herb Oil

A strongly aromatic oil is excellent for basting roast meat or poultry. Try it on a roast chicken, and use the cooking juices to dress an accompanying vegetable (green beans or spinach perhaps) or a green salad.

QUANTITY

Makes 1 pint/600ml
   herb oil

Put all the aromatics and the oil in a glass jar with a lid, seal and shake thoroughly. Ready in a week, it will be perfect in a month.

TIME

Preparation: 10 minutes

SUGGESTIONS

FENNEL OIL___Marinate a dried branch of fennel in a bottle of good olive oil for a month. The oil makes a delicious sauce for grilled fish.

1 sprig rosemary
2 pickling onions *or*
   1 clove garlic
1 sprig thyme (peeled
   and sliced)
1 bay leaf
6 black peppercorns
1 pint/600ml olive oil

UTENSILS

A storage jar

Basil Oil

Use this oil to dress a tomato salad, to sprinkle on pizza, to turn with pasta, or to finish a *minestrone*. Or use it in any dish to which you would like to give an Italian flourish.

QUANTITY
Makes 1 pint/600ml
　basil oil

TIME
Preparation: 10 minutes

2-3 sprigs fresh basil
2 peeled and crushed
　cloves garlic
2 sage leaves
1 pint/600ml olive oil
6 peppercorns

UTENSILS
A storage bottle

Put all the aromatic ingredients in a bottle and cover with the olive oil. Cork tightly and store in a cool dark cupboard. It will be ready in 2 weeks.

Paprika Oil

Use paprika oil to colour a mayonnaise for shellfish. Dribble a thread of the oil to decorate – Middle Eastern style – a salad purée such as aubergine or chickpea. Use it to add a little extra colour to *taramasalata* and to dress salads such as potato, red pepper or grated carrot. You can make chilli oil by using red chillies instead of sweet paprika.

QUANTITY
Makes 1 pint/600ml
    paprika oil

TIME
Preparation: 5 minutes

2 tablespoons powdered
    sweet paprika
1 pint/600ml olive oil
2 peeled and crushed
    cloves garlic

UTENSILS
A storage bottle

Mix all the ingredients in a bottle. Cork and store in a cool larder. Ready in 2 days.

Spiced Salts

Any powdered herbs can be used to make a seasoning salt – experiment with your own combinations and make up a few to suit your favourite recipes.

Oriental Salt

This used to be a commercial preparation available from good British grocers. Now that it seems to have been removed from the shelves, I have to make up my own. It is not an arduous task.

QUANTITY
Makes 8 oz/250g
    oriental salt

TIME
Preparation: 5 minutes

8 oz/250g fine salt
1 teaspoon freshly milled
    pepper
1 teaspoon powdered
    cumin
1 teaspoon paprika
1 teaspoon powdered
    coriander
1 teaspoon cayenne
    pepper (chilli)

UTENSILS
A storage jar

Mix the salt with the aromatics. Store in a screwtop jar. That's all. Oriental salt is the best of accompaniments to wild birds' eggs – particularly gulls' or plovers' eggs and farmed quail eggs. It adds sparkle as well to plain hard-boiled eggs or Scotch eggs.

Provençal Herb Salt

Use this flavour of the Mediterranean in a vinaigrette, a cream-cheese mix, stuffed tomatoes or aubergines – any dish which will be enlivened by the four aromatic sisters of the Provençal hills.

QUANTITY
Makes 8 oz/250g

TIME
Preparation: 5 minutes

1 lb/500g sea salt
1 clove garlic
1 teaspoon each dried
   rosemary, sage,
   oregano, thyme

UTENSILS
A pestle and mortar and
   a storage jar

Pound up a little of the salt with the herbs. Mix in the rest of the salt and put it in the jar with the garlic-clove buried in the middle. Ready in a week.

Celery Salt

Celery salt is perfect for seasoning roast or grilled meat, or poultry. Try it on a salad too – it has a natural affinity with potatoes or any root vegetables.

QUANTITY
Makes 8 oz/250g celery
   salt

TIME
Preparation: 10 minutes

8 oz/250g fine salt
1 teaspoon white
   peppercorns
1 tablespoon celery seeds

UTENSILS
A pestle and mortar, and
   a storage jar

Pound the salt with the celery seeds and peppercorns. Keep the salt in a screwtop jar. That's all. It adds spice to a salad dressing and character to a white sauce – and it is invaluable in a Bloody Mary.

4. Bottled Sauces, Relishes and Chutneys

'A great chef is witty, as well as cultured, in the choice of his sauces and impertinent in their use at the expense of dullard or unworthy dinners' wrote P. Morton Shand, a gentleman wise before his years, who had not yet reached the age of forty at the time (1927) of writing his delightful *Book of Food*. Here are a few bottles to sauce worthy dinners.

Worcestershire Sauce

Like many of Britain's favourite condiments, the recipe for this sauce seems to have been brought back from India by one of the Queen Empress's loyal servants. The second Baron Sandys of Worcestershire passed on the formula to Mr Lea of Lea & Perrins, who made his fortune from the brew.

QUANTITY
Makes 1 pint/600ml
sauce

TIME
Start the day before
Preparation: 20-25
minutes

1 pint/600ml vinegar
1 small piece whole
ginger
8 oz/250g black treacle
½ teaspoon chilli
1 clove garlic
1 teaspoon salt
1 teaspoon powdered
cloves

UTENSILS
A saucepan and storage
bottle

Boil all the ingredients together for 15 minutes. Leave to infuse overnight. Strain and bottle the sauce.

SUGGESTIONS

SPICED TOMATO SOUP___ You will need 8 oz/250g canned or fresh tomatoes, ½ small onion, 1 teaspoon flour, 1 teaspoon Worcestershire Sauce. Liquidize all the ingredients in a blender. Transfer to a small pan, bring to the boil and simmer for 5 minutes. Serve with hot croutons fried with a few cubes of bacon. Enough for 1.

Use the sauce to marinate meat for grilling. My local bar in Tarifa, on the southernmost tip of Spain, specializes in *pinchitos* well-spiced with Lea & Perrins Worcester Sauce. These all-meat kebabs are the star turn of the house tapas. This peculiarly British taste was probably inspired by the presence of Gibraltar just a cannonball away.

SPICED SARDINE FISHCAKES____ You will need 2 lb/1kg boiled potatoes mashed with 1 oz/25g butter, 1 can sardines, 2 eggs, 1 tablespoon Worcester Sauce. Beat the sardines (bones, oil and all), the eggs and the Worcester Sauce into the mashed potatoes. Add salt and freshly ground pepper. Fry spoonfuls of the mixture in shallow oil-and-butter. Turn once. Continue until all is used up. That's all. A fresh tomato sauce and a green vegetable will keep them good company.

Mushroom Ketchup

This should be made with those luscious flat black mushrooms, either field or cultivated, which have a richer, more developed flavour than the little white buttons. Use a drop of the ketchup in any recipe which calls for button mushrooms, to confirm the flavour.

QUANTITY
Makes 2 pints/1.2 litres ketchup

TIME
Start the day before
Preparation: 30 minutes

4 lb/2kg flat black mushrooms
1 teaspoon nutmeg
4 oz/100g salt
1 pint/600ml vinegar
1 teaspoon black peppercorns
1 small glass brandy
1 small piece mace

UTENSILS
A bowl, a plate, a pestle and mortar, a saucepan, a food processor (*optional*) and sterilized storage bottles

Wipe the mushrooms and layer them into a bowl, scattering salt between each layer. Weight with a clean plate and leave overnight to make juice.

The next day, crush the spices and bring them to the boil with the vinegar. Pour the vinegar over the mushrooms. Transfer the mixture to a large saucepan. Bring all to the boil and cook for 15 minutes.

Stir in the brandy. Either strain off the liquid and pour it, still hot, into sterilized bottles, and seal tightly. Or (and this is the way I like it) tip the whole mixture into the food processor and liquidize it into a thick dark sauce.

Bring back to the boil, and bottle it. Store the ketchup in a cool dark place, and transfer it to the fridge once opened.

SPICED KIDNEYS⎯⎯For 1, you will need 2 lamb's kidneys, 1 teaspoon flour, 1 table-spoon vegetable oil, 2-3 sliced button mushrooms, 1 tablespoon mushroom ketchup. Skin, core and slice the kidneys. Dust them with seasoned flour and fry gently in a little vegetable oil until they stiffen. Add the mushrooms and turn them in the oil. Sprinkle in a tablespoon of mushroom ketchup and a splash of water or cream. Bubble up. Finish with freshly milled pepper, very little salt, and, if you have it, a sprinkle of chopped spring onion. Eat with hot toast.

Use the ketchup to add flavour to a mushroom soup.

CAUCASIAN MUSHROOMS⎯⎯Serve these as a first course, or with game. To make them you will need 1 lb/500g large flat black mushrooms, 2 oz/50g butter, 1 table-spoon flour, 1 small carton soured cream, 2 tablespoons mushroom ketchup. Wipe and trim the mushrooms. Stew them gently in the butter until soft. Throw in the flour and stir it in the hot juices. Add the soured cream and the ketchup. Bubble all up, check and adjust the seasoning, and serve.

Tomato Ketchup

The English have always loved sweet relishes and fruit-based sauces with their meats and have a rich store of such recipes, reinforced by Indian spicing from the days of the Raj. Commercially prepared tomato ketchup seems to have escaped the attentions of the chemists and remains relatively additive – and preservative-free. Making your own allows you to adjust the seasoning to your own taste.

Use well-ripened tomatoes gathered towards the end of the season – the misshapen or undersized ones are fine. This is an excellent recipe for those who grow their own tomatoes.

QUANTITY
Makes about 2 pints/1.2 litres ketchup

TIME
Preparation: 20 minutes
Cooking: intermittent attention for 2 hours

8 lb/4kg tomatoes
8 cloves
½ pint/300ml white malt vinegar
1 short stick cinnamon
4 oz/100g sugar
1 small piece mace *or* 1 teaspoon freshly grated nutmeg
1 teaspoon salt
½ teaspoon white peppercorns
2-3 bay leaves

UTENSILS
A large saucepan, a sieve, and sterilized storage bottles

Wash and roughly chop the tomatoes. Put all the ingredients into a large saucepan and leave them to infuse for half an hour. Bring the pan to the boil, turn down to a gentle simmer and leave to cook gently over a low heat for at least an hour. It shouldn't need much attention as the tomatoes produce plenty of liquid at this stage, and there is little likelihood of the mixture sticking.

Push the tomato mixture through a fine-meshed wire sieve, leaving skin, pips and spice debris behind. Return the purée to the saucepan – at this stage it will probably be far too liquid. Bring back to the boil and simmer vigorously, stirring regularly, until the sauce is as thick as you like it – it will take 30-40 minutes to reduce satisfactorily. Taste and adjust seasoning. Bottle and cork tightly.

Experiment with different spices – coriander, cumin, ginger, paprika. Consider too the inclusion, French-style, of red peppers, onions, fresh chilli.

SUGGESTIONS

MEXICAN FRIED EGGS Into a helping of tomato ketchup stir a pinch of chilli, a scrap of finely minced garlic, a little chopped fresh coriander or parsley, and a sliced spring onion. Have it with a couple of fresh eggs fried in olive oil for the beautiful peppery flavour.

Stir a generous helping of ketchup into an oxtail soup or stew to add texture and spice.

MADEIRA SAUCE___Make this to serve with ham, tongue, or (best of all) a cold partridge or pheasant. I love it with cold breaded lamb cutlets – a very Victorian taste. For the sauce, you will need 2 glasses madeira or sweet sherry, ½ onion, 1 sprig thyme, 2 glasses water or clear stock, 2 tablespoons tomato ketchup, 1 small carton double cream. Put the wine and the peeled and chopped onion with the thyme into a small saucepan. Boil until the liquid is reduced by half. Strain and return the reduced wine to the pan. Add the water or stock and the ketchup. Bring all back to the boil. Stir in the cream. Serve the sauce warm.

Serve the ketchup with **VEGETABLE FRITTERS**. For 4, you will need 2 young courgettes, 4 branches broccoli, 1 aubergine, 1 green and 1 red pepper, a large handful fresh spinach, 1 artichoke. For the batter: beat until smooth, 8 tablespoons plain flour, ½ pint/300ml light beer, 1 teaspoon salt. Separate 1 egg. Stir in the yolk and fold in the whisked white. Slice the courgettes lengthways; separate the broccoli into small sprigs; hull and slice the aubergine; hull, seed and slice the peppers lengthways; remove the larger stems of the spinach and rinse well; trim the artichoke of its tough leaf points, remove the hairy chokes and slice the remaining hearts thinly (rub with a cut lemon to avoid blackening). Heat the oil until you can see a faint blue haze rising. Dust each piece of vegetable with seasoned flour, dip in the batter and deep-fry – not too many at a time. Serve the fritters immediately.

Almond and Garlic Sauce
Salsa de Picadilla

Literally, 'chopped sauce', this is a favourite sauce of the inhabitants of Spain's eastern seaboard. The main ingredient, the almonds, was one of the Moors' several contributions to Spain's well-being. The sauce is rather like a thin mayonnaise. You can include a slice or two of stale bread to replace a few almonds – this will add body to the sauce but is not suitable if you mean to keep it for more than a few days. The Bulgarians make the same sauce with walnuts instead of almonds.

QUANTITY
Serves 6-8

TIME
Preparation: 20 minutes

2 oz/50g blanched
  almonds
4 tablespoons wine
  vinegar
4 cloves garlic (peeled)
½ teaspoon salt
1 pint/600ml olive oil

UTENSILS
A liquidizer *or* pestle and
  mortar, and sterilized
  storage jars

Put all the ingredients in the blender and process to a smooth cream. Or you can do this in the traditional way with a pestle and mortar, pounding the almonds and garlic and adding the oil and vinegar slowly, but I don't think there is any perceptible difference. (I shall duck the flying cleavers of traditionalists from Valencia.) Pot and store in a cool place. It will keep for 2-3 weeks.

SUGGESTIONS

Use the *picadilla* to sauce a main dish of mixed plain-cooked vegetables – carrots, potatoes, cauliflower, broccoli, green beans. The Bulgarians serve their walnut version with potatoes and red peppers tossed with chopped dill.

In Spain the sauce traditionally accompanies poached or fried fish – it's delicious instead of an *aioli* with a fish soup. It even improves fish fingers.

Convert the recipe into a *salsa romesco*, an aromatic scarlet sauce in which Spaniards cook clams or mussels. Liquidize the *picadilla* mixture with a couple of large tomatoes, a glass of dry white wine or sherry, a tablespoon of paprika and ½ teaspoon chilli powder. Finish (*optional*) with a dash of *aguardiente* or any anis-flavoured spirit. Prepare the shellfish: soak them overnight so that they spit out their sand, and then put them to open in a tablespoon of olive oil heated in a lidded pan. Stir in the sauce and a handful of chopped parsley, let it all bubble up, and serve with bread and a salad.

Spanish Scarlet Sauce
Salsa Samfaina

This is a *ratatouille*-like mixture used in Spain as a sauce – the Spaniards and the French share more than the Pyrenees divide. The Hungarian preparation, *lecso*, is similar.

QUANTITY
Makes about 1
  pint/600ml sauce

TIME
Preparation: 15 minutes
Cooking: 30 minutes

1 large firm aubergine
4 tablespoons olive oil
1 lb/500g red and green
  peppers
salt and pepper
1 lb/500g tomatoes

UTENSILS
A shallow saucepan and
  sterilized storage jars

Wash, hull and chop the vegetables coarsely (de-seed the peppers and skin the tomatoes first). Warm the oil in a shallow pan and put in the chopped aubergine, peppers, and finally the tomatoes. Fry all together gently until you have a thick smooth sauce. Beat. Taste and add salt and pepper.

Pot, seal and store in a cool place. Ready to use immediately, it will keep for a fortnight in the fridge.

SUGGESTIONS

Use to sauce a grilled chicken joint, or cubes of pork fried in a little olive oil with garlic.

Samfaina makes a fine sauce for pasta – heat it with a little extra oil and freshly chopped herbs.

Serve the sauce with beans or chickpeas or lentils, strained from yesterday's bean pot, and 'refried' gently in a little olive oil in a shallow pan, until all their liquid has evaporated and you are left with a richly roasted bean pancake. Patience and slow cooking will produce the desired result, however soupy the original mix.

Spanish Green Sauce
Salsa verde

Salsa verde belongs to the Spanish kitchen's wide range of bread-thickened soups and sauces – a group which includes the well-known Andalusian cold soup, *gazpacho*. Spanish bread has had a reputation for excellence since Roman times and in a well-run household not a scrap is ever wasted.

QUANTITY
Makes approximately 1
   pint/600ml sauce

TIME
Preparation: 10 minutes

1 large Spanish onion
1-2 slices day-old bread
3 cloves garlic
2 tablespoons vinegar
1 bunch parsley
½ pint/300ml olive oil

UTENSILS
A liquidizer, *or* pestle
   and mortar

Process all the ingredients together in the liquidizer, or pound up in a mortar.

Pot and store in a cool place. Ready within an hour or two, it will keep for 2-3 weeks stored in a screwtop jar in the fridge.

SUGGESTIONS

This makes a delicious sauce for new potatoes or asparagus.

Serve with poached cod or salmon steaks and plain-boiled vegetables. Or with lightly poached scallops as a first course.

MUSSELS IN HERB SAUCE_____To make this for 4, put 2 pints/1 litre mussels, cleaned and scrubbed, to steam in a glass of white wine in a shallow, lidded pan. When the mussels are fully open, add a generous helping of the *salsa verde* and allow all to bubble up.

English Salad Cream

I can't resist including this peculiarly English sauce. It has been much neglected in favour of mayonnaise in recent years, perhaps because the recipe was abused by commercialization. Made with the best ingredients, it is a really excellent mixture. My copy of the little WI book, *Gleanings from Gloucestershire Housewives*, published in 1948, has nine recipes for the sauce, and not one for mayonnaise.

QUANTITY
Makes approximately 1½ pints/1 litre sauce

TIME
Cooking: 20-25 minutes

1 tablespoon flour
1 egg
½ teaspoon mustard powder
½ pint/300ml cream
1 teaspoon salt
½ pint/300ml milk
½ teaspoon freshly milled white pepper
¼ pint/150ml vinegar

UTENSILS
Liquidizer *or* bowl and spoon, saucepan, and sterilized storage bottles

Put all the ingredients in the liquidizer and blend thoroughly. If you have no liquidizer, mix the first 4 ingredients into a paste with a little oil. Then beat in the liquids. Bring all carefully to the boil, stirring well. Simmer for a few minutes until the mixture thickens like a custard.

Transfer to sterilized bottles and lid tightly. Keep in a cool place. Ready immediately, it keeps well, unopened, for months.

SUGGESTIONS

Delicious with new potatoes and hard-boiled eggs (bring to the boil in cold water, remove from the heat; leave 6 minutes, plunge into cold water and peel). Much better in Russian salad than mayonnaise.

Serve it with plain boiled asparagus.

Use to dress a warm salad of haricot or flageolet beans, chopped onion, tomatoes and cucumbers. Finish with crisply fried bacon crumbled over.

Cod's Roe Sauce

The noble cod was not just ordinary commons in Victorian times: no grand dinner table was considered well-dressed without its silver salver laden with a fine cod head-and-shoulders, boiled and served with quartered lemons, and a cod's roe, oyster or caper sauce. Mrs Beeton gives enthusiastic instructions for the preparation of the dish, and recommends the virtues of cod-liver oil for the treatment of consumption.

QUANTITY
Serves 4

TIME
Preparation: 5-15
  minutes
Cooking: 10 minutes

8 oz/250g cooked fresh
  cod's roe
1 teaspoon vinegar
1 teaspoon English
  mustard
6 oz/175g melted butter
1 teaspoon anchovy sauce
  or 2 anchovy fillets

UTENSILS
A food processor *or*
  pestle and mortar, a
  small saucepan, and
  storage jars

Skin the roe and put it with the rest of the ingredients in the food processor. Process thoroughly. Or you can pound up the roe in a mortar with the mustard and anchovy, and then mix in the rest of the ingredients. Put the resulting sauce in a small saucepan and simmer gently for 10 minutes to marry the flavours. Pot and cover tightly. It keeps in the fridge for 4 weeks.

SUGGESTIONS

Spread the sauce, cold, on toast and top with a poached egg.

Serve warm with plain steamed fish and vegetables.

The sauce, warmed, makes an excellent dip for raw vegetables, in the manner of the Italian *bagna cauda*.

Relishes

Relishes came into their own in the Victorian middle-class dining room. Abstemiousness had become a virtue – no longer was the Englishman's favourite spit-roasted haunch to be hacked to the bone at one sitting. Good manners dictated that there should be meat left over from the roasts which were the centrepiece of the family meal. Something had to be done to add interest to the cold cuts of the next day. Relishes and chutneys, based on the Indian style of eating enjoyed by the Queen Empress's subjects on the sub-continent, provided the perfect answer.

Pumpkin Relish

Autumn-ripening pumpkins keep well if stored in a cool larder, without recourse to salting or pickling devices. In my own centrally heated kitchen I find October to March is the limit. After that they fall off the dresser in a mushy heap. This relish, recommended by the Women's Institute in wartime, has a fine flavour and pretty colour. A paler pickle can be made with marrow instead.

. . . .

QUANTITY

Makes approximately
  5 lb/ 2.5kg relish

TIME

Preparation: 30 minutes
Cooking: intermittent
  attention for 1½ hours

3 lb/1.5kg pumpkin
  (prepared weight)
1 lb/500g brown sugar
1 glass water
1 level tablespoon salt
1 lb/500g apples
1 tablespoon powdered
  ginger
1½ lb/750g onions
½ teaspoon powdered
  cloves
4 oz/100g stoned raisins
1 pint/600ml malt
  vinegar

UTENSILS

A large preserving pan,
  and storage jars

Peel and scoop out the fibre and seeds from the pumpkin. Dice the beautiful orange flesh. Put the pieces in a large preserving pan with the water. Lid, bring to the boil, and stew for 10 minutes until the pumpkin pieces are soft. Remove the lid and evaporate any extra liquid. Take the pan off the heat and mash up the pumpkin.

Meanwhile, peel, core and finely chop the apples. Peel and finely chop the onions. Add the apples and onions, raisins, sugar, salt and spices to the cooked pumpkin in the pan. Pour in the vinegar. Cook all together gently for an hour until the mixture is thick and soft. Pot in sterilized jars and seal. Ready in a week, it keeps all winter.

SUGGESTIONS

Stir a spoonful into a winter vegetable soup.

Use it to thicken and spice the juices of cooked minced meat for a shepherd's pie.

Add a spoonful to an oxtail stew or steak-and-kidney pie.

Spiced Elderberry Relish

This is a fine sharp little Bavarian relish for cold meat. Like most such preparations, it was made with the gleanings of autumn hedgerows and orchards.

· ·

QUANTITY

Makes about 3 lb/1.5kg
relish

TIME

Start 1-2 hours before
Preparation: 40-50
minutes
Cooking: 30 minutes

1 lb/500g elderberries
1 lb/500g plums
1 lb/500g brown sugar
1 short stick cinnamon
1 lb/500g pears

UTENSILS

A bowl, a large saucepan,
a sieve, and storage jars

De-stem the elderberries and put them in a bowl. Crush them with the sugar and leave them to form a juice for an hour or two. Peel, core and chop the pears. Stone the plums.

Push the elderberry juice through a sieve into the saucepan and add the rest of the fruit, and the cinnamon stick. Stew all together for 30 minutes. Pot and seal.

SUGGESTIONS

Have the relish with grilled cheese on toast.

ELDERBERRY SOUFFLÉS (*cassolettes de sureaux*)_____To make these, stir 2 spoonfuls of the relish into the yolks of 2 eggs. Then fold in the stiffly whisked whites of the eggs. Spoon into 2 individual buttered soufflé dishes – don't fill them right to the top. Bake at 325°F/170°C/ Gas 3 for 10-12 minutes. Dust with icing sugar. Serve with cream or a sauce of melted spiced rowan jelly (see next recipe).

Mix with apple sauce (see page 70) and use as a pie or tart filling.

Spiced Rowan Jelly

The beautiful silvery-leaved rowan or mountain ash is very common in the Highlands of Scotland. Its clusters of berries ripen to luminous scarlet in the autumn. The berries look poisonous, but from them can be made a delicious bitter-flavoured jelly which provides the perfect accompaniment to game – particularly venison. The Highlanders themselves do not think much of the preparation, reckoning it a southerner's taste.

QUANTITY
Makes about 8 lb/3.5kg jelly

TIME
Start the day before
Preparation: 15 minutes
Cooking: about 40 minutes

4 lb/2kg rowan berries
1 stick cinnamon
2 lb/1kg sour apples *or* crab apples
approximately 6 lb/2.75kg preserving sugar
3-4 pints/2-2.5 litres water
6 cloves

UTENSILS
A large enamelled saucepan, either an upturned stool with a teacloth pinned to it and a bowl beneath to catch the juice *or* a pair of clean old nylon stockings *or* tights, and sterilized storage jars

Wash and pick over the berries. Put them in the saucepan.

Wash and roughly chop the apples and pour in enough cold water to cover all the fruit. Add the cloves and cinnamon, bring the mixture to the boil gently, turn down the heat and leave to simmer until the fruit is quite soft – about 20 minutes.

Tip all into the clean cloth pinned to the upturned stool. Leave overnight for the juice to drip into the bowl. The stocking method is almost simpler: find a hook from which you can suspend the stocking over a bowl, tip the contents of the pan carefully into the stocking and hang it up to drip overnight.

The next day, measure the quantity of ruby juice back into the preserving pan, and add 1 lb/500g sugar for each pint/600ml of juice. Bring back to the boil and turn down to simmer for 20 minutes. Test for set with a drop on a cold saucer. It should form a skin – obvious when pushed back with your finger.

Pot in sterilized jars and seal down when quite cool. A circle of greaseproof paper dipped in brandy placed on the surface of the jelly will keep mould from forming. If mould does form nevertheless, let it alone until you want to use the jelly, then lift off the whole little blue-green cap in one piece. The jelly should be perfectly good underneath.

SUGGESTIONS

Stir a spoonful of the jelly into a glass of cold water for a refreshing summer drink. Or make a hot winter toddy with a spoonful dissolved in a mug of hot water, spiked with a clove and a measure of whisky to keep out the cold.

Spread as the filling in a sponge cake, with a layer of whipped cream.

Use the jelly as the basis for a **CUMBERLAND SAUCE** to serve with a roast grouse or any wild game (it's good with cold ham and salt beef too). Redcurrant jelly is the more usual ingredient, but rowan jelly makes a superb sauce: you will need 4 tablespoons jelly, the finely pared rind of 1 orange and 1 lemon and a small glass of port. Cut the orange and lemon rind into very fine strips and simmer them in the port and jelly for 10 minutes or so, until the rind is soft. Serve the sauce cool.

Apple Sauce

The traditional accompaniment to roast pork, apple sauce does wonders, too, for bangers-and-mash. Pigs have a natural affinity with orchards in any event. In the days when the responsible English rural household kept its quota of domestic beasts, autumn saw the inhabitants of the stye turned loose to glean in the apple orchard.

QUANTITY
Makes about 5 lb/2.5kg
   sauce

TIME
Preparation: 40 minutes
Cooking: 40 minutes

6 lb/2.75kg well-
   flavoured apples
1 lb/500g sugar
½ pint/300ml water

UTENSILS
A preserving pan, a sieve
   and sterilized storage
   jars

Peel, core and quarter the apples. Put them in a preserving pan with the water and sugar. Lid and stew them gently on a low heat until the fruit is pulpy (20 minutes). Push the pulp through a nylon sieve. Return it to the pan and bring it back to the boil. Pour the pulp into hot, scalded, preserving jars. Stand the jars in a tray of boiling water and put them into a hot oven for 15 minutes. The contents should be at boiling point for 5 minutes to sterilize the fruit (this can be done on top of the cooker, but you will need a double floor to the boiling pot).

Keep in a dark cool place or in the fridge. The sauce will be good for 4-5 months.

SUGGESTIONS

APPLE EGGY-BREAD____Beat up a small egg with 2 tablespoons milk and a teaspoon sugar. Soak 2 slices of white bread in the mixture. Sandwich the slices with a tablespoonful of apple sauce. Serves 1.

WITCH'S CLOUD____This is a favourite with the children of Eastern Europe. Whisk a white of egg until light and fluffy (stop before it goes grainy). Whisk in 1 tablespoon castor sugar and fold in 4 tablespoons apple sauce. Whisk in the juice of ½ lemon. Serve with a crisp biscuit. For grownups, a small glass of Calvados or any apple brandy can be added with the lemon juice. Serves 1.

APPLE SAUCE CAKE____Take 12 oz/350g sugar, 6 oz/175g butter or lard, 1 lb/500g apple sauce, 1 lb/500g self-raising flour, 1 teaspoon ground cloves, 1 teaspoon ground cinnamon. Cream the sugar and the butter or lard until light and fluffy. Sieve the flour with the spices and fold it into the mixture, alternating with spoonfuls of apple sauce. Bake at 250°F/ 180°C/Gas 4 for 45-50 minutes, until well-risen and brown. Delicious served warm with cream. Serves 6.

Conserved Cranberries

The Scandinavians are the berry experts of Europe, and their woods and bogs all through the short summer are carpeted with the dark leaves of the mountain cranberry – also known in Britain as the ligonberry, the whortleberry and a host of local variations. Along with their blueberries, Arctic bramble and raspberries and, most valued of all, the succulent golden cloudberry, they form a valuable source of vitamin C in the winter. In pre-freezer days, barrels of berries stood in the corner of every Scandinavian larder for use throughout the winter. This method preserves the fresh flavour and brilliant colour of the summer fruit.

QUANTITY

Makes about 6 lb/2.75kg
preserve

TIME

Preparation: 20 minutes

4 lb/2kg cranberries
or blueberries or
cloudberries
2 lb/1 kg granulated or
preserving sugar

UTENSILS

A large bowl and a
storage crock or jar

Pick over the berries and discard any which are bruised (the Americans check theirs by bouncing them – a ripe cranberry, whose little air pockets for seeds are well developed, will bounce at least a foot high).

Put them into a large bowl with the sugar. Work berries and sugar together with your hands until the berries are foamy and the sugar completely dissolved. Pack the sugared berries into a sterilized stoneware or glass jar and cover loosely. Keep them in a cool larder or the refrigerator. They freeze well prepared in this way.

SUGGESTIONS

Preserved cranberries make a good filling for pancakes. Or serve them folded into whipped or soured cream for a delicious little dessert.

Accompany a grilled lamb or pork chop with a spoonful of preserved cranberries – the Scandinavians serve them instead of a vegetable.

Serve a bowlful of the scarlet preserve to accompany cold meats on a buffet – it is particularly good with turkey, ham or tongue. The Scandinavians like it with dried salted lamb and as an accompaniment to Swedish meatballs.

Apricot Chutney

We share with our northern European cousins a taste for fruit sauces with meat (serving apple sauce with pork, redcurrant jelly with lamb, prunes with bacon). The separation of sweet from salt flavours is a relatively recent kitchen prejudice, now being rapidly reversed by modern cooking trends. In the old days, the poor man had one pot in which to cook everything on his one heat source. The rich man did not serve his dishes in a sequence of salt and sweet courses, but heaped the table with the abundance of his larder, and ate in any order he pleased. Peaches or plums can replace the apricots in this recipe.

QUANTITY
Yields about 8 lb/4kg
  chutney

TIME
Start 1¾ hours
Preparation: 25 minutes

3 lb/1.5kg apricots (they
  do not have to be
  perfect – just cut out
  any bad bits)
12 cloves
1 teaspoon white
  peppercorns
3 lb/1.5kg apples
2-3 dried chilli peppers
1 lb/500g onions
1 tablespoon salt
1 lb/500g raisins
2 pints/1.2 litres vinegar
  (malt *or* cider will do)
3 cloves garlic
1 heaped teaspoon
  powdered ginger *or*
  small piece fresh root
2 lb/1kg soft brown sugar

A pestle and mortar, a

Stone the apricots and chop them roughly. Peel and core the apples and chop them too. Peel and chop the onions. Check the raisins for twigs and squeeze out their pips if necessary. Peel and chop the garlic. If you are using fresh ginger, peel it and mince it fine. Pound the cloves, peppercorns and de-seeded peppers in a mortar.

Put all the ingredients except the sugar into a large thick-bottomed pan. Bring all to the boil and simmer for 20 minutes until the fruit and vegetables are soft. Stir in the sugar: it is not added earlier or the solid ingredients will not soften. Bring the mixture back to the boil and cook the chutney gently until it is thick and dark. This will take about an hour. Turn up the heat to evaporate the moisture if the mixture looks too runny. Stir frequently to prevent sticking. If, in spite of all your best efforts, the chutney burns, just tip the whole lot into a new pan, leaving the burnt bits behind; add a little water and carry on.

Pot the mixture in sterilized jars while still warm. Seal and store in a cool dark larder. If you leave chutney in the light the colour fades.

UTENSILS

preserving pan – for chutney, it should be heavy and a good conductor of heat – and sterilized storage jars

Warm 1 tablespoon of the chutney with a splash of sherry or dry white wine to sauce a grilled gammon steak or a slice of ham.

EMPIRE EGGS___Mash 1 tablespoon of chutney and 1 oz/25g butter with the yolks of four hard-boiled eggs. Pile the yolks back into the whites. Cover with a white sauce flavoured with curry powder and another spoonful of chutney. Sprinkle with grated cheese. Grill or heat in the oven until the cheese is brown and bubbling.

Liquidized in the processor with a little water, this chutney makes an excellent sauce for **PEKING DUCK**. If you have made the chutney with plums, it would be almost perfectly Chinese.

Piccalilli

This relish first appeared in print in English in 1769 – born of *pickle* out of *chilli*. As the British expanded their Empire so the colonel's storecupboard filled up with these fiery preparations – as addictive in their fashion as anything that ever came out of the East.

QUANTITY

Makes approximately 8
  lb/4kg pickle

TIME

Start 24 hours before
Preparation: 1 hour
Cooking: 30 minutes

2 lb/1kg vegetable
  marrow
4 oz/100g plain flour
1 cauliflower
3 oz/75g mustard powder
1 lb/500g french beans
1 tablespoon turmeric
1 large cucumber
4 pints/2.5 litres vinegar
2 lb/1kg shallots *or*
  pickling onions
2 tablespoons sugar
8 oz/250g salt
1 teaspoon powdered
  ginger

UTENSILS

A large bowl, a
  preserving pan and
  pickling jars

Peel the vegetables as appropriate (string and chop the beans diagonally) and cut them up into small pieces. Lay the vegetables in a large bowl and submerge all in a brine made of 3 pints/2 litres water and the salt. Cover loosely and leave them for a day and a night.

The following day, drain the vegetables. Mix the flour, the mustard powder and the turmeric with a couple of tablespoons of the vinegar – enough to make a runny paste. Boil up the rest of the vinegar with the sugar and ginger, then allow the liquid to cool. Strain out the spices.

Mix the flour-turmeric-mustard paste into the spiced vinegar and bring all gently back to the boil, stirring as the mixture thickens. Add the vegetables. Cook them in the pickle for 10-15 minutes, until the vegetables are done but still retain a bit of bite. Allow the pickles to cool. Bottle and seal. The piccalilli will be ready in a few days.

SUGGESTIONS

Drain and chop a tablespoon of the pickle and mix it into 4 oz/100g fresh cream or curd cheese. Have it with hot biscuits, raw celery and mulled wine for supper.

Serve with **SIR HARRY LUKE'S HAMBURG STEAKS**___Chop 1 lb/500g braising steak finely with a knife. Work it with the contents of 1 all-pork sausage, a tablespoon of chopped parsley, a tablespoon of chopped raw onion and the yolk of an egg. Form into two flat patties and press lightly in fresh breadcrumbs. Fry in butter, turning once, until the patties are firm and cooked through. Top each pattie with a fried egg with piccalilli on the side.

Piccalilli is excellent with *suppli al telefono* (see page 164).

Green Tomato Chutney

The full crop of tomatoes rarely has a chance to ripen in an English summer. This pickle is the last resort of the gardener confronted with rows of green fruit as the days of autumn draw in. Nevertheless it is well worth making for its own sake. Town dwellers can prepare it with ordinary shop tomatoes, ripe or otherwise.

QUANTITY

Makes about 10 lb/4.5kg chutney

TIME

Start the day before

Preparation: 30 minutes

Cooking: intermittent attention for 3¼ hours

5 lb/2.5kg green tomatoes

1 stick cinnamon

salt

1 teaspoon coriander seeds

2-3 little dried chillis

12 peppercorns

2 pints/1.2 litres malt *or* cider vinegar

8 oz/250g onions

1 lb/500g brown sugar

1 lb/500g apples

UTENSILS

A large dish, a heavy enamelled preserving pan, and sterilized storage jars

Pour boiling water over the tomatoes to loosen their skins. Skin and slice them and lay them in a dish in layers, sprinkled with salt. Leave them overnight. Tie the spices into a small muslin bag and put them in the preserving pan with the vinegar. Bring the vinegar to the boil. Take it off the heat, cover and leave overnight to infuse.

The next day add the sugar and the onions, peeled and chopped finely, to the vinegar. Bring all to the boil. Meanwhile drain the tomatoes and chop them. Peel, core and chop the apples. Add tomatoes and apples to the boiling vinegar. Turn down the heat, lid and leave to simmer gently on a mat for 3 hours, stirring regularly. Chutney is a terrible sticker, so scrape the bottom carefully. Don't forget to remove the spice bag when the chutney is cooked.

Allow to cool a little before ladling the mixture into sterilized jars. Seal tightly. Ready to use in a week, it keeps all year.

SUGGESTIONS

Liquidize 2 tablespoonfuls of chutney with 1 tablespoon water as a dip for raw vegetables.

Serve as a relish for kebabs in pita bread – particularly good if you stir in a little chopped fresh coriander.

Stir a generous spoonful of the chutney into a fresh tomato sauce for fishcakes.

Apricot and Walnut Chutney

This is a delicious chutney, and very easy to make with fresh or soaked and dried apricots. Good with cold meat or cheese and summer salads.

QUANTITY
Makes about 6 lb/2.75kg

TIME
Start the day before if
   you use dried fruit
Preparation: 30 minutes
Cooking: 1½ hours

3 lb/1.5kg apricots *or* 1
   lb/500g dried apricots
1 lb/500g light brown
   sugar
8 oz/250g sultanas
1 lb/500g onions, peeled
   and chopped finely
2 teaspoons salt
1 teaspoon English
   mustard
1½ pints/1 litre cider
   vinegar
½ teaspoon powdered
   allspice
2 cloves garlic, peeled
   and crushed
8 oz/250g very roughly
   chopped walnuts
rind and juice of 2
   oranges

UTENSILS
A large preserving pan
   and sterilized jars

Split and stone the fresh apricots and chop them roughly. If you are using dried apricots, put them to swell overnight in water.

Boil the chopped onions for a few moments to soften them, otherwise you always seem to get a few hard bits. Drain.

Put all the ingredients except the walnuts into a large preserving pan and bring to the boil. Turn down the heat and cook gently, stirring regularly, for 1½ hours, until the mixture is thick and jammy. Stir in the walnuts. Pot while hot in warm sterilized jars. Seal.

5. Pickles and Conserves

Fresh pickles with a relatively short shelf life are much appreciated in Mediterranean countries. The purpose of the preparation is as much to add flavour through marinading as to conserve – perhaps because seasonal deprivations are not so acute or long-lasting as they are in northern Europe. These pickles are usually served as little appetizers with a glass of wine.

Mushrooms in Herbs and Oil
Manitaria tursi

Manitaria tursi are favourite Greek *orektika*, 'little desirables', sometimes known by the Turkish name of *meze*, with which the Greeks preface their meals.

QUANTITY
Makes approximately 2
   pints/1.2 litres pickle

TIME
Preparation: 20 minutes
Cooking: 30 minutes

2 lb/1kg button
   mushrooms
6 tablespoons wine
   vinegar
2 teaspoons salt
8 peppercorns, crushed
1 lemon
1 teaspoon dried oregano
2 glasses water
1 teaspoon dried thyme
½ pint/300ml olive oil

UTENSILS
1 saucepan and sterilized
   storage jars

Wipe the mushroom caps and trim the stalks. Put them in a shallow pan and sprinkle them with the salt. Squeeze the juice from the lemon. Cover the mushrooms with the lemon juice and water, and bring all gently to the boil. Turn down the heat and leave to simmer for 5 minutes. Drain the mushrooms thoroughly and pack them into sterilized jars to within two fingers'-breadth of the top.

Bring the oil, vinegar, crushed peppercorns and herbs to the boil. Pour the hot liquid over the mushrooms in the jar. Ready to use in a week, it will keep for a month in the refrigerator.

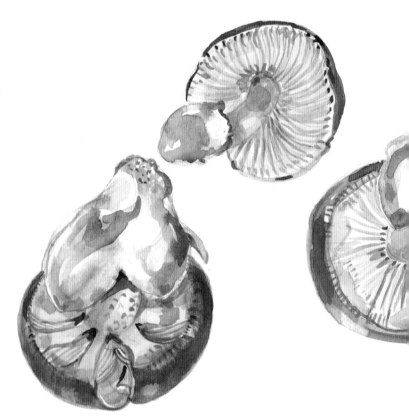

GREEK RAREBIT___To make this you will need 3-4 pickled mushrooms, 1 thick slice fresh bread, 1 tablespoon olive oil, 1 thick slice of a hard cheese – the Greeks would use *kefolotiri* or *kasseri*, but a strong Cheshire or Cheddar will do. Cover the bread with fine slices of pickled mushrooms. Slap the cheese into a hot frying pan with a trickle of oil, and let it fry until the edges are bubbling brown lace. Turn the cheese and fry the other side. Slip the sizzling cheese onto the mushroom bed. Finish with a squeeze of lemon juice. Eat it immediately. (You could grill the cheese, as for a Welsh rarebit, but it wouldn't have the same drama.)

STUFFED PICKLED MUSHROOMS___For these you will need 6 pickled mushrooms, 6 anchovy fillets, 1 tablespoon pitted chopped black olives, 1 tablespoon fresh bread-crumbs, 1 teaspoon chopped parsley. Mix all together and moisten with a tablespoon of the pickling liquor. Stuff the mushrooms with the mixture. Serve with tomatoes sliced and dressed with olive oil and basil.

Serve as part of the *meze*. Arrange pickled mushrooms on a bed of cos lettuce dressed with a trickle of the pickling liquor. Accompany with a few more little dishes: rosy radishes still in a bunch but well rinsed; 2-3 hard-boiled eggs sliced and served with a pickled fish (anchovies or the stiff spiky salt-cured herring the Greeks love); a dish of olives; a tomato, cucumber and onion salad dressed with oil, lemon juice and salt.

Marinated Squid
Calamari in conserva

Both the Greeks and the Italians are very fond of this pickle as an appetizer. Once you get the hang of preparing the oddly shaped creature, squid is the most delicious and rewarding of sea delicacies, particularly prepared with rice. Part of the charm of this particular recipe is the beauty of the mauve-tinged little fish in the jar. Chilli in the pickle complements the natural sweetness of the firm snowy flesh.

QUANTITY
Makes approximately 3
   lb/1.5kg pickle

TIME
Preparation: 20 minutes
Cooking: 30 minutes

2 lb/1kg squid (small to
   medium-sized)
1 pint/600ml white wine
   vinegar
6 tablespoons olive oil
2 cloves garlic, peeled
   and sliced
1 teaspoon salt
1 teaspoon coriander
   seeds
6 peppercorns, crushed
3-4 small dried red
   chillies
1 teaspoon dried
   rosemary *or* a sprig of
   fresh rosemary

UTENSILS
A saucepan and sterilized
   storage jars

Prepare the squid. First wash the fish thoroughly. Pull out the insides and remove the beautiful transparent bone. Discard the soft white innards and upper head with mouth and eyes, but reserve the tentacles and lower body as well as the cap. Scrape off the purplish outer skin – the fresher the fish, the purer white the flesh under the skin. Pay particular attention to the tentacles; they are equipped with marvellous little suction pads which have sharp cuticles – in the larger ones they are rather like toenails and should be scraped off. Slice the cap of the squid into rings, chop up the wings and the tentacles. Warm the oil in a saucepan and put in the cleaned chopped squid. Season with salt, peppercorns and rosemary. Lid and leave to stew gently for 30 minutes, until the squid is tender. Remove from the heat and stir in the vinegar, garlic, coriander and chillies.

The pickle can be made with octopus: the cleaned and scraped tentacles must be vigorously pounded for at least 20 minutes, preferably on a stone surface, although the kitchen table will do. Then cook as for the squid, in its own liquid, until the flesh is tender – it will take about an hour. Do not slice the tentacles into rounds until they are cooked. Bottle and seal and keep in a cool place. Ready after 2 days, it keeps for 2 weeks in the refrigerator.

DRESSED SQUID____Sprinkle the fish with a dressing of its own liquor, plus plenty of chopped fresh parsley and a little chopped garlic. Accompany the dish with a plate of hot chips, bread, quartered lemons and a salad of sliced fennel or celery with cucumber and onion.

SQUID AND HOT POTATOES____You will need 4 oz/100g pickled squid, 1 lb/500g potatoes, 2-3 spring onions or 1 small red onion, parsley, salt and pepper. Peel and slice the potatoes and cook them in boiling salted water, until soft (10-15 minutes). Meanwhile trim or peel the onions and chop them with the parsley. Drain the potatoes and dress them with the onions, parsley, seasoning and 2 tablespoons of the pickling liquor. Pile the squid on top of the hot potatoes. Serve with a green vegetable – young green beans or braised fennel.

RICE AND SQUID SALAD____For 4 you will need 1 lb/500g cooked rice, 6 oz/175g pickled squid, ½ red pepper, ½ small cucumber, 1 small onion, 1 stick celery *or* fennel, 1 tablespoon chopped parsley, salt and pepper. Toss all together and dress with a ladleful of the pickling liquor.

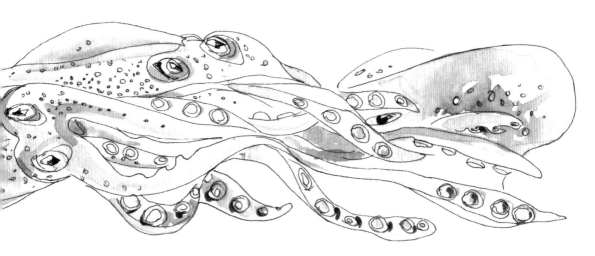

Artichokes with Fennel
Anginaves tursi

Vegetables form an important part of the Greek diet. In rural areas, a knot of excited shoppers forms whenever the travelling greengrocer parks his elderly, wheezing lorry and lets the tailgate down to reveal its contents: crates of scarlet tomatoes, bouquets of spiky mauve-blushed artichokes, firm purple aubergines, carmine-tinged onions, fine fat fennel bulbs, whatever is best of the season. The same pickle mix and method can be used to preserve beans, celery, fennel.

QUANTITY
Makes about 4 pints/2.5
 litres pickle

TIME
Preparation: 20 minutes
Cooking: 30 minutes

3 lb/1.5kg artichokes
1 teaspoon salt
juice of ½ lemon
3 tablespoons chopped
 fennel leaves
½ pint/300ml olive oil
2 bayleaves
1 pint/600ml white wine
 vinegar
2 sprigs thyme

UTENSILS
A large bowl, a saucepan
 and sterilized pickling
 jars

Prepare the artichokes. Cut off the stems (you can discard them or include them as you wish: if the latter, peel off the fibrous outer layer, and chop them into short lengths).

If you are using tender young artichokes, trim off the spikey tops of the leaves (they are a member of the thistle family, so their spines are sharp).

Cut each in half, nick out and discard the little hairy choke at the centre, and put the halves in a bowl of cold water acidulated with the lemon juice, while you prepare the rest. (If you don't do this immediately, the cut surface turns brown and remains brown throughout its pickled life.)

If the artichokes are larger, pull off the outer leaves and trim the rest of the leaves right down until you can see the 'choke. Cut out and discard the hairy centre – a sharp-edged spoon is the easiest instrument. Don't forget to put the cut artichokes into their lemon-and-water bath as you finish preparing them.

Drain the artichokes and transfer them to a roomy pan. Pour in the oil, vinegar and enough water to cover the vegetables. Add the salt and the herbs. Bring to the boil, turn down to simmer, lid tightly and cook for 30 minutes. The artichokes will then be quite tender. Pot and seal down. They will be ready in a day or two.

Stored in a cool larder or in the fridge, the artichokes will be good unopened for 1-2 months. For a pickle with a shorter life (a week in the refrigerator), replace the vinegar with the juice of 2 lemons.

Pickled artichokes are easily prepared as *stuffed artichokes*. Fill the cups with lightly cooked fresh green peas or young broad beans. This makes a delicious accompaniment to scrambled eggs or an omelette.

ARTICHOKE AND POTATO SALAD___To make this as a main dish for two, you will need: 4 pickled artichokes, 2 large potatoes or 8 oz/250g new potatoes, 2 eggs, 1 small green pepper, 2-3 spring onions, 1 tablespoon black olives. Slice the artichokes. Scrub the potatoes and boil them in salted water until tender (20 minutes). Add the eggs (still in the shell) to the simmering water 6-7 minutes before the potatoes are done – this is the lazy cook's way of hard-boiling eggs and saves on the washing-up. Meanwhile, seed and chop the pepper, trim and chop the onions. Roughly dice the potatoes (new ones need only be halved). Dress the potatoes with a ladleful of the pickling liquid. Peel the eggs, slice them thickly and toss them with the potatoes, the green pepper, onions and black olives. Taste and add salt and pepper, and extra pickling liquid if necessary. You could include anchovies and tunafish for a special treat.

Serve the artichokes sliced and sprinkled with more chopped fennel leaves and chopped parsley, flanked with lemon quarters, as part of the *orektiki* or *meze* – bearing in mind that enough of these little dishes of cold and hot appetizers makes a feast. Basic accompaniments are plenty of good bread, radishes, and perhaps a few Greek pickled olives, with a glass of ouzo and a glass of water to get the meal off to a good start.

Garlic-pickled Mushrooms

Funghi in conserva

The Italians find *funghi in conserva* a useful standby for an *antipasto*, when prepared with their favourite fungi, porcini (*boletus edulis*), which are wild-gathered and sold in the markets in autumn. Other varieties are available in spring and summer. To the Italian housewife, whose post-market snack in northern districts is a sliver cut off a huge side of whole roasted pig, the rounded domes of the shiny brown mushrooms look like little roast piglets, so they are known as *porcini*.

QUANTITY
Makes 4-5 pints/2.5-3
   litres

TIME
Preparation: 20 minutes
Cooking: 1 hour

4 lb/2kg penny bun
   boletus
4 cloves garlic, peeled
   and quartered
2 pints/1.2 litres wine
   vinegar
2 tablespoons dried
   oregano
1 pint/600ml water
2-3 blades mace
4 oz/100g salt

UTENSILS
A saucepan, a baking
   tray and sterilized
   storage jars

Cut the stems off the mushrooms level with the caps. Wipe the tops clean with a cloth dipped in vinegar – this rinses off the stickiness of the cap.

Make a brine with the rest of the vinegar, the water and salt, and bring it to the boil. Then pack the mushrooms into clean sterilized jars, layering in the garlic, oregano and mace.

Fill up the jars with enough hot brine thoroughly to sub-merge the mushrooms. Stand the jars in a baking tray full of boiling water and bake them in a low oven, 300°F/150°C/Gas 2 for an hour.

Ready to eat straight from the jar in 2 days, these mush-rooms can be stored in a cool place for 6 months – which should see you round to the next mushroom season.

CROSTINI CON PORCINI——As a supper for one, you will need 1 slice of good bread, 2 tablespoons olive oil, 2-3 chicken livers, ½ teaspoon chopped parsley, ½ clove chopped garlic and a pickled penny bun. Sprinkle the bread with a little oil, and toast it on both sides in the oven or under the grill. Clean the chicken livers and sauté them lightly in the olive oil. When they are stiff but still pink, remove them and put in the parsley, garlic and sliced penny buns. Turn all for a moment in the hot oil. Remove from the heat. Chop the chicken liver and add it to the mixture. Spread it on the *crostini* toast. A little salad and a glass of red wine will complete the pleasure.

PASTA AND PORCINI SALAD——For two, you will need 4 oz/100g short-cut pasta (*farfalle* or *conchiglie*), 3 tablespoons olive oil, 1 tablespoon wine vinegar, 2-3 preserved penny buns (chopped), 1 heaped tablespoon chopped fresh herbs (parsley/oregano/marjoram), 1 finely chopped clove garlic. Cook the pasta as usual. Drain and toss the pasta with the rest of the ingredients. Add salt and freshly-milled pepper to taste.

Preserved boletus make an excellent appetizer on their own. Or dress the mushrooms with a trickle of olive oil and a few capers – a very Italian seasoning – and accompany them with slices of *prosciutto*, bread (no Italian meal is complete without bread), a bunch of radishes and a tomato salad dressed with basil, olive oil and black pepper.

Larder Stores

The products of summer are still preserved for winter in many rural households throughout Europe. If you grow your own vegetables and fruit, pickling and preserving is an exciting alternative to freezing – enabling the creative cook to lay the foundation for a repertoire of quickly-prepared light meals and first courses. For city dwellers, there is always a good moment to take advantage of seasonal plenty, choosing the best when it is cheapest, and ensuring that larder stores are of the highest possible quality and contain the minimum of unwelcome additives.

Store pickles in a cool, dry place away from direct sunlight. An old-fashioned larder is ideal. Trust your eyes and nose – they will tell you whether the stores are good.

Bottling for the Larder

There are a few rules to be followed when bottling and sterilizing for the larder.

You should have a large, lidded sterilizing pan with a double base, in which the jars can be totally immersed in simmering water. A thermometer is a great help.

Use kilner-type jars which can be closed under pressure.

Make sure the pickling jars are not chipped or cracked.

Use new rubber rings each time.

Sterilize everything in boiling water just before you use it.

Only use the most perfect fruit and vegetables, and take great care in the cleaning and preparation of the raw materials. It is important to follow the directions, and not to cut short the sterilizing time. Calculate the timing from the moment the simmering water reaches the correct temperature.

Don't fill the jars right to the top. Leave 1 in/2.5cm space for the contents to expand in the heat.

Wrap the jars in cloth or newspaper so that they do not bump against each other during boiling.

Conserved Tomatoes

This is probably the most useful item in any storecupboard, invaluable for thickening and flavouring stews and soups and as the basis for sauces. Make it in August and September when home-grown tomatoes are in full season.

QUANTITY

Fills 1¾-pint/1-litre jars

TIME

Preparation: 15 minutes
Cooking: 30 minutes

4 lb/2kg tomatoes
2 bayleaves
4 peeled cloves garlic
1 tablespoon salt
8 oz/250g fresh shallots
2 tablespoons sugar
1 sprig thyme
1 teaspoon crushed white
  peppercorns

UTENSILS

Sterilized storage jars
  and a bain-marie

Scald and slip the tomatoes out of their skins. Skin the shallots and halve them if they are large. Pack all the ingredients into sterilized kilner jars. Seal and sterilize the jars, submerged in simmering water at 85°C, for 30 minutes.

SUGGESTIONS

Put a ladleful of the conserved tomatoes in the food processor with a tablespoon of olive oil and liquidize. Heat gently, stir in a pinch of chilli pepper, and use as a sauce for fried eggs and rice.

Use a ladleful as a topping for pizza (drain excess liquid first). Finish with grated cheese, anchovies and olives. Bake as usual.

Use as a sauce for pasta. Either just process the tomatoes with a little olive oil, or add to a *sofrito* made from a chopped onion, chopped carrot, chopped celery stick, a few chopped herbs (parsley, rosemary, sage), and minced meat, gently fried in olive oil. Stir in the tomatoes last and bubble up.

Conserved Flageolets or Haricots

Flageolet beans are small, pale-green members of the haricot family – all of whom are native to the Americas. They have a particularly delicate flavour and in France are eaten fresh when in season in June and July. The beans are usually conserved fresh, when the preliminary soaking is not necessary, and white haricot beans can be prepared in the same way as these flageolets. Both are useful larder stocks: the beans can be used straight from the jar, cutting out the long soaking and cooking previously completed.

QUANTITY

Fills 4 large (1¾-pint/1-litre) jars

TIME

Start 2 hours ahead
Cooking and sterilizing: 3 hours

4 lb/2kg beans
8 sage leaves
water
brine made with 1 oz/25g salt per quart/1 litre boiled water
8 oz/250g shallots *or* pickling onions
8 cloves

UTENSILS

A large saucepan and sterilized storage jars

Put the beans to soak in water for 2 hours. Drain and put them in a saucepan with the skinned shallots or pickling onions. Cover with fresh water to a depth of 2 fingers, and bring to the boil. Simmer for 1 hour, then drain.

Fill the sterilized kilner-type jars with the drained beans. Tuck 2 cloves and 2 sage leaves into each jar. Fill up with cold brine. Seal and sterilize the jars, submerged in simmering water at 100°C, for 2 hours.

SUGGESTIONS

Heat and serve the flageolets in traditional style with roast lamb (stir the cooking juices into the beans – particularly delicious if you have used garlic and herbs to season the meat).

Drain and toss a salad of flageolets with chopped onion, chopped tomato, chopped hard-boiled egg and chopped savory (the bean-herb in France). Dress with olive oil, wine vinegar, salt and freshly milled black pepper.

FLAGEOLET SOUP____Purée ½ pint/300ml of the beans with their own liquid and a dash of milk in the liquidizer. Add salt and pepper. Serve hot or cold, garnished with chopped spring onion or chives.

Conserved Peas

Petits pois en conserve

French housewives prefer *petits pois en conserve* to fresh peas. The flavour is quite different from that of the fresh vegetable – sweet and soft. The French find the British habit of cooking peas with mint very odd indeed. Prepare the peas young and tender in their high season.

QUANTITY

Makes approximately 4
   pints/2.5 litres

TIME

Preparation: 10 minutes
Cooking: 2 hours

3 lb/1.5kg shelled peas
2 teaspoons salt
approximately 1¾ pints/1
   litre water
2 teaspoons sugar

UTENSILS

Sterilized kilner-type jars
   and a bain marie

Fill the sterilized jars with the peas. Pour in enough water to submerge them (allow a finger's width of liquid at the top). Add the salt and sugar. Seal down and sterilize the jars, submerged in simmering water at 85°C, for 2 hours.

SUGGESTIONS

Cook a serving *en cocotte*, in a little ovenproof dish with 2 eggs and a spoonful of soured cream and a sprinkle of chopped fennel.

PEA SOUP____Put 1 pint/600ml of peas and their liquid in the food processor and liquidize. Stir in a knob of butter, a sprinkle of chopped savory, and serve with piping hot croutons fried in butter. Enough for 2.

Convert them into PETITS POIS À LA FRANÇAISE. Put 1 lb/500g peas in a saucepan with a ladleful of their own liquor. Add the shredded leaves of a small lettuce and an onion chopped fine. Lid and simmer for 10 minutes. Add salt and pepper, chopped parsley and chervil, and a small knob of cold butter worked to a paste with 1 teaspoon flour. Simmer for another 5 minutes to thicken the juices. Serve them French-style with rare-grilled lamb chops or steak and chips. Serves 4.

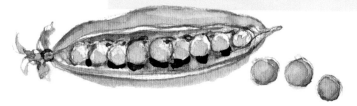

Bottled Asparagus

Asperges en conserve

The Traverse family of Villes-sur-Auzon in upper Provence replanted their hillsides with asparagus as a cash-crop to replace the olive trees killed in the hard winter of 1956. The terraced fields of Mont Ventoux are now well-established with mature crowns. In the asparagus season of May and June there are no Sundays or Bank Holidays for the family. The blanched shoots which the German market prefers grow with miraculous rapidity overnight, and will be spoilt by green tips if they are allowed to emerge from their sandy beds. Early every morning the night's crop is gathered with a special long-handled knife which can be thrust deep into the earthed-up crowns.

The business of washing, trimming, guillotining and bundling the asparagus takes the family the rest of the morning. The fat white spears have to be perfect if they are to fetch a good price from the German wholesaler. The British like their asparagus green, while the French housewife prefers hers tipped with the violet blush which appears on the young spears when they raise their heads into the Provençal sun.

When the wholesalers' prices dip too low in the high season, Madame Traverse conserves some of the crop as her own supplies for the winter.

QUANTITY

Fills about 4 1¾-pint/1-
   litre jars

TIME

Preparation: 30 minutes
Cooking: 1½ hours

4 lb/2kg short spears
   freshly-picked
approximately 4 pints/2.5
   litres water
white asparagus, peeled
4 oz/100g salt

UTENSILS

A saucepan, a bain marie
   and tall, sterilized
   storage jars

Blanch the carefully peeled fresh stalks for 10 minutes in sufficient boiling water to come just below the heads. Drain and rinse in cold water.

Bring 4 pints/2.5 litres of water to the boil with the salt, then leave this brine to cool.

Arrange the asparagus neatly, heads upwards, in sterilized jars. Cover them with brine. Seal and sterilize in a bain marie for 1½ hours at 100°C. Leave to cool. Store and use as required – this asparagus is particularly good in a cream sauce made to Madame Traverse's recipe (pages 170-171).

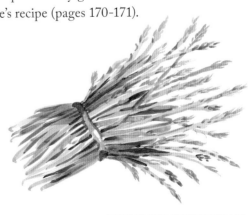

Baked Beans

The haricot bean came late to the European larder, being a native of Central America. Until Columbus had his great adventure, *fava* (broad) beans were the central ingredient in the *cassoulets* and *cocidos* of France and Spain. Europe has a relatively poor bean vocabulary, whereas there are hundreds of varieties of *Phaseolus vulgaris* on sale in any Mexican market: speckled or freckled, purple or green, yellow or red, white for pork, black for refrying. There is a bean for every occasion and every climate. The lima or butter bean was taken to Africa by returning slaves and it is now a major food source on that continent. Any dried beans can be prepared as in the following recipe.

QUANTITY

Fills 3 1¾ -pint/1-litre
  jars

TIME

Start 2 hours ahead
Preparation: 30 minutes
Cooking: 3 hours

4 lb/2kg dried haricot
  beans
cold water
4 cloves
2 lb/1kg fresh tomatoes
1 large sprig each thyme,
  parsley, and a bay leaf,
  tied in a bunch
2 onions
2 cloves garlic
boiling water
2 oz/50g butter
salt and pepper

UTENSILS

A soaking bowl, a large
  saucepan and sterilized
  kilner-type jars

Put the beans to soak in cold fresh water for 2 hours, then drain them. Scald and skin the tomatoes and chop them roughly. Peel the onions. Peel and finely chop the garlic.

Melt the butter in a large pan. Put in the onions and garlic and fry them gently until soft and golden. Add the soaked beans, chopped tomatoes, cloves and the bunch of herbs. Pour in enough boiling water to cover the beans to a depth of two fingers. Bring all to the boil, turn down the heat and simmer gently for 1½ hours. Remove the onions and the bunch of herbs. Taste and add salt and pepper.

Transfer the beans and their sauce to the jars. Sterilize them, submerged in simmering water at 110°C, for 1½ hours.

SUGGESTIONS

Have the beans on toast with crisp bacon on top.

To serve two, heat up 8 oz/250g beans with sliced frankfurters. Stir in, just before serving, a knob of butter and a clove of garlic chopped with parsley.

Make an instant CASSOULET by layering the beans with slices of all-pork sausage and pork steaks fried, if possible, in the fat from a piece of preserved or grilled goose or duck (which you also include). Top with fried breadcrumbs and garlic minced with parsley. Bake for 20-30 minutes in a moderate oven, 350°F/180°C/Gas 4.

Bottled Snails

If you collect your own livestock (and there can be few better ways of turning garden pest-control to your own advantage), starve the snails for two weeks in a clean container which allows air to circulate. Or feed them up on whatever delicious goodies you would like to flavour them with. The Spanish favour pennyroyal; the Romans recommended beefsteak and milk; I prefer bolted lettuce and mint. Clean them out every day – they make a lot of mess.

QUANTITY
Yields approximately 4
    pints/2.5 litres

TIME
Preparation: 30 minutes
Cooking: 3½ hours

100 snails
1 tablespoon salt
2 carrots, scrubbed and
    sliced
1¾ pints/1 litre water
2 onions, skinned and
    sliced
6 peppercorns

To de-froth
2 bayleaves
1 tablespoon vinegar

UTENSILS
A large saucepan,
    sterilized kilner jars
    and a bain marie

Wash the snails in several changes of cold running water, scrubbing the shells thoroughly.

When the snails are clean, put them in a large pan with enough water to cover them. Add the rest of the ingredients. Bring gently to the boil. Skim off the froth and throw in a tablespoon of vinegar.

Simmer the snails for 1½ hours. Drain, reserving the strained cooking broth. Take the snails from their shells and pinch off the little dark curl of intestine at the end of the body.

Pack the snails into the jars. Seal down and sterilize the jars for 2 hours at 100°C in a bain marie.

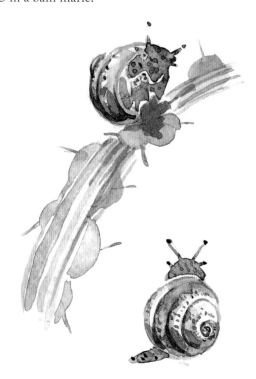

ITALIAN SNAILS——Sauté in a tablespoon of oil: 2 chopped button mushrooms, 1 teaspoon chopped onion, garlic, parsley, a pinch of rosemary, salt and pepper. Add 1 dozen prepared snails. Lid and simmer for 10 minutes. Stir in 1 tablespoon fresh breadcrumbs and 1 tablespoon chopped parsley. Top with a few slivered toasted almonds. Enough for 1-2.

SOMERSET SNAILS WITH CIDER——Drain 2 dozen snails. Make a white sauce with 1 large glass of cider and ½ pint/300ml snail broth or water brought to the boil and thickened with 1 tablespoon butter worked to a paste with 1 tablespoon flour. Stir in 1 chopped sage leaf, ½ teaspoon English mustard, 1 tablespoon double cream and a heaped tablespoon grated cheddar cheese. Bubble up and add pepper and salt and the snails. Lid and simmer for 5 minutes. Stir in 1 tablespoon chopped parsley and spread in a shallow gratin dish. Top with more grated cheese and gild under the grill. Enough for 2-3.

SPANISH SNAILS WITH TOMATO AND CHILLI——Drain 3-4 dozen snails. Sauté them in 3 tablespoons olive oil, 2 oz/50g chopped raw ham or bacon, 2 cloves garlic chopped with 1 onion, 1 chopped and de-seeded green chilli. Stir in 1 lb/500g chopped ripe tomatoes and bubble up. Splash in 1 glass red wine. Bubble up and stir in the snails. Simmer uncovered for 10 minutes, until the sauce is thick. Add salt and pepper and stir in 1 heaped tablespoon chopped parsley. Serves 4-6.

Salted Green Beans

Salting green beans gives infinitely better results than freezing them. If you grow your own you will know that they are all ready at once, so preservation is then the only answer. Even in the shops they become magnificently cheap in their season. Prepare them from July to September. Dwarf, French or Scarlet Runner beans all take kindly to the treatment. These instructions come from *The Country Housewife's Handbook*, an excellent little wartime WI publication which was reprinted three times from 1939-43.

QUANTITY
Makes 3 lb/1.5kg

TIME
Preparation: 1 hour

3 lb/1.5kg green beans
1 lb/500g
salt

UTENSILS
You will need an
    unglazed crock *or* jar
    and a heavy plate

Wash the beans, dry them, top and tail them, string them and slice into lengths if they are large. Put a layer of salt a finger-width deep in the bottom of the crock. Press in a layer of beans, then another layer of salt half a finger-width deep. Press the salt well down on the beans and press down each new layer. Repeat until all the beans are used up.

Finish with a double layer of salt. Cover with cloth or paper and tie it down when the crock is full.

For use, wash the beans thoroughly in hot water, then soak them for 2 hours only in fresh warm water. Strain and cook in the usual way, without salt.

Cook, toss with chopped ham and hard-boiled egg, chopped savory, oil and vinegar and serve as a warm salad.

BEAN GRATIN___Stir 8 oz/250g soaked beans into ½ pint/300ml cheese sauce: to make this, cook 2 tablespoons flour to a froth in 2 oz/50g butter, stir in ½ pint/300ml milk and cook, whisking to avoid lumps, until thick. Stir in 2 tablespoons grated cheese, reheat and add the beans. Cook for another 5 minutes. Taste and add freshly ground pepper. Sprinkle with more grated cheese and brown under the grill. Enough for 2.

SPANISH GREEN BEANS WITH HAM___Fry gently in 2 tablespoons olive oil: 4 oz/100g finely chopped gammon, 2 chopped cloves garlic and 1 chopped onion. Stir in 1 lb/500g ready-soaked beans, 1 glass dry sherry and 1 glass water. Bring to the boil, lid and simmer for 30 minutes. Remove the lid to evaporate excess moisture, stir in 1 tablespoon chopped parsley and marjoram and season with freshly ground pepper. You are not likely to need extra salt. Serves 4.

Salted Cabbage

Sauerkraut

All of northern Europe pickles its cabbage to make sauerkraut and *choucroute*. The salted cabbage accompanies the larderful of salted and smoked bacon, hams and sausages the prudent housewife stores away for winter. A German friend, a farmer's son from near Salzburg and still in his early twenties in 1988, can well remember his father donning a special pair of home-knitted white woolly socks in order to trample the freshly salted sauerkraut. There was always, he says, a flitch of bacon smoking in the chimney, and out on the lintel of the hay barn you can still see the twin hooks which were used to stretch the pig for gutting.

QUANTITY
Makes 20 lb/9kg

TIME
Start 1 month ahead
Preparation: 30-40
   minutes

20 lb/9kg white cabbage
1 tablespoon peppercorns
1 lb/500g salt
6 bayleaves

Remove any imperfect outside leaves and slice the cabbage as finely as possible. Put a layer of cabbage into the storage jar. Salt it and press it down. Continue, adding peppercorns and bayleaves at intervals, until all are used up and the jar is full to within a finger's breadth of the top. Press well down. Cover with a clean cloth and the weighted plate. Store in a cool larder. The sauerkraut will be ready in a month.

Sift it with your hands to avoid lumps when you reheat it. If the sauerkraut is good and sweet (trust your nose), do not rinse it – if it is very salty, at the end of winter, rinse it through in cold water before using it.

UTENSILS

There is a special sauerkraut-slicing utensil available in countries where housewives salt their own. It looks like a small wooden guillotine with a pair of fixed blades set diagonally across. For use, the instrument is straddled across a bucket or barrel and the cabbage, held in a square wooden frame, is grated across the blades. This produces very finely sliced cabbage. The job can of course be done by hand with a knife.

You will also need a large sterilized earthenware storage jar, a clean cloth and a sterilized weighted plate to fit inside the rim.

BULGARIAN SAUERKRAUT SALAD_____Toss a helping of drained sauerkraut with a handful of shredded lettuce. Grate an apple over the top and dress with a tablespoon of honey mixed with the juice of ½ lemon. Serves 1.

HUNGARIAN HANGOVER SOUP_____Heat 2 ladlefuls of chopped sauerkraut, 1 pint/600ml sauerkraut pickle, mixed half-in-half with plain water, and 4-5 slices boiling sausage. Mix 2 heaped tablespoons soured cream with a teaspoon of flour and a teaspoon of paprika. Stir this in and bubble it up. Soothes 2 hangovers.

Have the German pig-slaughtering meal, made in the evening after the hard work of preparing the household's porkers for the winter hams is over. The workmen tuck into a meal of pickled cabbage warmed in hot stock or water with a bay leaf, juniper berries and cloves to scent it; it is accompanied with fresh homemade pork sausages, grilled, mild German mustard and (most important) long pale strips of freshly grated horseradish.

Pickled Beetroot

Rødbeder

The Danes brew excellent beer, of which the spin-off is good malt vinegar for their pickles. The Tuborg factory dominates Copenhagen and ranks alongside the Little Mermaid and the Tivoli Gardens on the tourist itinerary. These *Rødbeder* are a favourite garnish for the *smørebrod*, the open sandwiches which in Denmark are synonymous with lunch. Prepare the pickle with fresh young roots available from June to October.

. . . .

QUANTITY
Makes 2 lb/1kg

TIME
Preparation: 20 minutes
Cooking: 1½-2 hours

2 lb/1kg young raw
   beetroot
2 heaped tablespoons
   sugar
1 pint/600ml malt
   vinegar
1 teaspoon mustard seed

UTENSILS
A large saucepan and
   sterilized storage jars

Choose whole, firm small roots – they should still be wearing a tuft of fresh leaves. Cut off the stalks quite close to the roots, leaving about ½ in/1cm of stalk attached – this ensures the root is not cut, which would cause it to 'bleed' when boiled. (Cook the leaves as fresh vegetables.)

Cover the roots to a depth of one finger with fresh water. Bring it to the boil, lid and turn down to simmer. The beetroots will be soft in 1½-2 hours – they do take rather a long time.

When they are cool enough, peel them and pack them into sterilized jars. Sprinkle in the sugar and the mustard seed – this keeps the beetroot from going mouldy. Cover with vinegar (you don't need to scald it first). If the beetroots are very large, slice them first. Cover them securely.

The beetroot will be ready to eat in a week and will keep in a cool larder or the refrigerator all year.

Serve, as in Scandinavia, MARINATED HERRING WITH BEETROOT. Mix 1 or 2 diced pickled beetroot with an equal volume of chopped pickled herring and a little chopped onion. Dress with oil and serve with soured cream and crispbread.

BEETROOT SALAD____Drain and slice the pickled beetroot and dress with a trickle of olive oil, plenty of chopped parsley and finely sliced garlic, Spanish-style. Serve as a first course, with cooked and cooled spinach dressed with lemon and oil, green olives and bread.

HOT BEETROOT AND POTATO SALAD_____Serve this with feathered game. For 4 servings you will need 2 lb/1kg potatoes, 2-3 pickled beetroots, 1 heaped tablespoon chopped chives or spring onions, and 3 tablespoons soured cream. Boil the potatoes and slice them while still hot. Dice the beetroot and toss them with the potatoes, the chives or spring onions and the soured cream. Season with salt and freshly milled black pepper. Serve the salad warm.

Pickled Cherries

This is a favourite of M. F. K. Fisher, America's finest food essayist (*The Art of Eating, With Bold Knife and Fork*, and so on). She always has French pickled cherries in her larder, and was planning, when I visited her in the autumn of 1987, on putting up that year's supplies.

QUANTITY
Makes 6-8 pints/3.5-4.5
   litres

TIME
Start 24 hours ahead
Cooking (intermittent
   attention): 30 minutes

4 lb/2kg firm white
   cherries
12 white peppercorns
4 oz/100g sugar
4 cloves
2 pints/1.2 litres white
   wine vinegar
1 short stick cinnamon,
   broken into pieces
1 teaspoon salt

UTENSILS
Sterilized storage jars
   and a saucepan

Pick over the cherries and discard any imperfect ones. Trim the stalks short, but do not remove them. Pack the cherries into sterilized jars and sprinkle with the sugar.

Bring the vinegar, salt and spices to the boil in a saucepan. Boil rapidly for 5 minutes. Remove from the heat and leave the mixture to cool, then pour it into the jars with the cherries. Cover lightly and leave for 24 hours. Drain out the vinegar juices from the bottles, add a glass of fresh vinegar, and reboil for 5 minutes. Let it cool and pour back over the cherries in the jars, making sure all are submerged. Seal and store. They will be ready in a month.

SUGGESTIONS

Have the cherries with a plate of *charcuterie*. Their sweet-sourness complements the rich meat perfectly.

Pit a handful of cherries and incorporate them with a ladleful of their liquor into a sauce for grilled duck or sautéed pigeon breasts – more interesting than raspberry vinegar.

Pickled cherries are used in France as an accompaniment to a *pot-au-feu*. They are excellent with any boiled dinner.

Pickled Cucumbers

Small cucumbers are grown especially for pickling – the very small ones are gherkins and can be pickled by the same method. Watch out for them in the shops in August.

Makes about 4 pints/2.5 litres

Start a day ahead
Cooking: 20 minutes

2 lb/1kg little pickling cucumbers
2 pints/1.2 litres white wine vinegar
4 tablespoons salt
12 peppercorns
2 onions
2-3 sprigs dill *or* fennel leaves

A large dish, a large saucepan, a draining spoon and sterilized storage jars

Rinse the cucumbers and put them in a dish. Sprinkle with the salt and leave overnight.

The next day, drain and dry the cucumbers. Peel and slice the onions. Bring the vinegar to the boil with the spices in a saucepan. Throw in the cucumbers and bring back to the boil. Remove the cucumbers with a draining spoon and transfer them to the sterilized jars, sprinkling in the slices of onion and the dill or fennel as you pack them down. Pour in the warm vinegar, making sure all the cucumbers are submerged. They will be ready in 2 weeks.

SUGGESTIONS

Make a Romanian dressing for new potatoes or a couple of hard-boiled eggs (bring to the boil from cold, remove from heat, leave for 6 minutes and plunge into cold water). Mix a tablespoon of chopped pickled cucumbers with 4 tablespoons soured cream, ½ teaspoon flour and a little chopped dill. Bring all to the boil. Use hot or cold.

Mix a tablespoon of chopped pickled cucumber with cream cheese, paprika and caraway seeds – delicious with good bread.

Make a stuffing for fish – herring, mackerel, trout – with a handful of breadcrumbs, an egg beaten with a little milk, a tablespoon of minced parsley, onion, dill and a tablespoon of chopped pickled cucumber.

Pickled Shallots

Shallots grow in chive-like clumps and until recently were reckoned a separate species from the usual pot-onion. The old instruction, 'plant on the shortest day, lift on the longest' remains good. Although shallots, like their bigger cousins, are now in the shops all year, they are at their best and cheapest in August. They are laborious to peel, but well worth the effort.

QUANTITY
Makes 2 lb/1kg

TIME
Preparation and
  cooking: 30-40
  minutes

2 lb/1kg shallots
2 cloves
2 pints/1.2 litres wine
  vinegar (it can be malt,
  but the flavour will be
  much stronger)
2 bayleaves
6 peppercorns
1 tablespoon salt

UTENSILS
A large saucepan, a
  draining spoon and
  sterilized pickling jars

Skin the shallots. Put the vinegar, cloves, bayleaves, peppercorns and salt in a roomy saucepan and bring all to the boil. Throw in the onions. Bring all back to the boil, and remove the onions with a draining spoon. Let the onions cool.

Pack the onions into sterilized jars and cover them with the now-cooled vinegar. Seal and store. They will be ready in a month.

SUGGESTIONS

Chop 2 pickled shallots finely and mix with yoghurt as a dressing for plain-cooked vegetables.

Stir a tablespoon of finely sliced shallots into a vegetable soup just before you serve it.

Mix a few chopped shallots into mashed potato or fish pie.

Sweet-Pickled Cauliflower

Cavoltiore in agrodolce

This is a favourite Italian pickle for serving as an *antipasto*. Artichokes, trimmed and sliced, can be prepared in the same fashion. Make double quantities of the pickle and do both at the same time – they are in high season in October.

QUANTITY

Makes approximately 3
  lb/1.5kg pickle

TIME

**Preparation and
  cooking:** 30 minutes

1 large cauliflower
  (2 lb/1kg trimmed
  weight)
1 lb/500g sugar
1 tablespoon mustard
  seed
2 oz/50g salt
2 short pieces cinnamon
  bark
1 pint/600ml water
½ teaspoon allspice
8 oz/250g onions
½ teaspoon cloves
1 pint/600ml wine
  vinegar
3 little dried red peppers

UTENSILS

A bowl, a drainer, a
  saucepan and sterilized
  storage jars

Trim the cauliflower and divide it into florets. Blanch the florets in boiling salted water for 5 minutes. Drain them and run cold water through them immediately.

Slice the onions and layer them with the cauliflower into clean sterilized jars.

Heat the vinegar with the sugar and spices, and pour the boiling mixture into the jars. The florets should be submerged. Cover and seal while hot. Ready to eat in a week, the pickle will keep in a cool place all year.

SUGGESTIONS

Make an *oeuf en cocotte*, very lightly cooked with a teaspoon of cream, and serve it on a plate with pickled cauliflower, sticks of cucumber, spring onions, and matchsticks of celery to dip into it.

Toss a few florets with a HARICOT BEAN SALAD dressed with olive oil, some of the pickling liquor, chopped garlic and parsley.

Serve them as part of an *antipasto* with olives and slices of salami.

Vinegar Pickles

All of northern Europe makes these vinegar, salt and water pickles, using spices, herbs, onion and garlic, and sometimes chillies to spice the brine. Wine or cider vinegar gives a gentler flavour than malt, although they can be used interchangeably. The proportions in the liquid can be varied from all water to all vinegar.

. . . .

QUANTITY
Makes 1 gallon/4.5 litres
of pickles

TIME
Start 2 hours ahead
Preparation: 30 minutes

1 teaspoon coriander
seeds
1 small cauliflower
1 teaspoon peppercorns
1 lb/500g young turnips
2-3 small dried chillies
1 lb/500g small pickling
cucumbers
2 pints/1.2 litres white
vinegar (see above)
1 lb/500g green beans
8 oz/250g shallots
2 pints/1.2 litres water
2-3 cloves garlic
2 oz/50g salt
1-2 fronds dill (optional)
1 lb/500g carrots

UTENSILS
A piece of cloth, a large
saucepan and sterilized
storage jars

Tie the spices into a scrap of clean white cloth. Bring the vinegar, the water and the salt, with the pickling spices, to the boil in a large saucepan. Take it off the heat and leave it to infuse for 2 hours.

Meanwhile trim the vegetables into bite-sized pieces: peel and cut the carrots lengthwise into quarters and chop the pieces into short lengths; divide the cauliflower into florets; peel and quarter the turnips; wipe over the small pickling cucumbers, leaving them whole if possible (larger ones should be cut into quarters vertically and chopped into short lengths); top and tail the beans and chop them if necessary; peel the shallots and garlic.

Pack the vegetables, shallots, garlic and dill into large sterilized jars. When the vinegar is infused and cool, pour it over the vegetables. Make sure all the pieces are submerged and push them down to release the air bubbles – oxygen is the enemy of all pickles.

Seal and store. Ready to eat in a month, these pickles will last all winter.

FRANKFURTERS AND HOT SPICED POTATOES____Peel and slice 1 large potato. Put the slices in a lidded saucepan with enough boiling salted water to cover. When the potato is nearly soft, put a pair of frankfurters on top to heat in the steam. Remove the sausages as soon as they have heated through or they will split. Drain the potatoes – they will be delicately flavoured with smoky frankfurter. Chop the vinegar pickles and toss them with the hot potatoes. Accompany with a spoonful of soured cream to sauce the hot salad, and freshly grated horseradish and mild German mustard on the side. Enough for one.

PICKLE-STUFFED TOMATOES____ To make these, chop 2 tablespoons pickled vegetables, turn them in a mild mayonnaise with 2-3 chopped raw button mushrooms and a spoonful of tuna. Use the mixture to stuff hollowed-out tomatoes.

SPICED POTATO SALAD____Drain and chop a ladleful of the pickles and mix into a warm potato salad dressed with chopped dill, oil and salt, or *salad cream* (see page 63). Top with sliced hard-boiled eggs and fine-cut bacon rashers fried crisp.

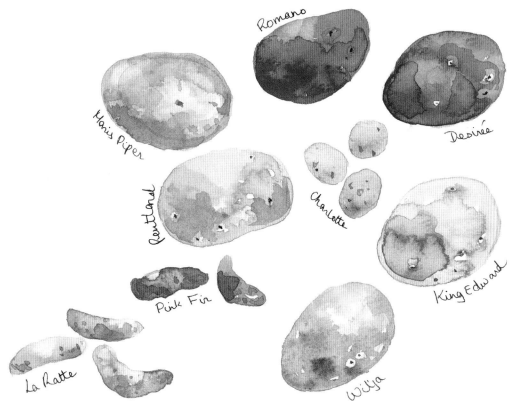

6. Potted Meats and Cheeses

Potted Meats

Potting is the process of sealing meats, fish, poultry, anything perishable, in an earthenware container under a coating of any edible fat. It was a useful method of preserving goods in pre-refrigeration days. It provided an alternative to salt-pickling and produced such delectable results that our modern fish and meat pastes, and preparations like the French *rillettes*, have survived for their own sakes.

Potted delicacies were transported from one end of Elizabethan England to the other without spoiling. Elvers, lampreys, game from the country estates of gentlemen resident in the capital – all would have been expected to remain good for a month at least, allowing two weeks on the road, whatever the weather.

In the seventeenth and eighteenth centuries potted meats and fish became fashionable at grand dinner parties, and no table was well-presented without at least one potted meat among the lighter dishes of the second remove. By the time Eliza Acton published her *Modern Cookery for Private Families* in 1845, the preparations had become sophisticated little pastes, although conservation remained a concern. She instructs that all meats (tender and well-roasted) to be potted must be free of all fat, skin and gristle and thoroughly pounded, not *rent*, before being mixed with, and sealed under, butter. Ham and salt beef will need, she says, more butter than roast meat. Miss Acton recommends mace, nutmeg, cayenne or white pepper as appropriate seasoning for white meats such as fish and poultry breasts, with a few cloves to be added to strong brown meats such as hare.

Potted Partridges, Pigeons, Grouse

Feathered game is excellent for potting. This is a recipe popular during the Second World War, when the country housewife was more likely to be able to come by wild game than any other meat. It is also suitable for rabbit – one little wild rabbit will replace 3 birds. If the birds are in feather, don't bother to pluck them, just take off the skin, feathers and all.

QUANTITY

Makes approximately 2 lb/1kg

TIME

Preparation: 30 minutes
Cooking: About 2 hours

3 old game birds (*or* 1 wild rabbit)
2 bayleaves
1-1½ pints/600-900ml water
1 blade mace *or* a teaspoon of nutmeg
1 teaspoon salt
1 teaspoon Worcestershire sauce (see page 55)
12 white peppercorns
1 sprig fresh thyme *or* 1 teaspoon dried
2 oz/50g lard *or* butter

UTENSILS

A large saucepan and small potting jars

Skin and clean the birds. Put them in a saucepan which will accommodate them neatly. Cover them with the water and add the salt, peppercorns, thyme and bay. Lid and bring to the boil. Turn down the heat and simmer for 1½ hours, until the meat is very soft and falling off the bones. Take the birds out, reserving the stock. Strip the meat from the bones and mince it finely.

Return the bones to the stock in the pan and boil uncovered until the liquid has reduced to ½ pint/300ml. Strain the stock onto the minced meat. Beat in 2 tablespoons softened lard or butter, the mace or nutmeg and Worcester sauce. Taste and add extra seasoning if required. Pot in small jars, leave until cold, and seal with a layer of melted lard or butter. Keep in the refrigerator. It will be good for 2 weeks at least.

SUGGESTIONS

Use, with breadcrumbs, chopped parsley and a beaten egg to stuff a baked marrow.

Potted Chicken

This is a nursery recipe from Northamptonshire, popular in the 1930s and perfect in sandwiches for a picnic or high tea. Miss Acton's seasonings (see the introduction to this chapter) have survived into these later recipes.

....

QUANTITY
Makes about 1½lb/750g

TIME
Preparation: 30 minutes
Cooking: 1-1½ hours

1 medium-sized chicken
1 bay leaf
approximately 1
    pint/300ml water
8 oz/250g butter
1 onion
½ teaspoon grated
    nutmeg
6 cloves
Salt and pepper
6 peppercorns
12 allspice berries

To finish
1 blade mace
1 oz/25g melted butter

UTENSILS
A saucepan and potting
    jars

Joint the chicken and skin it. Put it in a saucepan with enough water to cover, the onion stuck with the cloves, the peppercorns, allspice, mace and bay leaf. Lid, bring to the boil, turn down the heat and cook gently for 1-1½ hours, depending on the age of the fowl. When the meat is tender, take off the lid and boil fiercely to reduce the juices to ½ pint/300ml. Strip the meat off the bones and mince it finely. Strain the juices into the meat. Leave to cool. Soften the butter and beat it into the meat with the nutmeg. Taste and adjust the seasoning. Pot and seal with a layer of melted butter – leave this to settle a little before using, and take care not to pour in the whey as well.

Ready immediately, potted chicken keeps for 2-3 weeks in the refrigerator.

SUGGESTIONS

Stir into a thin white sauce for a delicious chicken soup.

Potted Crab with Cream

This recipe appears in my 1912 edition of Mrs Beeton's *Household Management*, although not in the original 1861 edition. The result is more perishable than earlier butter-pounded mixtures, perhaps because refrigeration was becoming more widely available. The mixture is so richly delicious that I cannot resist including it.

Take care to buy your crabs alive. Check for liveliness by picking up the tail flap to see if it snaps back neatly against the body – the female has a wider tail so that she can protect her eggs, and is considered the better meat. If possible, get the fishmonger to kill the creature for you. Take it home and cook it immediately in heavily salted water – 6 oz/175g salt to 4 pints/2.5 litres water. If the crabs are still alive, I start them in warm water and hold them under for 2 minutes. If you plunge live crabs into boiling water, they throw off all their legs, which is alarming for both perpetrator and (presumably) victim. Bring the water to the boil and boil gently for 15 minutes for the first 1 lb/500g, 10 minutes for each subsequent 1 lb/500g.

QUANTITY

Makes about 2 lb/1kg –
enough for 8 servings

TIME

Preparation and
cooking: about 1 hour

meat from 2 medium
crabs (a 2 lb/1kg
crab yields about 12
oz/350g meat)
3 egg yolks
¼ pint/150ml double
cream
2 oz/50g butter
½ teaspoon salt

Pull the undershell from the crab's carapace. Trim off the feathery grey lungs (dead men's fingers) and then pull off the little horny mouthpiece. Everything else (except the shell of course) is edible. Pick out all the meat from the shell, legs and claws – brown and white together.

Put the butter to melt in a saucepan, and stir in the crab meat and the seasonings. Cook gently, uncovered, for 15 minutes. Meanwhile, lightly whisk the egg yolks with the cream. Stir the cream mixture into the hot crab, and in turn stir this over a very low heat until the mixture thickens – over hot water if that is how you make your custard.

Pot in small earthenware jars and leave to cool. Cover with clarified butter. To clarify, melt the butter and leave the white whey behind when you pour the liquid butter over the potted crab. It keeps for a week in the refrigerator, but no more.

⟶

To finish

1 teaspoon paprika
  pepper
1 oz/25 g clarified butter
  (see page 111)
½ teaspoon cayenne
  pepper

UTENSILS

A saucepan and 4 small
  earthenware jars *or* pots

SUGGESTIONS

Stir a spoonful into a creamy white sauce for an instant crab sauce for fish. Or make CRAB FISHCAKES: beat a spoonful of potted crab into mashed potato beaten with an egg yolk, form into little patties and fry in butter. The mixture is delicious hot.

Potted Cod's Roe

Torskerognkaviar

The Norwegians catch a great deal of cod, particularly during the February-March cod-spawning season off the Lofoten islands. Most of the cod is salted and exported to the Mediterranean as *bacalao* – southerners all have a taste for 'mountain fish'. The fishermen in the old days used to waterproof the heavy leather coats they wore with cod-liver oil – the first oilskins. The Hanseatic merchants with whom they did business, although not themselves the most fastidious of men, reported that the pungent odour from the fishing boats could be detected long before the fleet sailed into Bergen harbour. The various tidbits – roe, tongues, livers (used to sauce fresh cod, and sweet as marrowbone) and cheeks – have always been enjoyed fresh.

This lightly preserved salted roe, *torskerognkaviar*, a modern preparation, has proved so popular throughout Scandinavia that it is now available in tubes for squeezing out directly onto the midday buttered bread. In the winter months, when the cod roes are fine, fat and plentiful, it is easy to make your own.

QUANTITY
Makes 1 lb/500g

TIME
Start 2 days ahead
Preparation: 30 minutes

1 lb/500g cod's roe (it
    should be at least one
    'wing' of roe, preferably
    both)
1 oz/25g sugar
2 tablespoons oil
1 oz/25g salt

UTENSILS
2 china plates, and
    potting jars

Wipe the roe, put it on a china plate, and sprinkle it, still in its membrane, with the salt and sugar, and rub the mixture in gently. Cover with a second plate. Leave the roe in the refrigerator for 2 days. Pour off all the juices and wipe the roe dry.

You can now either cold-smoke it for ½ hour, or prepare it raw. Whichever method you prefer, remove the membrane and mix the roe thoroughly with the oil. Taste it and add more salt if you wish. Pot in small jars, float a film of oil over the surface, and seal down.

The paste will keep for 2 weeks in the refrigerator (3 weeks if the roe has been smoked).

SUGGESTIONS

Potted cod's roe makes excellent fishcakes. Beat a spoonful into a helping of mashed potato. Beat in an egg. Season. Fry spoonfuls in hot butter and oil mixed. Serve with homemade tomato sauce.

French Potted Pork
Rillettes

The charcuteries of France all have their own special recipe for *rillettes* and *rillons*, a seasoned paste of slow-cooked fat pork. The meat for *rillettes* is pounded, whereas that for *rillons* is not. With good fresh bread, this is the best of midday snacks. In Spain the same preparation, unpounded, is coloured with paprika and perfumed with garlic and bay-leaves – it is my favourite Christmas treat.

QUANTITY

Approximately
  1½ lb/750g

TIME

Preparation: 20 minutes
Cooking: 3½ hours

1 lb/500g shoulder pork
  (without skin)
3 oz/75g salt
2 lb/1kg pork fat (not
  kidney)
1 teaspoon freshly milled
  pepper
1 glass white wine

UTENSILS

A heavy shallow pan, a
  wooden spoon, and
  small earthenware pots
  or jars

Cut the pork meat and fat into small dice. Put meat and wine to cook gently in a heavy pan over a very low heat for 3-3½ hours. Keep a careful watch for sticking – stir the pieces regularly with a wooden spoon. When the pork is very well cooked and golden, pour off some of the lard – about 4 tablespoons – and pound the rest up together with the salt and pepper until you have a rich paste. Pot in small earthenware jars and leave to cool. Seal with a layer of the reserved lard, melted. Ready to eat immediately, potted pork keeps for a month in the refrigerator.

Potted Liver
Leverpastej

Potted meat and fish preparations such as this Swedish *leverpastej* are common to northern countries whose climate, until the advent of centrally heated kitchens, allowed lengthy storage in reasonably cold temperatures. The refrigerator and freezer offer the modern alternatives to our grandmother's larder, which had only a wire mesh between it and the outside elements. We owe, in some measure, our highly developed chemical preservatives industry to central heating. This recipe includes anchovy – a neglected seasoning these days, but very popular in Roman times. Scandinavian anchovies belong to a different family from the Mediterranean sort, but they look and taste similar.

QUANTITY
2 lb/1 kg

TIME
Preparation: 30 minutes
Cooking: 2¼ hours

1 lb/500g pork liver
¼ pint/300ml cream
8 oz/250g fat pork belly
  (without the rind)
¼ pint/300ml milk
4 oz/100g flour
1 medium onion
1 teaspoon salt
6 anchovy fillets
1 teaspoon freshly
  ground pepper
3 eggs
1 teaspoon crushed
  allspice

UTENSILS
A sharp knife *or* food
  processor, a bowl and a
  loaf-shaped baking dish

Mince the pork liver and belly with a sharp knife or in the food processor. Peel and chop the onion and the drained anchovies. Mix with the meats. Beat the eggs with the cream or milk and stir them in. Work in the flour, salt and spices.

Pour the mixture (it is quite liquid at this stage) into a greased baking dish and cover with foil. Set the dish in a pan of boiling water and bake it in a low oven 300°F/150°C/Gas 2 for about 2¼ hours, until the 'loaf' feels firm to your finger and a knife-point pushed through the centre comes out clean.

Leave it to cool, tip it out of its dish (unless you want to store it in the same container) and wrap it in foil.

It makes good sandwiches, or an excellent cold meat. The potted liver will keep for 2 weeks in the refrigerator, and freezes adequately, although I find it goes a little grainy when defrosted. Serve it with a sweet relish and pickled cucumbers or onions.

Swedish Liver Pudding with Rice and Raisins

Leverpudding med ris

The Swedes like both their liver sausage and their black pudding made with raisins and sugar and rice – all imported luxury items intermittently available to the Viking-descended sea traders. The division between salt and sweet is far less defined in Scandinavia than it is elsewhere in Europe, and the Swedes came late and enthusiastically to the delights of sugar. I include this recipe, even though it must be reckoned somewhat of an acquired taste for non-Scandinavians, since it much resembles our own culinary tastes in medieval times. English Christmas mincemeat (which once included meat as well as suet) is an annual reminder of this lost preference.

QUANTITY
Makes about 2 lb/1kg

TIME
Preparation: 10 minutes
Cooking intermittently:
   2 hours

4 oz/100g rice
4 oz/100g fat pork belly
½ pint/300ml water
1 large onion
1 pint/600ml milk
2 tablespoons molasses
1 oz/25g raisins
2 teaspoons salt
1 lb/500g calf *or* pork
   liver
freshly milled white
   pepper

Pick over the rice and put it in a large saucepan with the water. Bring the water to the boil, then turn the heat down and leave the rice to simmer until all the water is absorbed. Pour in the milk and bring that to the boil. Turn it down to simmer, cover and leave to cook gently for 20-25 minutes until the rice is soft (stir it every now and again – rice pudding mixtures stick and burn easily).

Put the raisins to soak in a little warm water.

Mince the liver and the pork belly together finely with the peeled and roughly chopped onion. Mix in the raisins, molasses, salt and plenty of pepper. Add the cooked undrained rice and work all well together. Pour the mixture into a loaf tin, put it into a larger roasting tin or baking dish and pour in hot water to come within 3 fingers of the top. Lid the dish with foil. Put it to bake in a medium oven, 350°F/180°C/Gas 4, for 1 hour 10 minutes, until the mixture feels firm to your finger.

Serve the liver pudding hot with preserved cranberries (see page 71) and a jug of melted butter (the most readily available sauce in the dairy farmer's storecupboard). It will keep for a week in a cool larder, longer in the refrigerator, and freezes well. Cut it in slices, fry it and serve with cranberries as for the just-cooked pudding.

A large saucepan, a small bowl, a mincer or food processor, a large bowl, a loaf tin and a large roasting tin

Potted Head-cheese

Pressylta

Swedish *pressylta* is a standby of the serve-yourself *smörgåsbord* which is the favourite Scandinavian way of entertaining. The whole of Europe makes these head-cheeses with that most of awkward of joints, the pig's head. The reward for your trouble is a delicious cold meat, set in its own well-flavoured jelly. The Hanseatic League, a union of Hamburg merchants who controlled Baltic trade in varying degrees from the fourteenth until the nineteenth century, supplied Sweden with her Eastern flavourings. Norway had a thriving trade with the Dutch, and even the smallest harbour town tucked away at the foot of the fjord had a wood-built store whose shopkeeper supplied the rural population with spices. Pepper, allspice, nutmeg, cinnamon and cloves are common seasonings in the Scandinavian kitchen, prized for their ability to lift an otherwise somewhat limited repertoire of ingredients.

QUANTITY

Yields about 2 lb/1kg

TIME

Start a day ahead
Preparation: 30 minutes
Cooking: 4 hours

1 pig's head

To finish
water
2 egg whites
salt
½ teaspoon powdered
  cloves
6 cloves

Have your butcher split and prepare the pig's head. Leave it to soak overnight in a bowl of cold fresh water. Save the brains for a savoury.

The next day, put the head in a large pan and cover it with water, plus ½ teaspoon of salt for every pint/600ml of water used. Add the whole spices.

Bring the water to the boil, then lid the pan and turn the heat right down so that the water is only just moving. Leave the pig's head to simmer for 3-4 hours, until the meat is very soft. Remove the joint from the broth and put aside to cool.

Pour about 2 pints/1.2 litres of the broth into a small saucepan (save the rest for a soup – it will make a wonderful *minestrone*) and boil it rapidly until the volume of liquid is reduced by half – this will give you a good strong jellied stock.

Meanwhile, as soon as the head is cool enough, sort carefully through the skin and bones, and take out the meat and all the edible pieces. Discard the skin and fat, but do not neglect

½ teaspoon ground
   pepper
1 small piece dried
   ginger root
½ teaspoon ground
   allspice
6 allspice berries
6 peppercorns

A large bowl, a large
   saucepan with a lid, a
   small saucepan, and a
   3-pint/2-litre pudding
   basin

the tongue (that will need to be skinned) and the white meat in the cheeks which looks very like fat. Cut the meat into nuggets – you should get at least 1 lb/500g meat off a pig's head – sprinkle in the powdered spices, and arrange the meat neatly in a 3-pint/2-litre pudding basin. Taste and adjust the seasoning of the reduced broth, boil it up again and whisk in the egg whites to clarify the liquid. Strain. Pour enough broth into the basin to submerge the meat.

Cover the head cheese and leave it in a cool place to set. It will keep in the fridge for a week, and freezes beautifully if you want to keep it longer. It is very good in sandwiches, and delicious on its own with mustard and pickled beetroot (see page 100).

You could omit the spices and replace them with *plenty* of chopped parsley. The brawn will not keep so long, but the flavour will be excellent.

Potted Cheese

Potted Cheese with Marc
Concoyottes

The farmers of Burgundy appreciate these pungent little potted cheeses made with rinds and remnants. They are taken with bread and wine as a midday snack.

QUANTITY
Serves 6

TIME
Preparation: 20 minutes

8 oz/250g remnants of
   hard and soft cheeses

To finish
1 oz/25g clarified butter
1 small glass *marc*
a little unsalted butter
   or fresh cream cheese
   (*optional*)

UTENSILS
A food processor *or*
   pestle and mortar
   and small stoneware
   moulds

A mixture of the scrapings and rinds of Brie or Camembert together with a few remnants of hard cheese – Comté, Munster, Beaufort – gives the best results. Grate the hard cheese and then pound it up with the soft cheeses. Work in the *marc* and taste the mixture. If it is really too strong (remembering that this is not a preparation for faint hearts) work in a little unsalted butter or fresh cream cheese. Pot in little moulds (those stoneware ones for individual portions of butter would do fine), and seal with a thin layer of clarified butter. Keep in a cool larder. It gets a little stronger every day. Best eaten within a fortnight.

Potted Cheese with Roquefort

Le Cachat

This is a powerful preparation much appreciated by the shepherds of the sparse mountain pastures of the Causses. Those who live near Roquefort add a little of the local speciality, the monarch of all blue cheeses, to the mixture.

. . . .

QUANTITY

Serves 4

TIME

Start 8-10 days ahead
Preparation: 15 minutes

2 well-drained fresh
  tommes *or* fresh goat's
  cheese
1 tablespoon wine
  vinegar
1 tiny glass *marc, or*
  other white spirit
  (vodka will do)
2 *picodons* – matured
  tommes *or* mature
  goat's cheese
2 oz/50g Roquefort
1 clove garlic
salt and pepper
1 tablespoon chopped
  parsley

UTENSILS

A food processor *or*
  pestle and mortar and
  a storage jar

Pound the cheeses well together in a mortar or food processor. Pack the mixture into a salt-glaze earthenware jar and lid it tightly. Leave the cheeses to ferment together for 8-10 days in a cool larder.

Mix in the rest of the ingredients and add salt and pepper to taste. Serve with thickly sliced toasted country bread (if possible, grilled over a flame so that the bread chars lightly – Mediterranean market stalls sell a purpose-made contraption for gas cookers).

Marinated Goat's Cheese

Tommes á l'huile

Trays of tommes, delicate-flavoured fresh curd cheeses made from rennetted goat's milk, are to be found on sale in all the markets of Provence. The preparation remains largely a home-farm industry, and the seller is often the cheesemaker in person. The tommes are either sold fresh; or prepared with the fragrant local herbs, or parsley and garlic; or they are sold in various stages of maturity with a chalky dry crust, or with a 'flower' of rich dark mould. The composition of the cheese has by law to contain more than 45 per cent fat. The herbs and leaves which have pastured the goats flavour their milk: a seasoned palate in its own home area expects to be able to distinguish between cheeses made from a flock pastured on one or other side of the mountain.

QUANTITY

6 cheeses

TIME

Preparation: 10 minutes

6 well-drained goat's
  cheeses (weighing
  about 2 oz/50g each)
1 teaspoon tarragon
½ teaspoon juniper
  berries
1 heaped teaspoon dried
  savory
1 sprig rosemary
1 teaspoon dried thyme
approximately 3 pints/2
  litres olive oil

UTENSILS

A large sterilized jar
  (rinsed out with brandy
  or any strong spirit)

Drop the savory and thyme into a large jar. Lay in the cheeses, sprinkling in the tarragon and juniper berries as you go. Lay the rosemary branch on top. Pour in the oil to cover – the cheeses must be completely submerged. Cover tightly and store in a cool place.

These cheeses will keep for a long time, and can be replaced with new ones as you empty the jar. The oil is deliciously fragrant – use it to dress salads when you tire of replacing the cheeses.

Serve the cheese with a few drops of its own olive oil. It is particularly delicious with a salad of the large sweet tomatoes of Provence, dressed with olive oil, salt and a sprinkling of fresh summer herbs – basil or marjoram are perfect.

Top a halved baked potato with a slice of pickled cheese and a sprinkle of chopped chives.

WARM CHEESE SALAD____Prepare a *mesclun* of as many different salad leaves as you can find, including a little rocket for its mild mustard flavour. Divide the salad between 2 plates. Split two cheeses in half and grill them until the surface bubbles and softens. Slide the hot cheese onto the salad leaves, and trickle on a little of the pickling oil and a sprinkle of freshly-ground black pepper.

Top a pizza dough with slices of fresh tomato and slices of the pickled cheese. Sprinkle with chopped oregano and a spoonful of the pickling oil and bake as usual.

Bavarian Potted Cheese
Obatzter

Obatzter **is a delicious potted cheese from Bavaria. An overripe Camembert responds well to the same treatment.**

QUANTITY
Enough for 4

TIME
Preparation: 10 minutes

4 oz/100g butter
1 tablespoon caraway seeds
8 oz/250g Limburger *or*
   Brie
freshly ground black
   pepper
2 pickled onions
1 tablespoon paprika
To finish
1 oz/25g melted butter

UTENSILS
A food processor and a
   storage pot

Soften the butter. Remove the rind from the cheese and mash it thoroughly, either in the processor or with a fork. Chop the onions. Mix all the ingredients together thoroughly. In Bavaria this would be served piled in a pyramid on a wooden plate.

Pot and seal under a layer of melted butter (don't pour in the whey). Ready immediately, the potted cheese will keep in a cool larder for a week at least.

Accompany with pickled gherkins or cucumbers and black bread, with a Bavarian white wine – a Federweisser for example – to balance the richness.

Serve it after a lentil or pea soup in winter. It is delicious too in summer as part of a cold table with sliced German sausages, mild mustard and a warm potato salad.

Potted Stilton

I make this every year with the end of the Christmas Stilton. You can use the parings, all but the chalky exterior. It's quite delicious with any of the homemade biscuits on pages 222-227.

QUANTITY
Makes 1½ lb/750g

TIME
Preparation: 20 minutes

1 lb/500g well-matured
   Stilton
1 glass brandy
8 oz/250g unsalted
   softened butter
1 teaspoon
   Worcestershire sauce
   (see page 55)
½ teaspoon dry mustard
½ teaspoon chilli pepper
melted butter to finish
½ teaspoon powdered
   celery seeds

UTENSILS
A food processor *or*
   pestle and mortar and
   a potting jar

Trim the rind of the cheese so that there are no gritty flakes on it. Pound it up with the butter and the spices. Work in the brandy and the Worcester sauce. If you make this in a food processor, it is easier if you liquefy the butter first. Pot and seal with a layer of melted butter (don't pour on the whey).

7. Jams and Preserves

The preparation of beautiful jewel-clear jams and preserves is a special British skill. Antoine Carême, who in 1815 transferred his extraordinary culinary genius from the Paris kitchens of the diplomat M. Talleyrand to the Prince Regent's Pavilion at Brighton, acknowledged this strength. 'The essentials of English cooking,' he remarked, 'are the roasts of beef, mutton and lamb . . . fruit preserves, puddings of all kinds.'

Eliza Acton's 'General Rules and Directions for Preserving' in her *Modern Cookery for Private Families* of 1845 – a period when all conscientious housewives made their own preserves – gives clear directions.

1____All utensils must be clean and dry – especially jars and bottles.

2____Sugar sticks and burns easily, so keep the bottom of the preserving pan away from contact with direct heat – use a simmering mat.

3____After the sugar is added, stir the preserves gently at first and more quickly towards the end. But keep watch throughout.

4____All preserves should be perfectly cleared of the scum as it rises.

5____Fruit to be preserved with sugar must first be blanched, macerated or lightly cooked to soften its exterior enough to allow syrup to be absorbed – or you will have hard little bullets instead of juicy fruit.

6____For a clear, true-flavoured jam, do the rapid boiling to reduce *before* the sugar is added.

7____Use a *wooden* spoon to stir the jam. As you get more experienced, setting-point can be judged by the way the drop forms on the spoon edge when lifted from the pot.

8____Use special preserving sugar as it will throw up less scum.

9___If you gather your own fruits, pick them on a dry day, after the morning dew has dried, well away from dusty roads. Use the fruit on the day you pick it. Otherwise, freeze it immediately and make your jam at your leisure.

To summarize: the golden rule is to marinate or cook the fruit *slowly*, with or without water, *before* adding any sugar. *Stir* while the sugar is dissolving. Once the sugar has melted, boil the jam *quickly*. Test for set after 10 minutes of quick boiling.

Strawberry Jam

European gardeners did not find it necessary to improve on the varieties available from the wild (in Britain *Fragilaria vesca*), contenting themselves with merely transplanting native plants into the kitchen garden, until well into the nineteenth century – long after raspberries, currants and other soft fruits had been cultivated and cross-fertilized to produce bigger and better crops. Until then the tiny fragrant scarlet berries were predominantly a wild crop, picked by children and gypsies and offered for sale at the roadside, or hawked round the cottagers' back doors and the town markets. The berries were sold by the handspan, strung like beads on a length of straw – which may perhaps account for their name.

It was the New World species of the plant (greeted by the hungry settlers in Virginia with astonished enthusiasm) which produced the modern large-berried cultivar.

Strawberries are short of pectin (the naturally-present gelatine which permits the jam to set). Strawberry jam remains runny, unless it is stewed for long enough to break up the fruit and thus release the pectin. This spoils the flavour and destroys the chief delight of a well-made berry jam – beautiful whole berries suspended in clear fresh-flavoured juices. The inclusion of redcurrants, high in pectin, improves the set and compensates for the low acidity of the fruit.

QUANTITY
About 10 lb/4.5kg

TIME
Preparation: 30 minutes
Cooking: 30 minutes

5 lb/2.25kg strawberries
　(not too ripe)
5 lb/2.25kg preserving *or*
　granulated sugar
1 lb/500g redcurrants

UTENSILS
A large preserving pan, a
　sieve or liquidizer, and
　sterilized storage jars

Hull and wipe the strawberries. Strip the redcurrants from their stalks, push them through a sieve (or liquidize them and then strain), and measure the juice – you will need 1 pint/600ml of it.

Weigh the jam pan and keep a note of the weight. Rub the bottom of the pan with a thin skim of butter – this helps prevent sticking and burning, the bane of jam-makers. Put in the strawberries with the sugar. Heat gently, stirring so that the sugar dissolves thoroughly. When the sugar has melted, add the redcurrant juice.

Bring all to the boil and cook, stirring regularly, until the contents of the pan have reduced to a weight of 10 lb/4.5kg – it has to evaporate 1 pint/600ml of juice.

Allow the jam to cool to finger-heat before you pot it – there is then a good chance of the fruit remaining suspended throughout instead of rising to the top.

Before you seal down, cover the surface of the jam with a circle of waxed paper dipped in brandy – this inhibits the growth of mould to which this lightly-cooked preserve is vulnerable. If it does grow a furry blue layer, don't disturb it. The furry fungus acts as a perfectly efficient airtight seal. It can be lifted off and the rim of the jar carefully wiped clean when you are ready to use the jam. We all worry much too much about such things these days.

Potted Raspberries

Raspberries, sometimes called hindberries and native to Britain and northern Europe, have been cultivated in our gardens for 500 years. This recipe dates back to the seventeenth century, so it is tried and true.

QUANTITY
About 10 lb/4.5kg

TIME
Preparation: 30 minutes

5 lb/2.5kg raspberries
5 lb/2.5kg caster sugar

UTENSILS
2 large bowls

Warm the oven to 300°F/150°C/Gas 2. Put each ingredient into a separate bowl and put both to heat in the oven for 20 minutes, until the berry juice begins to run. Tip the berries into the sugar and stir all well together until the sugar dissolves.

That's all.

Pot in sterilized jars as usual. Top with circles of paper dipped in brandy. The fruit will probably drift to the top – but no matter, the jam will taste magnificent. It does not keep as well as longer-cooked jams – best to store it in the fridge once opened.

Bilberry Jam

Bilberries are the native European blueberry. They ripen in Britain during July and were until recent times one of the most prized of our wild-gathered fruits. The indigo berries have a plum-like soft blue bloom, and they make the best of jams. Shakespeare knew their inky juices well. In *The Merry Wives of Windsor*, Pistol instructs the goblin Cricket, despatched to check on slatternly Windsor housemaids, to 'pinch the maids as blue as bilberries'.

QUANTITY
About 6 lb/2.75kg

TIME
Start a day ahead
Cooking: 30 minutes

4 lb/2kg blueberries (wild *or* cultivated)
juice of 2 lemons
3 lb/1.5kg preserving *or* granulated sugar

UTENSILS
A large bowl, preserving pan, and sterilized jars

Pick over the berries and discard any that are not perfect. Mix the blueberries with half the sugar and the lemon juice in a large bowl, and leave overnight for the juice to run. The next day strain the juices into a preserving pan, reserving the fruit. Add the rest of the sugar to the juices and bring to the boil, stirring until the sugar is dissolved. Skim and then stir in the berries. Bring back to the boil, turn down the heat and simmer for 10 minutes, when the jam should have reached setting point.

Pot in sterilized jars – 20 minutes in a low oven will sterilize them. German housewives rinse their jam jars round with alcohol as a sterilizing measure.

SUGGESTIONS

Bilberry jam is delicious with yoghurt or a fresh curd cheese.

Stir a few spoonfuls into the filling for an apple pie. Or use the preserve to top a cheesecake or fill a spongecake.

BLUEBERRY ICE CREAM___Stir a cupful of blueberry jam into 1 pint/600ml unsweetened custard and freeze as usual.

Greek Cherry Preserve

Vyssino glyko

Vyssino glyko is the most delicious of all the Greek sweetmeats when made with bitter morello cherries. The Romans planted cherry trees all over Europe – deliberately on the edge of common woodlands, or inadvertently when the legionaries spat out the stones as they marched up the ruler-straight new roads which linked their provinces from Romania to Britain.

QUANTITY
Makes about 5 lb/2.5kg

TIME
Start a day ahead
Cooking: 50 minutes

3 lb/1.5kg sour cherries
juice of 1 lemon
3 lb/1.5kg granulated
    sugar

UTENSILS
A large bowl, a
    preserving pan and
    sterilized storage jars

De-stalk and stone the cherries and layer them into a big bowl with the granulated sugar. Cover and leave overnight to make juice.

The next day, transfer the cherries and their juice to a heavy preserving pan. Bring gently to the boil. Skim off the foam and then simmer gently for 10 minutes. Remove the cherries with a draining spoon and put them aside. Continue to boil the syrup, uncovered, for about 30 minutes, when it should be at the large thread stage.

Stir in the cherries and the lemon juice. Allow to cool. Pot and seal in sterilized jars. Keep in a cool dark larder.

These Greek jam-like sweetmeats are celebration treats, offered in a little saucer with a spoon. Welcome guests are regaled with them on arrival, with a glass of water and a tiny cup of bitter coffee to accompany.

For the Greeks' favourite refreshing drink, *vyssinada*, stir a spoonful of cherry preserve (with or without the solid fruit) into a glass of water. Mix well and finish with an ice cube.

Marrow and Ginger Jam

This is a lovely, fresh-tasting pale golden jam – particularly good for breakfast. Marrows are a good storecupboard vegetable. Like pumpkins, they will last all winter stored on a shelf or suspended in a sling. Melon can be substituted for the marrow in the recipe.

QUANTITY

Makes about 6 lb/2.75kg
   jam

TIME

Start a day ahead
Intermittent attention:
   1¼ hours

4 lb/2kg marrow
   (prepared weight)
thinly pared rind and
   juice of 4 lemons
4 lb/2kg granulated *or*
   preserving sugar
1 oz/25g butter
1 oz/25g fresh ginger
   root

UTENSILS

A bowl, a large
   preserving pan, a
   hammer, a scrap of
   clean muslin, and
   sterilized jars

Peel the marrow and scoop out the seeds. Chop the flesh into neat small chunks – the pieces remain whole after the jam is cooked, so you will get out what you put in.

Put the marrow chunks into the preserving pan and sprinkle over 1 lb/500g of the sugar. Cover and leave overnight (well out of range of ants and other hungry insects) to form plenty of juice.

Next day, bash the ginger with a hammer and tie it up with the lemon rind in a scrap of muslin. Add the bag and the lemon juice to the marrow in the preserving pan, and bring all to the boil. Turn down the heat immediately (gentle cooking is the key at this stage) and simmer the fruit for ½ hour.

Remove the pan from the stove. Stir in the rest of the sugar. Carry on stirring patiently until all the gritty little crystals have dissolved.

Put the pan back on the heat and add the knob of butter – it helps to clarify a transparent jam like this. Bring to the boil, turn down the heat, and allow the jam to bubble gently for another ½ hour. Test for setting point after 20 minutes – drop a little jam in a cold saucer and see if it jells. Or use a sugar thermometer – the reading should be 235°F/115°C.

Pot in sterilized jars while hot. If you are using glass vacuum jars, seal them immediately. Otherwise let the jam cool, top with a circle of wax paper, and cover.

Marmalade

Marmelo – from which derives the English name for our favourite breakfast preserve – is Portuguese for quince, a fruit which is still used to make a sweetmeat popular all round the Mediterranean as a Christmas treat. The quince cheese pioneered by the Portuguese – who brewed the fruit pulp into a thick paste with sugar – was soon applied to plums and damsons, apples and medlars, strawberries and pears.

Citrus fruits were not actually used to make marmalade until the mid-eighteenth century. By then the British were beginning to separate their marmalade from their jam, and instructions start to appear in household books for the making of a sweetmeat with oranges and lemons which contained the peel sliced into long strips. In the Latin countries of Europe, fruit jams remain marmalades, leading to bemused disappointment among modern British tourists and confusion among their hosts.

QUANTITY

Makes about 10 lb/ 4.5kg
  marmalade

TIME

Preparation: 1 hour
Cooking intermittently:
  1¼ hours

12 Seville oranges
approximately 4 pints/2.5
  litres water
3 sweet oranges
approximately 4 lb/2kg
  preserving sugar
3 lemons

UTENSILS

A large preserving pan,
  sieve and clean cloth,
  and sterilized jars

Wash the fruit and pare off all the rind as finely as you can with a very sharp knife or potato peeler. Cut the rind into thin slivers and put aside. Weigh the fruit, and then peel off and discard its white pith. Cut up the flesh roughly and put it in a large heavy pan with the water. Boil it steadily for ½ hour, stirring every now and again.

Strain the pulp through a sieve lined with a clean linen cloth. Measure the liquid and add 1 lb/500g sugar for each pint/600ml of juice. Put the juice and sugar and the rinds back into the preserving pan on the heat. Stir until the sugar melts. Turn up the heat and boil the mixture for 30-35 minutes until the jelly is at setting point. Let it cool so that the rind sinks. Pot as usual.

Lemon Curd

This is my absolute favourite spread for toast and scones and to fill sponge cakes. It is also everyone else's, it seems. The jars never last out the week in my household.

QUANTITY
Makes about 3 lb/1.5kg curd

TIME
Preparation: 15 minutes
Cooking: 40 minutes

6 lemons
1½ lb/750g sugar (granulated *or* preserving)
8 oz/250g butter
8 eggs

UTENSILS
A grater, a bowl with a saucepan into which it will fit, another bowl and a whisk, and sterilized storage jars

Wash the lemons and grate the peel finely. Squeeze the juice. Put the juice and the grated lemon peel into a bowl with the butter, chopped into small cubes, and the sugar. Set the bowl over a pan of simmering water and leave the ingredients to dissolve together gently.

In another bowl, whisk the egg yolks and whites together. Pour in the melted sugar, butter and lemon, whisking steadily as you do so. Return the mixture to the bowl over the simmering water and continue to whisk as the mixture cooks and thickens. Don't let it boil.

When the curd has a slightly jellied, thickened look, it is done. This will take 20-30 minutes. It will thicken further as it cools and the butter solidifies. Pot as usual. Best kept in the fridge.

Peach Jam

Mermelada de melocoton

This is my favourite non-English jam. Perhaps we do not make it much in Britain because it is best prepared with those fine sweet yellow-fleshed fruits which need a Mediterranean sun to ripen perfectly. The scent will tell you if the fruit is ripe – the peach will come easily away from its twig when it is ready. This is the Spanish version.

QUANTITY
Makes about 8 lb/4kg
jam

TIME
Preparation: 30 minutes
Cooking: 40 minutes

4 lb/2kg ripe yellow
peaches (de-stoned
weight)
4 lb/2kg sugar
¼ pint/150ml water

UTENSILS
A preserving pan and
sterilized storage jars

Peel and stone the peaches (crack and reserve a few of the kernels to add their delicate almond flavour to the jam). Dice the flesh and put the pieces in a preserving pan or saucepan with the water. Lid and cook gently for 20 minutes. Stir in the sugar and the peach kernels and reheat gently, stirring. When the granules are dissolved, turn up the heat. Boil rapidly for 15 minutes and test for set. Pot and seal as usual.

Quince Honey

Quince trees are quite common in old orchards in England – Thomas Tusser includes them in his list of garden fruits. The quince was originally imported by the Normans – the conquerors thought highly of the furry yellow fruit and planted quinces in the royal gardens at Westminster.

Quinces should be left on the tree until mid-November, like medlars they *blett* with a frost. Store them in a cool larder for 2 or 3 weeks after gathering until they are soft.

This unusual preserve is delicious on bread and makes a good sauce, melted down, for steamed puddings.

QUANTITY

Makes about 8 lb/4kg
   preserve

TIME

Preparation: 20 minutes
Cooking: 30 minutes

4 lb/2kg quinces
1 pint/600ml water
4 lb/2kg sugar

UTENSILS

A large preserving pan,
   a grater and sterilized
   storage jars

Wipe the quinces but do not peel them. Make a syrup by boiling the sugar and water together, stirring until all the crystals are dissolved. Grate the quinces straight into the hot syrup. Boil for 30 minutes. Pot and seal in the usual way.

Damson Cheese

Damsons probably had their name from Damascus, where these dark bitter little plums with an incomparable flavour have been cultivated since pre-Christian times. This is what should be done with the crop when you have made all the tarts and compotes you want (it makes the best of fruit pies). Use slightly underripe damsons for jam. If you pick your own, do so on a dry day.

QUANTITY
Makes about 6 lb/2.75kg

TIME
Preparation and
  cooking: about 1 hour

4 lb/2kg damsons
approximately 4 lb/2kg
  sugar
water

UTENSILS
A large saucepan *or* a
  preserving pan and
  sterilized jars

Stone the fruit. Put the damsons to boil, with enough water to cover them, in a roomy pan. When they are soft and pulpy (about 20 minutes), push them through a sieve. Weigh the pulp and allow 1 lb/500g sugar for each 1 lb/500g fruit.

Put the sugar in the pan with just enough water to allow the sugar to melt. Bring to the boil, stirring as the sugar granules dissolve. Boil for 5 minutes. Stir in the fruit. Boil again for 20-30 minutes, stirring, until the cheese is thick. If you want a traditional stiff damson cheese, cook it until the mixture leaves the sides of the pan. Pot as usual.

Mulberry and Apple Jelly

Mulberry trees are the last remnants of a very ancient trade. In 1984, Mademoiselle Louise Morell, born *circa* 1900 at Buis-les-Baronnies in upper Provence, told me why there are still old mulberry trees in the yards and streets of Mediterranean villages:

'My neighbour told me I should tell you about the silkworms. Not many people are interested in how it was. The world has changed so fast.

'There was one thing that all the neighbours had in common. They all kept the same cash crop – until the invention of nylon killed the trade. Each kitchen had its tray of silkworms. Each terrain had its mulberry tree, and Buis-les-Baronnies boasted three working silk mills.

'They were lovely, those little caterpillars. You bought them from the merchant when they were tiny little creatures. You laid out your tray with a very clean white cloth, then you picked some fresh clean mulberry leaves, and you put the little worms on them. And how they ate and how they grew! They made little nibbles up and down the leaves, up and down all day, until there was nothing left but the stem. And every day you had to clean them, which was easy – you put in the new mulberry leaves, and they hopped on them straight away to start eating. Then you could pick them up on the leaves and pop them onto a new cloth. Then, suddenly, after about a month, when they had moulted three or four times and grown so big, one of them would get the idea and they would all start to spin. Then you had to run and hang them on the kitchen beam – we did not have much room you know – and they would all spin their cocoons. Three colours, they had: there was a white, and a yellow and a beautiful rose-colour. Then you sold them to the merchant in the market. But they had to be clean, very fresh, or they were worthless.'

Teresa Stratilesco observed the same industry in Hungary in 1906 and wrote about it in *From Carpathian to Pindus*:

> The peasant woman grows silk – an industry that was universal once upon a time . . . she buys in town the silkworm seed, then produces worms on the best bed of the house, or if there is no room, then under the bed, on mulberry leaves, changed daily. They will produce a fine or coarse silk. . . . With silk they weave stuff for shifts and head-veils, sometimes wonderfully thin and beautiful, with stripes or delicate designs in white cotton.

Mademoiselle Morell's trees had only white berries. The dark berries are the ones to be used for jams. Mulberries ripen in Britain at the end of August. If you have your own tree and there is grass beneath, let the fruit fall and gather it from the ground: mulberries have to be fully ripe for their flavour to develop.

→

Makes about 10 lb/4.5kg
   jelly

TIME
Start a day ahead
Preparation: 40 minutes
Cooking intermittently:
   1 hour

3 lb/1.5kg mulberries
approximately 6
   lb/3kg granulated *or*
   preserving sugar
3 lb/1.5kg cooking apples
approximately 6 pints/3.5
   litres water

UTENSILS
A large preserving pan,
   a jelly bag *or* a clean
   tea-towel firmly pinned
   by each corner onto a
   well-washed upturned
   stool, and a large bowl
   to catch the juice, a
   sugar thermometer,
   and sterilized storage
   jars

Rinse and de-stalk the berries – it doesn't matter if some bits of stem are left. Chop up the apples – skin, pips and all. Put the fruit into a large preserving pan and cover it to the depth of one finger with cold water. Bring all to the boil, turn down the heat and simmer until apples and berries are mushy – about 30 minutes will be enough. Mash the fruit a little as it cooks and keep stirring to avoid sticking.

Put the pulp to drip through a jelly bag or clean tea-towel overnight. Don't squeeze or stir the pulp, or the jelly will be cloudy.

The next day, measure the juice back into the pan. Stir in 1 lb/500g sugar for every pint/600ml liquid. Bring all gently to the boil, stirring constantly until the sugar is dissolved. Boil until setting point is reached – that is 220°F on the sugar thermometer. The test without a thermometer is a drop of the hot jelly on a cold saucer – setting point has been reached when the liquid remains a drop without running. Pot while still hot. Cover with a circle of waxed paper when cool. Seal and store away from the light.

Gooseberry and Elderflower Jelly

'Muscat jelly' is an old country preserve with a delicate pink colour and the delicious fragrance of elderflowers. Prepare it in June and July, when both the ingredients are in season. Elders thrive in our cities as well as in country copses and hedgerows.

QUANTITY
Makes about 10 lb/4.5kg
 jelly

TIME
Start a day ahead
Preparation: 10 minutes
Cooking intermittently:
 2½ hours

4 lb/2kg gooseberries
approximately 4 lb/2kg
 preserving sugar
approximately 4 pints/2.5
 litres water
12 heads elderflowers

UTENSILS
A large preserving
 pan, jelly-straining
 equipment, a piece
 of clean muslin, and
 sterilized storage jars

Wash the gooseberries, put them in a large preserving pan and cover them with water. Bring to the boil, turn down the heat and simmer for 2 hours. Strain through a jelly cloth overnight.

Tie the elderflower heads in a piece of clean muslin.

Next day measure the juice and add 1 lb/500g sugar for each pint/ 600ml liquid. Bring all to the boil in the preserving pan, stirring until the sugar is dissolved. Boil for 10 minutes. After 7 minutes, plunge in the bag with the elderflower heads. Simmer for another 3 minutes, take out the bag and pot the jelly as usual.

Prune and Raisin Jam

Papette

Papette is a larder standby of the Swiss valleys, delicious on brown toast or as a filling for little jam tarts.

QUANTITY

Makes about 4 lb/2kg
  preserve

TIME

Start a day ahead
Preparation: 20 minutes
Cooking: 30 minutes

1 lb/500g prunes
4 oz/100g blanched
  almonds
1 lb/500g raisins
3 cloves
1 lb/500g currants
1 lemon
1 pint/600ml hot strong
  tea
1 glass *eau-de-vie, or*
  brandy
1 lb/500g dark brown
  sugar

UTENSILS

A large preserving pan
  and sterilized storage
  jars

Stone the prunes and roughly chop them. Crack the stones and add the kernels to the fruit. Put the prunes, raisins and currants in a bowl. Pour in the hot tea and leave to soak overnight.

Transfer the soaked fruit to a large preserving pan. Stir in the sugar, the almonds roughly chopped, the cloves and the grated rind and juice of the lemon. Heat gently, stirring as the sugar melts. When the sugar has dissolved, bring the mixture to the boil and cook it for 30 minutes, until you have a thick sticky jam. Stir in the *eau-de-vie* or brandy.

Pot in warm sterilized jars and seal while still hot. Keep in a cool larder. It will be ready in 2 weeks.

Have it with yoghurt and *muesli* as a delicious breakfast.

Make a quick dessert: stir 2 spoonfuls of *papette* into whipped cream folded with an egg white whisked stiff with a spoonful of caster sugar.

Use the *papette* to make a **PANADE**, the Provençal open tart served at the Christmas Eve fasting supper. The tart can be filled with quince paste, apple sauce, chestnut purée, or spinach stewed with butter, flavoured with lemon peel and sweetened with sugar. For the pastry you will need 4 heaped tablespoons flour, ½ teaspoon salt, 1 tablespoon sugar, 2 oz/50g butter, 1 tablespoon hot water, and 1 egg. Mix the flour, salt and sugar in a bowl. Melt the butter in the water. Lightly beat the egg. Work the melted butter and the egg into the flour mixture until you have a soft malleable paste. Roll the pastry out into a large circle and lay it in a 8-9-in/20-23-cm tart tin. Trim carefully, saving the scraps. Spread the *papette* over the pastry. Finish the tart with ribbons of pastry cut from the scraps and criss-crossed over the filling in a lattice design. Bake in a moderate oven, 350°F/180°C/Gas 4, for 20-25 minutes, until the pastry is crisp and golden.

Prunes in Red Wine

If ever a fruit had a reputation to recover, it must be the prune. The dried plum fell from grace in Victorian times, and has never really staggered back from the medicinal nursery prunes-and-custard routine. A pity, since a dish of stewed prunes can be a great treat. This Swiss version of the old nursery staple is spiced with cinnamon and cloves.

QUANTITY
Serves 4

TIME
Start a day ahead
Preparation: 15 minutes
Cooking: 15 minutes

1 lb/500g best prunes
4 cloves
1 bottle full-bodied red wine
4 tablespoons sugar
1 stick cinnamon bark

UTENSILS
A large saucepan and a bowl

Cut the prunes in half and remove their stones. Bring the wine, the cinnamon and the sugar to the boil in a roomy saucepan. As soon as the liquid is boiling, add the prunes. Remove from the heat immediately. Leave the prunes in their juice in a cool place overnight. Or put them in sterilized jars and keep them in a cool larder. Serve with cream.

A whole prune makes a delicious stuffing for roast feathered game.

SUGGESTIONS

Make **ZWETSCHGENPAVESEN**, German prune fritters. Sandwich slices of white bread with a spoonful of the purée, dip the sandwiches in egg-and-milk or a pancake batter, and fry them in butter until crisp and golden.

8. Suppers

Bread Suppers

Unleavened breads made without the assistance of yeast still provide home bakers with the basic recipes for quickly made solid food to add substance to an evening meal. Self-raising flour and baking powder – a mix of bicarbonate of soda and cream of tartar providing alkali and acid respectively – now add leavening where before light fingers had to be sufficient. I have also included here a recipe for a quickly baked yeast-raised bread very popular in southern France and Switzerland.

Don't throw away old crusts and ends of loaves – they can be sliced and put to dry in a very low oven for half an hour or so to make rusks. If the basic bread is good, these have a fine flavour, can be stored in a tin almost indefinitely and provide an excellent accompaniment to cheese or butter-and-jam, or to add body to soups. Crush them either in a clean tea-cloth with a rolling pin, or in the food processor whenever you need homemade toasted breadcrumbs.

Cream Girdle Scones

Scones and soda-breads often replace yeasted bread as the daily accompaniment to a meal in the Celtic corners of Britain – Wales, Ireland and Scotland. Betsy Ingram of Killiemor on the Isle of Mull makes scones for her shepherding family daily. Any leftovers are toasted rather than reheated – or split, buttered and filled with cheese or homemade bramble or strawberry jam as a 'piece for the pocket' to be taken back out onto the hill by the working shepherds. The 'cream' is a reference to the richness of the mix, and Betsy likes to include new-laid eggs from her own foraging hens. She explains that purists would not approve of the inclusion of sugar in the mix. Girdle scones are baked on both sides on an ungreased iron girdle or griddle, over a top-heat. They should have a smooth, flat brown-gold skin top and bottom – the sign of a well-made girdle scone.

QUANTITY
Makes 2 rounds

TIME
Preparation and
  cooking: 20 minutes

8 oz/250g self raising
  flour
1 oz/25g butter
¼ teaspoon salt
¼ pint/150ml milk
  (soured is best)
1 oz/25g sugar
1 large egg

UTENSILS
A sieve, a bowl, a fork,
  rolling pin and pastry
  board, and a girdle/
  griddle *or* heavy iron
  frying pan

Sieve the flour with the salt into a bowl and sprinkle in the sugar. Rub in the butter with your fingertips.

Beat the egg and milk lightly together with a fork. Use the fork to mix the liquid into the dry ingredients. Fork well until all the dry flour is wet – the wetter the mix, the softer the scone.

Meanwhile, put the girdle, ungreased but dusted with flour, over direct heat.

Scatter plenty of flour on the pastry board and tip the soft mixture onto it. Dust all surfaces well with more flour. Halve the dough pat into ½-in/1-cm thick rounds the size of a side-plate – handle the dough as little as possible. Cut each round into quarters – called farls in Scotland – and transfer them to the girdle. Give them 4 minutes each side, turning once – they may need more or less time. Keep the scones warm, wrapped in a cloth. Use as you would your own daily bread.

Welsh Cakes

Mrs Dorothy Thomas runs the post office, shop and tearoom in Rosebush, the highest village in Pembrokeshire – and her Welsh cakes are famous. Until the arrival of her recently acquired electric griddle, the cakes were baked on a Welsh *planc* – as this heavy iron cooking plate is called in Wales.

The post office itself is accommodated in a roomy, comfortable old house with a little provisions shop and the sub-post office incorporated into a front room. The doctor runs a surgery here every week, and the previous owners had a tradition of giving cups of tea to the hill walkers. The house is built of beautiful thick bricks, unmortared, of blue-grey slate from the quarry, worked out in 1910, to which Rosebush owes its existence. A neat terrace of cottages flanks the road to the disused workings – small hills of broken slate and rock clothed patchily in heather and grass and gorse make an intimate small-hill landscape. North Wales slate has the reputation for quality, but slate from the Rosebush workings roofs St Margaret's chapel in the Houses of Parliament.

QUANTITY

Makes about 20 cakes

TIME

Preparation and cooking:
20-25 minutes

1 lb/500g self-raising
flour
4 oz/100g sultanas and
raisins mixed
2 oz/50g butter
2 eggs
4 oz/100g sugar
⅓ pint/200ml water

UTENSILS

A sieve, a bowl, rolling pin
and pastry board, a 2 ½
-in/7-cm diameter shell-
edged pastry cutter,
and a *planc*/griddle *or*
heavy frying pan

Rub the fat into the flour in a bowl, and stir in the fruit and sugar. Mix the water and the eggs together with a fork, and with it make a soft dough just a little firmer than that for the girdle scones (see previous recipe). Tip the dough on to a well-floured board and roll it out to ½ in/1cm thick. Cut the dough into rounds with the pastry cutter.

Heat the *planc* – get the heat up into it gently and thoroughly, and do not let it overheat. Bake the Welsh cakes on the *planc* or griddle (as for the girdle scones in the previous recipe) turning once, until well-risen and brown. They will take about 5 minutes a side. Lovely with butter and honey.

Drappies or Scotch Pancakes

Scotch pancakes were my birthday treat as a child, and the first thing I ever learnt to cook. A neighbour in the Hebrides recommends that the sugar be replaced by a 'knife-ful' of golden syrup (draw a clean blade through the syrup tin and then through the mix). She says this gives a fine bronzed surface to the dropped scones.

QUANTITY

Makes about 20
    pancakes

TIME

**Preparation and
    cooking**: 20-25
    minutes

1 lb/500g plain flour
about ¾ pint/450ml milk
    (soured is best, but if
    using it cut down on
    the cream of tartar)
½ teaspoon salt
½ teaspoon bicarbonate
    of soda
1 teaspoon cream of
    tartar
butter to grease (it is
    traditional to use a
    lump of suet held in a
    cloth)
1 tablespoon caster sugar
1 egg

UTENSILS

A sieve, a bowl, wooden
    spoon, and griddle *or*
    heavy frying pan

Sift the flour into a bowl with the salt, bicarbonate of soda, cream of tartar and sugar. Make a well in the flour and work the egg in with a wooden spoon. Beat in enough milk to make a thick cream. Beat it some more until it bubbles. Now the chemicals are beginning to work, so the mixture will not wait.

Heat a griddle or heavy frying pan. Grease it lightly with butter. When it is hot but not too hot, pour on spoonfuls of the mixture. Let the pancakes cook. They are ready for turning when the bubbles which form on the surface burst. Turn and cook on the other side. Continue until the mixture is all used up.

The hot pancakes should be piled up with butter in between, but eaten separately, not cut through like a cake. Have a good thick soup to start the meal, and strong milky tea to accompany the scones.

Potato Scones

Every farmer on the island of Mull has a potato patch – the Hebrides are famous for their potatoes. A late-planted crop used to be grown on the hilltop in 'lazy beds' – earthed-up furrows. The tattie crop is important even today, and news of who has lifted the first 'earlies' travels fast. These scones are made with main crop full-grown potatoes.

QUANTITY
Makes 2 rounds

TIME
Preparation: 15 minutes
Cooking: 20 minutes

8 oz/250g cooked
   potatoes mashed with
   1 heaped tablespoon
   plain flour
½ oz/12g butter
flour for dusting
2 tablespoons milk

UTENSILS
A bowl, rolling pin
   and pastry board and
   griddle *or* heavy iron
   frying pan

Mix the mashed potatoes, the milk and the flour together lightly with fingers or a fork – use enough flour to stiffen up the potato mixture.

Dust the table or pastry board with *plenty* of flour. Tip the mixture into the floury bed. Pat it into a circular shape with well-floured hands. Divide into two. Press each piece into a ball and press it gently with a rolling pin into a round ¼-in/5-mm thick and about the size of a dinner plate. Cut each round into quarters.

Bake on a hot, but not overheated, griddle dusted with flour. Turn the scones when the bottom surface is golden. Finish cooking on the other side. Wrap the scones in a clean towel until needed. They are delicious split and sandwiched with a rasher of crisp-fried bacon or cheese. To reheat them, fry in butter.

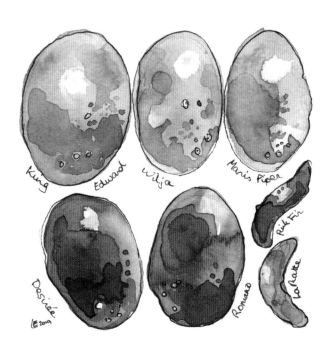

Italian Bread Pudding
Panada alla fiorentina

Panada alla Fiorentina can be cooked on top of the stove like a porridge. Michaela, the cook in the *pensione* in Florence where I spent six months while a student, baked a *panada* every Monday with the bread we English girls had not eaten over the weekend. She could never accept our limited capacities for the most important Mediterranean foodstuff of all. 'If you were Italian *ragazza*,' she would complain as she grated the leftovers, 'you would be eating bread with everything, and you would have cheeks as round as peaches.'

QUANTITY
Serves 4

TIME
Preparation: 20 minutes
Cooking: 40-50 minutes

4 oz/100g fresh
  breadcrumbs (not
  toasted)

To finish
tomato sauce made
  with 1 lb/500g
  ripe tomatoes (*or* a
  1-lb/500-g can). *Or*
  homemade tomato
  ketchup (see page 58)
4 oz/100g grated
  Parmesan cheese
nutmeg
4 eggs
1 pint/500ml chicken
  stock (homemade)
salt
olive oil

Mix the breadcrumbs in a bowl with the cheese and season with a grating of nutmeg. Beat the eggs with the stock and mix all in with the breadcrumbs. (Michaela would sometimes add a handful of peas, green beans or chopped green peppers.) Taste and add salt.

Spread the mixture in an oiled baking dish and trickle a little more oil on top. Bake in a moderate oven, 350°F/180°C/Gas 4, for 40-50 minutes, until the mixture is firm, brown and bubbling.

Meanwhile, scald, peel and chop the tomatoes. Put them into a little pan with a tablespoon of olive oil, a little chopped onion and garlic, and let them melt down into a thick sauce.

Cut the *panada* into squares and serve it warm, with a spoonful of the tomato sauce.

UTENSILS

A bowl and shallow baking dish and a small pan for the sauce

Crackling Bread
Fougasse aux grattons

Fougasse aux grattons is made by the bakers of France and Switzerland. *Grattons* or *greubons* are the little pieces of crisp crackling which are sieved out from clarified lard. Continental pork butchers usually have them for sale, as did English butchers until recently. In Britain a similar preparation is now sold in packets like crisps – heavily salted and prepacked as 'pork scratchings'. Most of Europe has similar recipes for crackling breads, often prepared after the autumn pig-slaughter. Make your own with a piece of pork belly, cubed and rendered slowly in a frying pan over a gentle heat. Stir paprika, salt and pepper into the liquid lard and save it for sauté potatoes or to stir into a bean dish.

QUANTITY
Makes 1 loaf

TIME
Start about 1 hour ahead
Preparation: 20 minutes
Cooking: 30 minutes

1 lb/500g flour
1 oz/25g fresh yeast (½ oz/12g dried)
1 teaspoon salt
¼ pint/150ml warm milk
2 oz/50g lard *or* butter
2 eggs
8 oz/250g homemade pork scratchings

UTENSILS
A sieve, a bowl and a baking tray

Sieve the flour and salt into a warm bowl. Add the lard of butter, chopped in small pieces, and rub it into the flour. Make sure the scratchings are well broken up, and stir them in. Make a well in the centre.

Dissolve the yeast in a little of the warm milk and leave it for a few minutes to froth up. Beat up the eggs with the rest of the milk (reserve a spoonful for gilding the top of the bread) and stir in the yeast liquid.

Pour the mixture into the well in the flour. Work the flour into the liquid with a circular movement of your hand. Knead thoroughly until you have a soft dough which no longer sticks to your fingers – you may need a little extra milk.

Form the dough into a ball, cover it with a damp cloth (an alternative is a plastic bag ballooned around it and loosely tied: this works on the greenhouse principle) and put it to rise in a warm place for an hour or so – until it has doubled in size.

Preheat the oven to 450°F/230°C/Gas 8.

Knock the dough down to distribute the air bubbles, and then roll it out into a large rectangle about ½ in/1cm thick. Grease a large shallow baking tray well with lard or butter and then dust it with flour. Lay the rolled out bread dough into the tin. Slash the dough into 2-in/4-cm wide strips and paint them with the reserved egg and milk.

Put the bread to bake in the preheated oven for 20-30 minutes (depending on the thickness of the dough), until well risen and golden.

Eat the *fougasse* fresh from the oven on a cold autumn evening, with a glass of mulled cider.

If you would like to try a sweet version of this bread, add 4 oz/100g sugar to the mix, plus a little grated lemon peel.

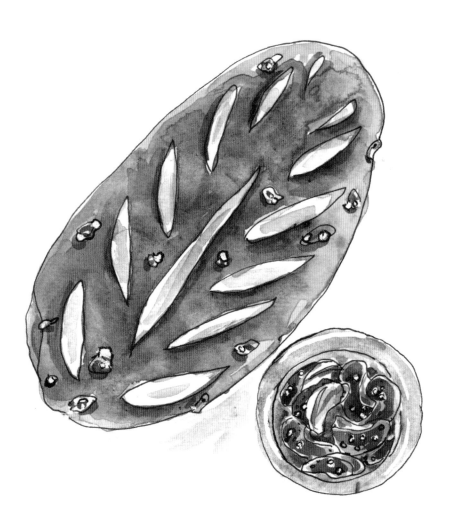

Spanish Doughnut Fritters

Churros

Churros are long thin doughnuts made sometimes with wheat flour, and sometimes with potato and flour. They are sold by weight and piping-hot from a frying kiosk in any Spanish market. Each *churro*-fryer has his or her own special skill with the mixing of the paste and deft handling of the oversize piping syringe. Certain stands in large markets where there is a choice are always much better patronized than others.

More sophisticated town-vendors will make single circles of fritter, which are then strung on green reeds and sold in bunches. The *churro*-man will also make batches of potato *churros*, which are pushed through a star-shaped nozzle and chopped off in finger-lengths. Rural *churro*-makers prefer to make long cartwheels, concentric circles of dough, which are scissored into lengths for weighing and wrapping in brown sugar-paper. The purchaser then takes her paper-wrapped bundle to the nearest bar for a cup of thick hot chocolate, or a large glass of always-excellent coffee in which to dunk her *churros*. Quite delicious – it is no wonder the middle-aged Spanish housewife is inclined to rotundity.

In the north *churros* are often sold sugared. In the south, although they are dunked in sweet beverages, *churros* are salted. The stalls are always closed down by midday – although the *churrerias* may open again at around 7 p.m. to fry crisps for the evening *tapa* and cinema trade. The Spaniards love their street life, whether in a small *pueblo* or the big city. Everyone comes out for the ritual evening *paseo* – still, in rural communities, the only time when boy can meet girl without compromise.

. . . .

QUANTITY
Makes about 20 fritters

TIME
Preparation: 20 minutes
Cooking: 20 minutes

1 pint/600ml water
same volume of flour as
   water (approximately 8
   oz/250g)
1 tablespoon oil
½ teaspoon salt
oil for frying

Bring the water, oil and salt to the boil together in a roomy saucepan. When they are boiling, stir in the flour. Turn down the heat and cook the paste until it forms a ball and leaves the sides of the pan. Allow to cool a little. (This is a *choux* pastry without eggs). Put the paste into a large biscuit-dough syringe: the instrument will need to be quite large and tough – an icing syringe is unequal to the task. The star nozzle should be about the diameter of a thumbnail – in Andalusia a spread star is used for the wheat-flour *churro*, a sharper-pointed star for the version when half the flour is substituted by mashed potato.

Heat frying oil in a deep-frying pan.

Pipe out a few *churros* in 4-in/10-cm lengths on a clean, floured cloth – don't do them all at once or they form a skin and don't expand properly when they are fried. If you pipe straight

A large bowl, saucepan,
biscuit syringe and
deep fryer

into the oil, you end up with greasy hair and a red face, explained the elderly lady in the Valencia market who sold me my *churro*-maker and supplied the recipe.

When the oil is smoking hot, drop in the *churros* (not too many at a time) and fry them golden. If the oil is too hot, the centres will remain raw; if the oil is too cool, the *churros* shatter.

Drain the fritters well: *churros* are always sold wrapped in absorbent sugar paper – a courtesy which serves the same purpose as that accorded to fish and chips in Britain.

Serve immediately – they must be eaten piping hot as they come out of the pan, with a big cup of frothy chocolate or milky coffee to dunk them in.

Fried Milk

Leche frito

Leche frito is simply a very thick custard, breadcrumbed and fried. It, and its close cousin the *flan*, is to the children of Spain as rice pudding is to the children of Britain.

QUANTITY
Serves 4

TIME
Start an hour ahead
Cooking: 30 minutes

1 pint/600ml milk
1 oz/25g butter
4 tablespoons flour
2 tablespoons sugar
3 egg yolks

To finish
1 whole egg
2 tablespoons milk
4 oz/100g breadcrumbs
oil for frying
sugar and powdered
  cinnamon

UTENSILS
A liquidizer, whisk,
  saucepan and shallow
  dish, 2 plates and a
  frying pan

Put all the ingredients except those needed for the finishing in the liquidizer and process thoroughly. The butter will make the mix seem somewhat lumpy, but no matter – it melts down.

Heat the mixture gently in a saucepan over a low heat. Keep whisking and stirring so that it doesn't stick. Just as it comes to the boil, turn down the heat and simmer until the mixture is thick and no longer tastes of raw flour.

Pour it into a lightly oiled dish in a layer about ½ in/1cm thick. Let it cool and cut it into 2-in/5-cm squares.

Beat the egg in a plate with 2 tablespoons milk. Spread the breadcrumbs on another plate. Dip the squares in the egg-and-milk to coat them. Press them gently all over in the breadcrumbs.

Heat a finger's width of oil in a heavy frying pan. When it is hazed with blue, carefully fry the squares, a few at a time, turning once. Drain them on kitchen paper. Arrange them on a warm plate, sprinkle with cinnamon and sugar, and serve immediately.

Queen of Puddings

As far as I can judge, this seems to be a descendant of College Pudding, so it is quite right that it was the only dish I ever liked at school. I still do. It makes an excellent private little supper.

QUANTITY
Enough for 4

TIME
Preparation: 15 minutes
Cooking: 35-45 minutes

2 eggs
1 oz/25g butter
1 pint/600ml milk
4 heaped tablespoons
    strawberry *or* raspberry
    jam
2 oz/50g caster sugar
½ pint/300ml untoasted
    white breadcrumbs

UTENSILS
A bowl and a pudding
    dish

Separate the eggs. Beat the milk with the egg yolks and 1 oz/25g of sugar and pour the mixture over the breadcrumbs in a bowl.

Preheat the oven to 300°F/150°C/Gas 2.

Butter a pudding dish and spread the jam in the bottom of it. Cover with the soaked breadcrumbs. Bake in the preheated low oven for 30-40 minutes until set and slightly brown.

Beat the egg whites until stiff and fold in the remaining 1 oz/25g sugar. Pile this meringue in peaks on the pudding, turn up the oven heat and pop it back for 5 minutes to brown. This is a soft meringue and does not need to be baked crisp.

Delicious with single cream.

Cheese Suppers

Homemade farmhouse cheeses stocked the larders of rural Europe until well into the last century. Many eastern European and Mediterranean country farmwives still make their own cheese: some to be sold as the housewives' essential small cash-crop, her corner-of-the-apron money, some to be stored as a winter fast-food. In peasant communities cheese often replaces meat in a meal, adding protein to a bowl of soup or a vegetable dish; and in communities where daily baking is a ritual it completes a quickly made bread as a light evening meal.

The nature of the finished cheese is dictated by three factors: first, the raw materials – the milk and the curdling agent; next, the preparation of the curds; finally, the treatment of the finished cheese.

In Europe the milk may come from cows, goats, sheep or buffalo (further east, milk-animals include camel and yak). The traditional rennet for curdling, when not a modern commercial preparation, can be either animal in origin – an infusion from the lining of a ruminant's stomach, a piece of curd from the stomach of milk-fed kid or lamb – or the curdling agent can be one of a delightfully wide variety of vegetable substances. These are often identified by some local name which indicates their use: the glaucous leaves and root of butterwort *Pinguicula vulgaris* were used to turn curds in Britain and Scandinavia within living memory – those who remember it describe the wonderful long strings of the curd it makes, like knitting wool. Others included the chokes of wild and cultivated artichokes and fig-tree resin – each community has its own special knowledge. In the dairy regions of Spain an infusion of artichoke hearts was used to make *cuajada*, a thick sheep's milk junket much appreciated around Burgos. It is delicious with honey and toasted almonds.

The curds when converted to a thick junket are cut, kneaded and drained (for Mozzarella the curds are not cut after draining, which accounts for the long strings). The curds can be cooked or left raw depending on the cheese to be made; and then, in the case of hard cheeses, they are 'cheddared' – chopped – a process whereby the curds are squeezed of all whey. The resulting cheese can be eaten fresh, or it can undergo a period of storage and maturing – damp or dry, salted, rubbed with aromatics (my neighbour in Spain used to rub her homemade matured goat's cheeses with olive oil and paprika), injected with mould or matured with surface bacteria.

Cheese remains a valuable larder staple and there are plenty of supper dishes, apart from the simple toasted cheese and rarebits, which can be made with it.

Cheese Fritters

Malakoffs

Malakoffs was the nickname given to the Swiss mercenaries who fought for the French during the Crimean War after they stormed the fort of Malakoff-Sebastopol. These delicious fritters, rather like a Swiss fondue dipped in batter, commemorate the famous victory.

QUANTITY
Serves 4

TIME
Start 2-3 hours ahead
Intermittent attention:
   45 minutes

1 lb/500g hard cheese
   (Jura, Gruyère)
¼ pint/150ml milk
1 large glass white wine
1 tablespoon oil
6 oz/175g flour
oil for deep-frying (lard
   or butter are more
   traditional – but that
   is true of all these
   northern deep-fried
   foods)
1 teaspoon salt
3 eggs

UTENSILS
A bowl for soaking,
   another bowl for
   mixing, a blender
   would be useful, and a
   deep fryer

Cut the cheese into fingers about the length of a thumb. Put the fingers to soak in the white wine for 2-3 hours.

Make the coating batter about 30 minutes before you are ready to cook: sieve the flour into a bowl with the salt. Make a well in the middle and break in the eggs. Pour in the milk and oil. Incorporate the flour into the liquid gradually with a wooden spoon. Beat the mixture until smooth, then beat it some more to incorporate air. (You can do all this in a blender.) Leave it to rest for 20 minutes or so.

Put the oil on to heat in a deep-fryer. When it is hazed with a faint blue smoke, drop in a cube of bread as a tester – when the oil is hot enough, the bread cube will be golden in a few seconds. If it blackens, the oil is too hot and must be taken off the heat for a minute or two to cool down.

Remove each cheese finger from its wine bath (not an unfamiliar situation for a victorious mercenary), dip it in the batter and drop it into the hot oil. Continue with the rest of the fingers – do not do more than 4 or 5 at a time or the oil temperature will drop too much. When the *Malakoff* fritters are crisp and golden, remove them with a draining spoon and transfer them to absorbent paper.

Serve the fritters piping hot, with more chilled white wine to cool your burning tongue. Accompany the meal with a green salad of interesting leaves – Good King Henry, dandelion, lamb's lettuce – to commemorate the French soldiers and their Swiss brothers-in-arms who picked and ate the wild greens which they found in the Crimean fields. Unlike their British allies, neither French nor Swiss suffered from scurvy.

Do-it-yourself Liptauer

The Hungarian spiced cream cheese, Liptauer, was named for the fresh curd sheep's milk cheese from Lipto in northern Hungary. The spread is popular in Austria as well, where it was often made with Brimsen, a rich cream cheese from over the border in Czechoslovakia. The Italians of Trieste, part of the Austro-Hungarian Empire until the end of World War I, made a similar mixture with Mascarpone and Gorgonzola – the basis for the layered combination now sold ready prepared under the name of *torta*.

QUANTITY

According to numbers: 8 oz/250g cream cheese is enough for 2

TIME

Preparation: 10 minutes

Set out these ingredients for mixing according to preference
caraway seeds
salt and pepper
beer
fresh sheep's milk cheese
  or cream *or* curd cheese
unsalted butter
chopped onion
paprika

Optional but worthy of addition
mild mustard, capers,
  gherkins, anchovies,
  chopped chives, caviar

UTENSILS

Plates and knives

The proportion of cheese to butter should be 2-1. Make your own mixture and moisten it with a little beer. Accompany with dark rye bread, radishes, and a stein of good German beer.

Cream Cheese with Herbs

Tommes fraîches aux herbes

This is a kind of southern Liptauer made in upper Provence with fresh goat's or sheep's milk cheese. Experiment with your own mixtures of herbs in season. Fresh green peppercorns are a lovely addition. Try dill and tarragon, sage and chopped capers, thyme and chopped olives, rosemary and chopped walnuts.

QUANTITY
Makes 1½ lb/750g

TIME
Preparation: 15 minutes

1 lb/500g curd cheese
1 tablespoon chives
8 oz/250g thick cream
   (the slightly soured
   French *crème fraîche*
   is best)
1 tablespoon chervil (or
   extra chives)
1 teaspoon salt
1 clove garlic
½ teaspoon freshly
   milled black pepper
1 tablespoon parsley

UTENSILS
A mixing bowl, a
   draining mould *or* a
   cloth and a sieve

Mix the curd cheese with the cream in a bowl. Peel and chop the garlic finely with the herbs. Work the herb mixture and the salt thoroughly with the cream and cheese.

Pack the mixture into a draining mould or a cloth suspended over a basin. Leave to drain overnight in a cool place – the longer the cheese is left to drain the firmer it will be.

Eat it fresh with a glass of light Rhône wine accompanied by a salad – lamb's lettuce, young dandelion and rocket (these mildly mustard-flavoured leaves are excellent cooked like spinach).

A spoonful makes an excellent sauce for fresh pasta.

Greek Fried Cheese

Saganaki

This very simple Greek appetizer takes its name from the little two-handled frying pan in which it is prepared. I tasted it first in a small family restaurant in Alexandroupolis, a port only a few miles from the perennially sensitive Turkish-Greek border. The sizzling little morsel and the tiny tumbler of *ouzo* which accompanied it went a long way towards soothing travellers battered by 6 hours spent negotiating the customs posts.

QUANTITY
Serves 2

TIME
**Preparation and
   cooking**: 10 minutes

8 oz/250g Kefalotiri
   or Kasseri cheese (*or*
   mature Gruyère, *or*
   Italian Pecorino)
1 tablespoon olive oil
1 lemon

UTENSILS
A griddle *or* heavy frying
   pan

Cut the cheese into 2-in/5-cm squares ½ in/1cm thick. Heat the pan and brush it with oil. Slap on the cheese squares and fry them first on one side and then on the other, until they have a crisp brown crust.

Serve piping hot, with quarters of lemon to squeeze over them and thick slices of country bread to accompany.

Cheese Fritters

Mozzarella in Carozza

The best and original Mozzarella is that made with buffalo milk. These days, however, even the Italians have to make do with Mozzarella made from cow's milk and marketed sealed, with its own whey, in a plastic envelope. These little egg-shaped balls of fresh cheese have a rubbery consistency which cooks into characteristic long strings. *Mozzarella in carozza* is a favourite snack throughout Italy. Every Italian housewife seems to possess and use a deep-fryer, and can turn out a variety of similar little fried snacks.

. . . .

QUANTITY

Makes 2 sandwiches

TIME

Preparation and
  cooking: 15 minutes

4 oz/100g Mozzarella
1 heaped tablespoon flour
4 slices bread
2 tablespoons milk
1 small egg
oil for deep-frying
salt and pepper

UTENSILS

A small plate and a deep-
  fryer

Cut the Mozzarella into 4 slices. Make 2 sandwiches with the sliced Mozzarella and the bread. Beat the egg lightly in a small plate, seasoning with a little salt and pepper. Season the flour and spread it out on another small plate. Sprinkle the milk over both sides of the sandwiches.

Heat the oil until a faint blue haze rises from the surface. If you have no deep-fryer, then a finger's width of oil in a small frying pan will do. While the oil is heating, dip both sides of the sandwiches quickly in the egg and then in the flour.

Fry the sandwiches until both sides are crisp and golden. Serve them as soon as they are ready, and enjoy the little stringy 'telephone wires' which pull out as you bite into the creamy centre.

Complete a delicious little supper with an orange and watercress salad: peel 1 orange, pith and all, with a sharp knife, and then slice it horizontally. Toss with watercress leaves and dress with freshly milled black pepper.

Include a slice of tomato or ham in the sandwich filling.

Accompany the sandwiches with a little fresh tomato sauce. Make this very simply with 1 lb/500g fresh tomatoes skinned and chopped, 1 crushed clove garlic, 1 tablespoon chopped fresh herbs (basil, oregano, marjoram, sage), and 2 tablespoons olive oil. Simmer all together for 5 minutes in a small pan and leave to infuse for another 10 minutes before serving.

Cheese-and-rice Croquettes

Supplí al telefono

The best reason to make plenty of risotto is so that you have enough over to make *supplí al telefono* tomorrow. Italian family cooking always anticipates unexpected guests, large families being attuned to expandable feasts – so there is a wide range of delicious recipes to cope with the leftovers. An Anglo-Italian schoolfriend of one of my daughters, who spends his summers in Sorrento near Naples with his Neapolitan cousins, loves rice balls like this made with rice cooked really soggy with tomato sauce, then breadcrumbed and deep-fried. Stuff the balls with a few chopped mushrooms cooked in olive oil with garlic and parsley (the Italian favourite boletus are best) as well as the cheese.

QUANTITY
Enough for six

TIME
Preparation and
cooking: 30 minutes

1 lb/500g cooked rice
2 oz/50g Mozzarella, *or*
    Provatura *or* Gruyère
    cheese
2 eggs, lightly beaten
½ teaspoon salt
2-3 slices ham
black pepper
4 oz/100g breadcrumbs
oil for deep-frying

UTENSILS
2 bowls and a deep-fryer

Mix the cooked rice well with the lightly beaten eggs, and season with salt and 3-4 turns of the pepper mill. Dice the cheese and ham.

Fill a basin with water so that you can rinse your hands while you work. Squeeze the rice into egg-sized balls. Push a hole into the middle of each. Tuck in a cube of cheese and one of ham and close the gap neatly. Roll the balls in breadcrumbs.

Tell your guests to come to table – *supplí* wait for no man. Heat the oil in a deep pan. When you can see a faint haze rising and a cube of bread tossed in will gild in seconds, start frying the *supplí*. Drain them as soon as they are golden.

They must be eaten immediately. The beauty of these rice croquettes lies in the way the cheese melts into long elastic strings which wrap themselves from teeth to fingers. Children love them, particularly with homemade tomato ketchup (page 58).

If anyone is still hungry you can always fry them some chips in the hot oil.

Pizza Cheese Turnovers

Calzone

Calzone are the perfect family food – filling, delicious, easily made and cheap, requiring the minimum of saucepans and washing-up. They are the favourite supper of the large families of Naples. Complete the meal Italian-style, with red wine and water on the table, a bowl of fresh fruit to finish, and strong black coffee for the digestion. The *calzone* can be made without a filling – just as bread-dough fritters with tomato sauce.

The quantities given will feed 8-10. If you have fewer people to feed, make the leftovers into pizzas for freezing. Roll out the leftover bread dough into thin rounds, top it with leftover tomato sauce, a few anchovies and a sprinkling of grated cheese, and bake it in a hot oven for 10-15 minutes until the edges of the dough are blistered and crisp.

QUANTITY

Makes about 24 *calzone*

TIME

Start an hour ahead
Preparation: 30 minutes

2½ lb/1.5kg strong white
   flour
1 teaspoon salt
1½ oz/40g fresh yeast
water
1 teaspoon sugar
3 whole Mozzarella
   cheeses (10 oz/300g)

4 tablespoons corn *or*
   sunflower oil
oil for frying

UTENSILS

A large mixing bowl,
   rolling pin and pastry
   board, and a deep-fryer

Sieve the flour into a large bowl and put the bowl into a low oven for the flour to warm.

Warm a mug with hot water. Tip out the water and put in the yeast and sugar. Cream the two together (it's marvellous how the yeast liquidizes with the sugar). Fill up the mug with warm (not hot) water.

Make a well in the middle of the warm flour. Measure in the oil and sprinkle in the salt. Pour in the yeast mixture. Stir it round and add enough warm water to make a soft dough – about 1 pint/600ml. Knead thoroughly, working it well with your fists (very therapeutic – get an exam-taking child to do this). When the dough is smooth and no longer sticky put the empty mixing bowl back into the low oven until it is warm again. Settle the doughball in the warm bowl and put the whole thing into a plastic bag. Tie the bag loosely and leave the dough to rise for an hour.

Meanwhile, cube the Mozzarella small.

When you are ready to cook, break off small pieces of dough the size of a pigeon's egg and roll each out into a thin disc on a well-floured board. Put a little pile of cheese into the middle of each disc, wet the edge of the dough and fold over into a semi-circle to enclose the filling. Press the edges together. Continue until all the dough is used up.

Heat the oil in a deep-fryer until the surface is shimmering. Test to see if a bread cube sizzles and browns immediately. Fry the *calzone* until puffed and golden – a matter of moments. Serve immediately with tomato sauce or homemade ketchup (page 58).

Fried Cheesecakes
Quarkkeulchen

Quarkkeulchen come from Saxony in Northern Germany. The Saxons are hearty eaters and would regard these little treats as a light midmorning snack.

QUANTITY
Serves 4

TIME
Preparation: 10 minutes
Cooking: 10 minutes

8 oz/250g cold mashed
   potatoes
1 oz/25g raisins
1 oz/25g flour
grated rind of 1 lemon
1 egg
butter to fry
8 oz/250g curd cheese
cinnamon and sugar to
   finish

UTENSILS
A bowl and a frying pan

Mash the first six ingredients together very thoroughly in a bowl with a fork. Form into little patties, and fry in butter in a hot pan.

Sprinkle with sugar and powdered cinnamon. Serve with stewed apples or other stewed fruit, or after a vegetable soup.

Vegetable Suppers

My Scottish grandmother used to store the vegetables from her kitchen garden. They lasted out the winter and always seemed sweet and full of flavour. In the school holidays I would sometimes go to stay with her, and my help was always welcome – nimble young fingers were better than old at sorting peas and stringing onions.

Large onions were stored in a chicken-wire hammock slung from the rafters in the shed, little pickling onions were bunched with string and hung from a nail. Pumpkins went on the beam, and marrows were hung in canvas slings beneath. Potatoes were stored in large wooden boxes lined with dry beech leaves and covered from the light by a layer of old sacking. Carrots were buried in a sand-heap in one corner – winter carrot soup always had a few grains of sand in the bottom of the bowl.

Vegetables in Spiced Breadcrumbs

Legumes à la barigoule

The housewives of the fertile Rhône valley and upper Provence bottle and preserve their vegetables for the winter. This way of preparing them *à la barigoule*, coats the vegetables in a wonderfully aromatic rich sauce. The dish can of course be prepared with fresh or frozen vegetables, but for the last you will have to decrease the cooking time a little. If you would like the dish to be vegetarian, omit the ham or bacon and include finely chopped mushrooms.

QUANTITY
Serves 4 as a main dish

TIME
Preparation: 20 minutes
Cooking: 30-40 minutes

2 lb/1 kg prepared
   vegetables – choose
   well-matched pairs of
   cauliflower florets and
   chopped green peppers
or quartered artichokes
   and shelled broad
   beans
or peas and tiny new
   potatoes
or green beans and
   carrots

For the sauce
1 glass white wine
4 oz/100g olives (un-
   pitted weight)
1 glass water

Pit and chop the olives. Peel and chop small the onion, garlic, carrot and celery. Put these aromatics to fry gently until soft in 4 tablespoons of olive oil. Splash in the white wine and water. Turn the vegetables in this fragrant sauce. Add the ham or the bacon, prepared vegetables, thyme and sage. Allow all to bubble up. Lid and leave to simmer for 30-40 minutes until the vegetables are tender. Stir in the parsley and enough fresh breadcrumbs to take up the liquid. Over the heat, turn the vegetables to coat them thoroughly. Serve with bread and the good red wine of the Rhône – Chateauneuf du Pape would not come amiss.

1 large onion

2 oz/50g ham *or* lean
   bacon

2 cloves garlic

½ tablespoon thyme

1 carrot

2 crumbled sage leaves

1 stick celery

approximately 3
   tablespoons fresh
   breadcrumbs

4 tablespoons olive oil

1 tablespoon chopped
   parsley

Pinenuts

UTENSILS

A casserole with a lid

Rice with Raisins and Pine Nuts

Riso con ueta e pignoli

Riso con ueta e pignoli is a speciality of Venice – the raisins and pine nuts which flavour
it give the dish, quite properly for a port trading with the East, an oriental flavour. The
mixture can be used for stuffed vine leaves – the dolmades of which the Greeks and Turks
are so fond. Include, if you like, a little chopped oregano, marjoram or a sage leaf. This
recipe can be adapted for any risotto mixture – peas or sliced artichoke hearts can replace
the raisins and pine nuts. So can dried boletus mushrooms (soak them first in warm water,
and use the soaking liquid to replace some of the cooking water).

QUANTITY

Serves 4

TIME

Preparation: 20 minutes

Cooking: 20 minutes

1 lb/500g round-grain
   rice

Pick over the rice. Peel and chop the onion and garlic. Chop
the parsley.

Heat the oil gently in a shallow pan. Throw in the pine nuts
and let them take colour for a minute. When they are golden,
take them out and reserve.

Stir the rice into the hot oil and turn it until the grains go
a little transparent. Add the wine and bubble it up to evaporate
the alcohol. Stir in the raisins and two-thirds of the stock or
water. Bubble up again, then turn down the heat – there are

3 oz/75g raisins

1 onion

2 pints/1.2 litres water *or*
  homemade stock

2 cloves garlic

1 small bunch parsley

salt and pepper

3 tablespoons olive oil

1 oz/25g butter

2 oz/50g pine nuts

grated Pecorino *or* fresh
  Parmesan

1 glass white wine

those (with time on their hands) who fuss over adding the liquid very gradually to Italian rice dishes. Busy cooks put most of it in at once. Move the rice if it looks like sticking (not a problem if your pan is well-seasoned) and add the rest of the liquid as necessary – when it dries too much, the surface will pit like the bubbles in volcanic lava. Cook the rice over a gentle heat for 20 minutes – by which time the grains should be tender but still slightly chewy in the middle. Bite a grain between your front teeth to make sure. Season the rice with salt and pepper and stir in the butter, chopped into little pieces. Scatter in the pine nuts. Hand round the grated cheese separately.

You can replace the raisins with fresh white grapes – but stir them in at the end along with the pine nuts.

UTENSILS

A large heavy frying pan

Asparagus in Aromatic Cream Sauce
Asperges à la crème

The Traverse family of Villes-sur-Auzon have tilled the mountain's lower slopes for more generations than the grandmother cares to remember. The local cash-crop used to come from the olive trees for which the area has been famous since Roman times. But after the disastrous winter of 1956 killed off most of the trees, the family replanted their fields with asparagus for export to Germany, and cherries for the markets of Lyons and Paris. Grandfather, grandmother, son and daughter-in-law and their two small children live, as is usual in rural Provence, in a little community of dwellings surrounding the farmyard and vegetable patch. The family grow all their own vegetables: garlic, onions and potatoes alternate with aubergines, tomatoes and peppers, lettuce, beans and melons. There is no need to plant the great aromatic herbs since rosemary, thyme, sage and marjoram spring untended from the hillside.

Madame Traverse keeps the broken asparagus spears for her own table, and gave me a big basket of them for my supper. 'When we harvest the first asparagus of the year,' she explained, 'the stalks are so young and tender we like to eat them raw: well-washed, sliced as fine as a one-franc coin, and tossed in vinaigrette, made with our own olive oil and wine vinegar. But for that they must be no more than an hour or two out of their beds.'

This is how she prepares her winter supplies of bottled asparagus.

Serves 4

Preparation: 30 minutes
Cooking: 10 minutes

2 lb/1kg asparagus
3 oz/75g chopped
Bayonne *or* Parma
ham (*or* cooked ham
will do)
2 oz/50g butter
2 oz/50g flour
2 chopped hard-boiled
eggs
1 pint/600ml milk
1 small carton soured
cream
2 heaped tablespoons
chopped parsley
salt and pepper
2 finely chopped cloves
garlic
3 oz/75g grated cheese

A small saucepan and a
gratin dish

Rinse the asparagus and chop the stalks into lengths. If they are raw, first cook them upright in boiling salted water for 10 minutes, refresh in cold water and drain.

Melt the butter in a small saucepan, stir in the flour and fry for a few moments without allowing the mixture to brown. Beat in the milk gradually and bubble gently until the sauce is thick. Stir in the parsley, chopped garlic, ham and chopped hard-boiled eggs. Simmer for a few moments. Take off the heat and stir in the soured cream. Taste and add salt and pepper.

Lay the asparagus in a gratin dish, and pour the sauce over them. Sprinkle with grated cheese, and put in a hot oven for 10 minutes to heat all through and gild the top.

Precede with a little salad, and serve the asparagus *gratin* with plenty of bread, and a light red wine from the Luberon or Mont Ventoux itself.

Vegetable Bread Pudding
Lasagne al verde

An Italian Lenten dish, this can be made in large quantities for a party. This version is made with bread – very easy and delicious.

QUANTITY
Serves 4

TIME

Preparation: 20 minutes
Cooking: 30-35 minutes

8 slices buttered bread
  (not too fresh)
salt and pepper
1 large carrot
3 tablespoons grated
  cheese
1 onion
2 tablespoons chopped
  nuts
2 cloves garlic
1 red pepper
For the sauce
1 aubergine
¾ pint/450ml milk
2 courgettes
3 eggs
4 tablespoons oil
salt and pepper
1 level teaspoon dried
  mixed herbs
a scrape of nutmeg

QUANTITY

A frying pan and a gratin
  dish

Cut the bread into fingers. Scrape the carrot and dice it. Peel and chop the onion and garlic. De-seed and chop the pepper. Hull and cut the aubergine and the courgettes into small chunks. Fry all the vegetables lightly in the oil, starting with carrot and adding the courgette last. Season with herbs, salt and pepper. Leave the vegetables to simmer together for 5 minutes.

To make the sauce, beat the eggs up in the milk. Season and add the nutmeg.

Cover the base of a gratin dish with bread fingers, buttered side down. Pour in one-third of the milk-and-egg, sprinkle with a little cheese, then spread on half the vegetables and a spoonful of chopped nuts. Repeat the layer with the rest of the ingredients, reserving enough bread, milk-and-egg and grated cheese to make a final layer.

Bake in a moderate oven, 350°F/180°C/Gas 4 for 30-35 minutes, until golden and bubbling.

Stuffed Peppers

Pimientos mellenos

This is a speciality of the Venta del Pilar in the hills above Alicante in south-east Spain. They serve mountain food with Moorish spicing – nutmeg, cinnamon, cloves. The saffron milk-cap *Lactarius deliciosus* is the local mushroom picked and sold in the markets. These are very dramatic in colouring – orange staining blue – but those who gather them and offer them for sale do so with as much confidence as we gather our own field mushrooms.

Big thick-fleshed peppers, red or green, are used for the dish. The Spaniards use these peppers for stuffing and for slicing into salads and grow special thin-fleshed varieties for frying.

QUANTITY
Serves 4-6

TIME
Preparation: 30 minutes
Cooking: 1 hour

8 large red or green
  peppers
3 cloves garlic, peeled
  and chopped
4 tablespoons olive oil
handful of parsley,
  chopped
8 oz/250g mushrooms
  (they *should* be saffron
  milk-caps, but no
  matter)
2 lb/1kg tomatoes,
  skinned and chopped
4 oz/100g chopped
  salt-dried ham *or* lean
  bacon
1 lb/500g round rice
  (Italian or Spanish)
1 teaspoon salt

Wipe the peppers and cut off a lid round the stalk end (leave the stalk in place). Empty out the seeds.

Make a *sofrito* by heating the oil gently in a frying pan. Throw in the mushrooms (wiped and chopped), ham or bacon, spices, and chopped garlic and parsley. Let it cook for a few moments until the garlic is soft. Stir in the tomatoes. Let the mixture bubble up, then stir in the rice, salt and saffron or turmeric.

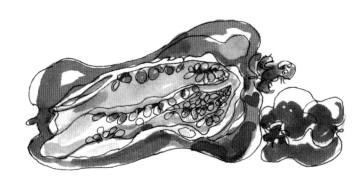

1 teaspoon grated
   nutmeg
6 threads saffron
   (infused in hot water
   and crushed) *or* 1 flat
   teaspoon turmeric
1 teaspoon powdered
   cinnamon
1 tablespoon paprika

UTENSILS
A frying pan and a
   casserole

Preheat the oven to 450°F/230°C/Gas 8. Use the rice mixture to stuff the peppers – only half-full as the rice needs room to swell. Arrange the peppers upright, mouths pointing heaven-wards, in a dish which will just accommodate them. Replace their lids. Cover and cook in a hot oven for about 1 hour. Test by biting a grain of rice: the rice on top will have to be very soft if the middle is to be properly cooked. Serve hot or cooled to room temperature.

Valencian Vegetable Stew
El Bullit

This green vegetable stew is the traditional Valencian 'boiled dinner' served as the evening meal in many households. The ingredients change with the season and each household has its own recipe, but it seems to be one of those humble home-cook's dishes, dependant for its excellence on well-chosen ingredients, which never appear on Spanish restaurant menus or in cookbooks. Rice meals, such as the *paella* and *arroz a banda* for which Valencia is famous, are only eaten at midday.

QUANTITY
Serves 6-8

TIME
Preparation: 20 minutes
Cooking: 30 minutes

1 large onion
4 tablespoons good olive
   oil
1 stick celery
1 lb/500g peas
1 large green pepper

Peel and chop the onion. Wipe and chop the celery. Wipe, hull, de-seed and chop the green pepper. De-stalk and rinse the spinach or chard and chop the leaves roughly. Wash and scrub the potatoes. Wipe, hull and slice the courgettes (not too thinly). Top and tail the green beans or young broad beans, and chop them into short lengths.

Put all these prepared ingredients in a large saucepan or casserole. Add the water and a teaspoon of salt, and bring all to the boil.

Stir in the oil (olive oil is here used as a seasoning, so the quality is important) and turn the heat down to simmer. Lid and leave the stew to cook for 15-20 minutes, until the pota-toes are tender. Add the peas 5 minutes before the end of the

1 lb/500g leaf spinach or chard

To finish
1½ lb/750g small new potatoes
4 spring onions *or* fresh garlics (chive-like, with a gentle flavour)
8 oz/250g courgettes
8 oz/250g green beans *or* baby broad beans in the pod
1 tablespoon chopped parsley
1 tablespoon wine vinegar
1¾ pints/1 litre water
freshly milled black pepper
salt

UTENSILS
1 large casserole

cooking time. The consistency of the *bullit* should be midway between a stew and a soup.

To finish, chop the spring onions (or fresh garlics) and the parsley. Stir these and the vinegar into the stew. Bring the stew back to the boil. Taste and add extra salt if necessary, and freshly milled black pepper.

Serve the *bullit* in deep bowls. Accompany with plenty of good fresh bread, roughly chunked, and a garlicky mayonnaise.

Complete the meal, as would a native Valencian, with fresh fruit. Or make a bowl of sliced oranges topped with toasted slivered almonds – in spring Valencia floats in a scented sea of almond and orange blossom.

Stuffed Cabbage

Poule Verte

This is a dish from the Languedoc, where I lived for a year with my young family. It was our usual supper on a Friday evening – cheap and delicious, leaving money and appetite for the Saturday market.

QUANTITY
Serves 4-5

TIME
Preparation: 30 minutes
Cooking: 2-2¼ hours

1 large green cabbage
salt and pepper
1 large onion
1 lb/500g mushrooms
2-3 old carrots
2-3 rashers of bacon
bunch parsley, thyme,
    rosemary, bay leaf
8 oz/250g fresh
    breadcrumbs
¼ pint/150ml milk
1 pint/600ml homemade
    stock *or* water and
    white wine
3 eggs
nutmeg
2 tablespoons lard *or*
    goose fat

UTENSILS
1 large cooking pot with
    a lid, a colander, and
    string

Trim the cabbage and cut a cross in the stalk end. Put it into a large saucepan of salted cold water. Bring the water to the boil and then lift out the cabbage. Drain in a colander, then cut out the heart-leaves and chop them.

Wipe and chop the mushrooms. Chop the bacon finely. Soak the breadcrumbs in the milk and then squeeze out any surplus liquid. Make a stuffing with the mushrooms, bacon, bread, chopped cabbage heart, and a seasoning of nutmeg, salt and pepper. Bind this mixture with the eggs, lightly beaten together. Form the mixture into a large dumpling, and put this into the empty heart of the cabbage. Fold the leaves over the stuffing.

Truss the cabbage with string, parcel-fashion, as if it were a chicken for the pot. Settle the 'hen' in a lidded casserole which will just accommodate it comfortably. Peel and roughly chop the onion and carrots and tuck the pieces, together with the herbs, down the sides. Pour in enough stock to come halfway up the cabbage. Dot with pieces of lard or goose fat. Lid tightly and put to cook in a moderate oven, 350°F/180°C/Gas 4. The total cooking time – until the *poule verte* is soft – will be 2-2¼ hours, depending on the size of the cabbage. Take care towards the end to see that it does not stick and burn.

Serve the 'green hen' in its glory surrounded by its vegetables. It reheats beautifully.

Cabbage Rolls

Sarma

Certain dishes – *pot-au-feu* to a Frenchman, *bangers-and-mash* to the Englishman – can bring tears to the eyes of expatriates. *Sarma* has the same effect on the wandering Serb. This recipe comes from a Yugoslav family now living in New York. The salt or 'sour' cabbage, *kisele kupus*, which is the essential ingredient, is easily bought in the markets of northern Yugoslavia, and indeed throughout the Balkans and into Germany and Alsace, but many families prefer to make their own when living abroad.

They make it by placing whole heads of fresh cabbage in brine in a closed plastic container and storing it in a cool place. The consistency of the brine should be midway between seawater and a soup – about 3 oz/75g salt to 2 pints/1.2 litres fresh water. *Sarma* is a winter dish, and my friends the New Yorkers store the cabbage on the balcony in the cold winter air – where it will be sour enough in about 2 weeks. There are many versions of *sarma*. Some say tomatoes should be included, some recipes have mushrooms, some only smoked meat, some have herbs – it is as variable a recipe as meat balls.

....

QUANTITY

Enough for 4 for two days (it's better rcheatcd on the second day, and even better on the third)

TIME

Start 2 weeks ahead if you make your own cabbage

Preparation: 30 minutes

Cooking: 1½ hours

1 large onion

3 lb/1.5kg whole salted cabbage (if you use fresh cabbage, blanch it in boiling water first)

1 tablespoon oil (maize

Peel the onion and chop it finely. Warm the oil in the frying pan and put in the onion. Leave it to fry gently until transparent and golden.

Meanwhile mix the ground meats with the bacon, cut into small squares, the rice, the peeled and finely chopped garlic, salt and pepper, and add the fried onions with their oil. Mix all well together.

Remove the core of the cabbage head. Peel off the cabbage leaves and trim off the thick ribs at the base. Save any trimmings or parts of leaves. Rinse the leaves and taste a little piece. If it tastes too sour/salt, boil the cabbage leaves for a few minutes.

Form the meat mixture into oblong shapes about 1½ in/4cm long and about 1 in/2.5cm thick. The size of the meat shape should match the size of the cabbage leaf in which it will be rolled, the larger ones being used in the outside leaves and the smaller ones in the inner leaves. Place each meat pattie in the centre of its appropriate cabbage leaf. Roll the leaf over the meat from the left side, and fold over one end. Finish rolling and tuck in the free end.

or vegetable oil)

1 lb/500g lean ground
beef

8 oz/250g ground pork

8 oz/250g smoked
pork or dried smoked
sausage
(Polish Kabanos)

2 thick slices bacon

4 oz/120g rice

2 cloves garlic

To finish

1 teaspoon salt

2 tablespoons oil (maize
or vegetable oil)

1 teaspoon freshly
ground black pepper

1 tablespoon flour

1 teaspoon sweet paprika

Water

UTENSILS

A frying pan, mixing
bowl and a heavy,
lidded pot or casserole

Line the bottom and sides of the pot or casserole with cabbage leaves, about 2 or 3 leaves thick. Place the cabbage rolls side by side in the pot (like laying bricks, says Hrvoje, who gave me this recipe) to form layers. Between the layers tuck in roughly chopped pieces of the smoked pork or dried sausage. Use finely chopped reserved scraps of cabbage to fill in the voids.

To finish, heat 2 tablespoons of oil in the frying pan. When it smokes, stir in the flour and paprika to make a thick paste. Add about a pint/600ml of water and pour this sauce over the cabbage rolls. Add water to the pot until the level is about ½ in/1cm below the top layer of rolls.

Bring the liquid to the boil, cover the pot and simmer slowly for 1½ hours. Serve with bread, and choose a good Yugoslav wine, white or red, to accompany the dish.

Yugoslav Chopped Salad
Sõpska

Sõpska is the classic salad of the Balkans. The amount of cheese used varies according to the means of the cook. Some districts like more chilli, some leave it out altogether.

QUANTITY
Serves 4-6

TIME
Preparation: 10 minutes

1 lb/500g tomatoes
salt and pepper to taste
8 oz/250g peppers (red *or*
   green *or* both)
6 oz/175g crumbly strong
   white cheese (Greek
   Feta, white Stilton *or*
   Cheshire are fine)
1 large sweet onion
5-6 tablespoons vegetable
   oil (olive or sunflower)
1-2 small green chillies
   (*optional*)
1-2 tablespoons wine
   vinegar

UTENSILS
A serving bowl

Thinly slice the tomatoes round the middle. De-seed and cut the peppers into strips. Peel and slice the onion finely. Mix all well together in the serving bowl with the oil, vinegar and seasoning. Grate or crumble the cheese over the top, and scatter on a few rings of sliced chilli if you like your salad piquant.

Serve the salad on its own, with sliced salami, or as a side-dish with barbecued meat.

Pumpkin Cake

Torta di zucca

Torta di zucca is a recipe from Venice, where the New World vegetables arrived via the Spanish Main – often to be re-exported to the Ottoman Turks. Pumpkins keep well, even in our modern central-heated kitchens. In peasant communities the seeds are saved and spread out in the sun to dry for nibbling by children instead of sweets, or ground to give a very dark but surprisingly light-flavoured oil.

QUANTITY
Serves 4-6

TIME
Preparation: 25 minutes
Cooking: 1 hour

1 lb/500g piece of
   pumpkin
1 teaspoon cinnamon
8 oz/250g runny honey
½ teaspoon freshly grated
   nutmeg
6 tablespoons nut *or* seed
   oil (pumpkin if you can
   get it)
½ teaspoon salt
2 tablespoons raisins
   soaked in a little
   brandy
3 eggs
8 oz/250g flour
juice and grated rind of 1
   lemon

Oil and line the base of the cake tin with a circle of greaseproof paper.

Peel and chunk the pumpkin and put it to cook in boiling water for 20 minutes, until soft. Drain well, and either purée it in a liquidizer or push it through a sieve.

Preheat the oven to 350°F/180°C/Gas 4.

Beat the oil and the honey into the pumpkin pulp.

Separate the eggs and beat the yolks into the pumpkin mixture. Reserve the whites.

Sieve the flour and fold it into the mixture, along with the spices, salt, raisins, lemon rind and juice.

Whisk the egg whites until stiff and fold them in lightly.

Tip the mixture into the cake tin and bake for an hour. It is done when well risen and brown and firm to the finger. Leave it to settle for 5 minutes before easing it out to cool on a wire rack.

Serve after a thick soup as a light supper, or a special occasion to finish a party meal.

UTENSILS

An 8-in/20-cm diameter cake tin and greaseproof paper, a medium lidded saucepan, a sieve *or* liquidizer, a whisk, and a wire rack

Fish Suppers

Salt fish played a very important part in stocking the inland larders of Europe until modern times, when freezing and refrigeration took over the storage problem. Cod from the cold waters of the Atlantic was salted and dried into large stiff planks, and traded throughout the Mediterranean. Salted, dried and smoked salmon and tuna added protein to local winter dishes. Herring and mackerel and various little fishes including sardines and anchovies were all barrelled, layered with salt and stored for use throughout the winter storms.

Some of these preparations have survived in altered forms in the modern kitchen. Modern cures for salmon, herring and fish roes are now so light that the shelf life of the fish is a week or two where once it was months. Salt cod – *bacalao* – is now a luxury where it was once essential fast-day food in Catholic Europe, although the taste for the fish still remains very much alive. The smaller salted fish such as anchovies and sardines now come in tins in modern British supermarkets and are very useful larder stores for little meals. The rest of Europe can still buy their salt fish straight from the barrel or from gigantic tins, and have it with bread in south and central Europe, and with plain-boiled potatoes (dressed with dill, chives or onion and accompanied by soured cream) in the north.

Mediterranean markets usually have at least one stall selling tuna and anchovies by weight, along with the tubs of pickled olives and brined vegetables. All contribute to the array of little appetizers which the inhabitants of the sunny littoral love to pick at as they take their evening glass of wine.

Fresh-pickled Sardines

Sardines en marinade

This is the Provençal version of a favourite Mediterranean way with the most plentiful local catch. Sardines are an oily fish and their flavour deteriorates fast. Fish pickles were, obviously enough, a way of preserving highly perishable goods without refrigeration – the technique produces such good results that pickled fish is often preferred to the day's catch of sparkling silver-flanked fresh fish. Don't be afraid of the quantity of garlic – it is only about ½ clove per medium-sized fish. Any other small fish can substitute – as can mackerel, herring or trout cut into bite-sized chunks.

QUANTITY
Serves 4

TIME
Start 2-3 days ahead
Preparation: 30-40
    minutes

1 lb/500g fresh sardines
2 tablespoons fresh
    mixed herbs (rosemary,
    savory, marjoram,
    thyme, salt, oregano)
2 heaped tablespoons
    flour
3 tablespoons olive oil
2 bayleaves
1 medium onion
½ teaspoon roughly
    crushed peppercorns
1 large old carrot
4 cloves garlic
½ pint/300ml wine
    vinegar

Gut and clean the sardines and dust them with the flour, seasoned with a little salt. If the fish are small, pinch them together in threes by the tails (they stick neatly and are easier to handle).

Heat the oil in a shallow frying pan. When it is lightly smoking, put in the sardines and fry them golden in batches – don't let the oil overheat or the flavour will be spoilt. As soon as the fishes are cooked (a few minutes only – depending on their thickness), transfer them to a wide shallow dish.

Meanwhile, peel and slice the onion. Scrape and cut the carrot into small sticks. When all the fish are cooked, fry the onion gently in the oil which remains in the pan (add a little more if you need it). Add the carrot and the cloves of garlic, unpeeled, along with the parsley and other herbs, and the bayleaves and peppercorns, roughly crushed. Allow the aromatics to fry gently for a few moments so that the flavours blend. Add the wine vinegar and water, stir in the cayenne and a little salt, and allow the mixture to bubble up. Scrape in all the bits that stick to the bottom of the pan. Pour this warm, scented bath unstrained over the waiting fish.

Cover loosely with a clean cloth, and leave the dish in a cool place. Ready to eat in 2-3 days, it is delicious as a light supper with a warm salad of potatoes dressed with olive oil, and a side-dish of fried peppers or baby artichokes. Accompany with a *vin gris* – my favourite summer thirst-quencher from the salt marshes of the Rhône basin. To finish, sweet rosy-cheeked white cherries served from one of those pretty white pottery colanders the French use for rinsing and presenting their soft fruit.

1 heaped tablespoon
  chopped parsley
1 glass water
½ teaspoon cayenne

UTENSILS
A frying pan, a wide
  shallow dish and a
  clean cloth

Sweet-Sour Cod
Baccalà in agrodolce

Much of the salt cod sold round the Mediterranean is imported from the Norwegian Lo-foten Islands. The Norwegians themselves like the flavour of the salt fish raw and will chew it like pemmican – fast food to fuel a Viking longship, both as provisions and as barter. The trade in salt cod is very ancient – in medieval times it was controlled by the merchants of the Hanseatic League based in Bergen. These days the Lofotens' salt cod industry sells direct to its markets and the salesmen have a chance to sample other nations' dishes prepared with their raw materials. Ulf Ellingsen, director of the Svolvaer fishmer-chants' association, makes a sales trip to Italy every year so that he can enjoy the Italian salt-cod dishes – this is his particular favourite.

QUANTITY
Serves 4

TIME
Preparation: Start a day
  ahead
Cooking: 30 minutes

Soak the salt cod for 24 hours, changing the water once or twice. Remove any bones and skin. Cut the fish into bite-sized squares and roll them lightly in the flour. Peel and slice the garlic and onion.

Put the olive oil to heat gently and then add the garlic and the onion. Stew these gently until they soften. Push them aside and add the floured fish pieces. Cook the fish over a low heat until it is lightly browned. Add the pine nuts and let them take colour. Add the vinegar, water and herbs. Let all bubble up for a few minutes.

1 lb/500g salt cod (1½ lb/750g fresh cod can substitute)

1 tablespoon pine nuts

5 tablespoons wine vinegar

1 tablespoon flour

5 tablespoons water

2 cloves garlic

1 teaspoon chopped fresh basil

1 onion

1 teaspoon chopped fresh mint

5 tablespoons olive oil

Serve with bread or *polenta*, a bowl of ripe tomatoes, rough red wine and a jug of water to mix with the wine, Italian-style.

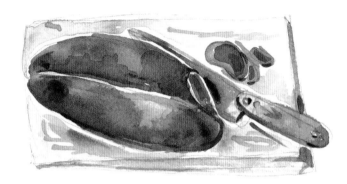

Salt Fish and Red Peppers
Esgarradet

This is a fast-day dish from the Levante of Spain. It is eaten with bread and made with *bacalao* – the locals call the salt cod 'mountain fish' as it has for centuries been a staple of the shepherding communities. The vegetables and fish were originally blistered directly on the embers of the fire, which gives the dish its deliciously sweet roasted flavour. When fresh peppers were not available in the winter months, dried peppers, *ñoras*, were used instead. Roasted aubergines sometimes replace the *bacalao*.

QUANTITY
Serves 4

TIME
Start ½ hour ahead
Preparation: 20-30 minutes

Put the gridiron or iron pan on to heat.

Wipe the red peppers but do not hull them. Roast them on the dry iron, turning regularly, until the skins blister black and the flesh softens.

Don't soak or skin the cod, but cut it into squares and smack the pieces onto the hot metal and let it blister black. Turn once.

1 lb/500g ripe red
  peppers
4 tablespoons olive oil
1 lb/500g salt cod
  (*bacalao*)
½ teaspoon cayenne
  pepper
1 whole head garlic

UTENSILS

A gridiron *or* a heavy
  iron frying pan, and a
  bowl

Divide the head of garlic into separate cloves and put them on the grill to roast until the papery skin is burnt black and you can see the soft cream flesh.

Tear the fish (avoiding the skin if you prefer) and the peppers into small flakes with the fingers – no nonsense with knives. Chop the garlic. Toss all the ingredients together. Sprinkle with olive oil – and a little cayenne pepper to spike. Leave to infuse for half an hour or so. Serve with a salad of chopped cos lettuce dressed with sliced onion, salt, olive oil and vinegar.

Salt Fish and Spinach Soup Stew
Borreta

Borreta is a Spanish *bourride* – as here, a spinach soup with *bacalao*. It was originally a shepherd's dish which can be made with just the *bacalao* and a green vegetable – including a variety of wild-gathered greens. Jose Luis Gregorio serves this version in the Venta del Pilár below the mountain town of Alcoy, in the province of Alicante.

QUANTITY
Serves 4-5 for supper

TIME
Start a day ahead
Preparation: 15 minutes
Cooking: 1 hour

1 lb/500g *bacalao*
1 small glass olive oil
2 pints/1.2 litres water
1 clove garlic
1 tablespoon *pimentón*

Soak the *bacalao* overnight, drain and pat it dry. Rinse the spinach well (and the chard if you are using it) and chop the leaves roughly.

Chop the *bacalao* into bite-sized pieces and put it in a large saucepan with the water. Stir in the spinach, the peeled garlic, the *pimentón* and the dried red peppers torn into little pieces (or add extra *pimentón* if you have not managed to find any *ñoras*). Bring to the boil and add the potatoes, peeled and cut into bite-sized chunks. Stir in the olive oil. Allow to come back to the boil. Turn the heat down and add the optional fresh fish after 10 minutes' cooking.

Simmer until the soup thickens – about half an hour in total. The consistency should be midway between a stew and a soup. To finish, stir in the fresh or mature garlic, chopped, then

2 lb/1kg spinach with
a few chard leaves
(*optional*)
3 dried red sweet peppers
(*ñoras*), torn into pieces
(if unobtainable, use
an extra spoonful of
pimentón)

optional additions:
monkfish, squid and
cuttlefish (*or* other
firm-fleshed fish)

To finish
3-4 stalks fresh garlic
shoots *or* 1 extra clove
garlic
1 tablespoon wine
vinegar
salt
1½ lb/750g potatoes
1 egg per person

the vinegar. Bring back to the boil. Taste and adjust the seasoning. With a ladle, make hollows in the surface of the hot stew and slide in an egg per person. Let the eggs poach for a minute or two, basting them with hot soup, until the white sets.

Serve in deep bowls, with an egg in each portion. Accompany with chunks of bread and a salad of cos lettuce, chunked cucumber and sliced mild onions seasoned with olive oil, salt and vinegar.

Tuna and Vegetable Stew
Giraboix

Giraboix is a vegetable soup-stew which takes its name from the mortar in which the sauce is made. It can be made with *bacalao*, or with the salted locally-caught tuna which was a major industry of Valencia and the east coast of Spain. It is a popular dish in the mountains of Jijona, where the nougats of Spain are made. The air of the high hills brings a chill in winter and diners huddle happily for hours round the *mesa camelia*, a round table which hides beneath its woollen skirts a metal dish filled with hot charcoal.

QUANTITY

Serves 4

Peel and chop the onions and potatoes. Top and tail the beans. Slice the cabbage. Wipe the chilli. Put all these ingredients

Preparation: 30 minutes
Cooking: 1 hour

1 lb/500g onions *or* leeks
1 lb/500g potatoes

8 oz/250g green beans
(*or* cardoons, chopped)
¼ small cabbage (*or* 2
smallish artichokes,
quartered and with the
chokes removed)
2 pints/1.2 litres fresh
cold water

To finish
All i olio made with
6 cloves garlic, ½
teaspoon salt, and
approximately ½
pint/300ml olive oil
8 oz/250g ripe tomatoes
4 slices day-old bread
8-oz/250-g tin tuna in
brine, drained and
flaked
1 hot red chilli (called
a *guindilla* – 'little
cherry' – a nickname it
shares with the village
policeman)
1 tablespoon toasted pine
nuts (*optional*)

A large casserole with
a lid and a pestle and
mortar, and a deep
serving dish

into a casserole or stewpot with the water. Bring to the boil, lid, turn down the heat and leave to simmer gently for an hour.

While the stew cooks, settle down with a pestle and mortar to make the *all i olio* (garlic and oil). Made by hand, this is a soothing process which envelops the maker in the delicious fumes of fresh garlic.

Peel and crush the garlic in the mortar with the salt. When the garlic is well pounded, start adding the oil in a thin stream. Keep pounding with the pestle and trickling in the oil until the mixture is good and thick.

If you are in a hurry, make the *all i ollio* in the liquidizer, with a peeled boiled potato, or a crust of stale bread, soaked and squeezed, to stabilize it. Those uncertain of good results can make it with an egg yolk, like a garlic mayonnaise – which gives a richer but less piquant mix.

Find the chilli, remove it from the soup and chop it up with the tomatoes (skinned or not, as you please).

Toast the bread. It is particularly delicious if you do this Spanish-style on a grill over a flame (the bread grills well enough if put straight on an electric ring turned low). This is more of a quick blister-blacken than real toasting and gives a special caramelized flavour to the bread.

Strain the vegetables from the soup and transfer them to a warm deep dish. Lay the tuna flakes on top so that they heat in the steam. Sprinkle on the pine kernels if you are using them. Put a slice of the toasted bread into the bottom of each soup plate (some cooks tear the bread first). Pour a ladleful of hot soup into each plate.

Serve the soup first, and then the vegetables and tuna. Hand round the tomato/chilli mixture to spice the soup, and the *all-i-olio* mix to eat with the vegetables and fish.

This is a robust winter dish which should have a strong red wine to accompany it. Complete the meal with a fruit salad of sliced oranges topped with matchsticks of their own fine-pared peel simmered in a little sugar syrup.

Sausage and Bacon Suppers

The autumn pig-killing remains a very important event in those peasant communities which still survive in the modern world. In Britain slaughtering is no longer allowed on the farm for health and safety reasons, although those smallholders who still keep a pig do not necessarily agree that this is for the best. The family pig, during his lifetime an admired and cossetted member of the household, is perhaps not well served by being transported in discomfort miles from his home territory to meet his end.

The pig, unlike sheep and cattle, is not a migratory animal. The presence of pigs is the sign of a settled farming community. Nomads could not keep the creatures as they resolutely refuse to be herded. The pig prefers instead to go his own sweet way, hurtling round his own home territory making the best of the local products – acorns, apples and all manner of roots and tubers. Those who keep pigs will always inspect with an eye to their own stew pot any new foodstuff which their charges find palatable – which is probably how the delights of the first truffle were discovered.

The homemade sausages of Central Europe often have vegetables such as cabbage and leeks added to the chopped pork. To reheat a precooked sausage (a boiling ring, frankfurters and other smoked sausages): first bring a saucepan of water to the boil. Put in the sausage (without pricking it) and let the water just return to the boil – one large belch is enough. Remove from the heat and let it sit in the hot water on the side of the stove for 10 minutes to heat through. If you prick the sausage first to stop it bursting, you can simmer it gently for 5 minutes. This method is faster, but you will lose some of the juices to the water – which is fine if you are going to make a soup with the cooking water.

Smoked Pork and Sauerkraut
Tsarfion

Tsarfion is one of Switzerland's favourite pork and cabbage dishes. All of central Europe makes these boiled dinners. Breadcrumbs can replace half the sausage meat. Cider, cream or milk can replace the wine.

QUANTITY

Serves 6 hearty Swiss
appetites

TIME

**Preparation and
cooking**: 1 hour

6 smoked pork chops
(gammon steaks can
substitute)
8 oz/250g mushrooms
(wild if possible – the
Swiss collect a wide
variety)
4 oz/100g smoked
streaky bacon in a piece
1 tablespoon bacon fat
1 egg
4 oz/100g green streaky
bacon in a piece
1 tablespoon flour
6 prunes
1 glass white wine
1 lb/500g sauerkraut
salt and pepper
1 lb/500g sausage meat

UTENSILS

A large casserole, a
colander and a small
saucepan

Wipe the first 3 meats and put them in a roomy casserole with the prunes. Cover all to a depth of one finger with water. Bring the water to the boil, then turn it down to simmer. Lid and leave to cook gently for 30 minutes, until the meats are tender.

Rinse the sauerkraut if it tastes too salty. Put it in a small saucepan with a ladleful of the liquor from the meat. Leave it over a gentle heat to simmer for 30 minutes.

Meanwhile, wipe and chop the mushrooms. Fry them in a little bacon fat. Work the sausage meat well with the mushrooms, egg, flour and wine, seasoning with a teaspoon of salt and a few turns of the pepper mill. Form the mixture into prune-sized dumplings.

Remove the meats and prunes from the casserole (keep them warm) and drop the dumplings into the simmering liquid. Bring all back to the boil, turn the heat and poach the dumplings for 15-20 minutes, until they are quite firm. Remove them with a draining spoon to a large warm dish.

Slice the meats, drain the sauerkraut, and arrange all, including the prunes, on the dish with the dumplings. Hand a jug of the cooking broth separately.

Serve with potatoes boiled in their skins, and plenty of cold white wine.

Tripe Sausages

Andouillettes de Troyes

Tripe sausages are a particular speciality of Troyes in the Champagne district of France, although plenty of other areas make them too. Waverley Root tells a fine story about them in *The Food of France*: when the city was under attack from Royalist troops in the sixteenth century, the invaders happened upon a great store of the sausages. So delighted were they by the excellence of the preparation that they gorged themselves and, as is proper after a heavy meal, fell asleep replete and insensible. The defenders, leaner and keener, were then able to fall upon their enemies, put them to the sword and save the city – a rare victory for the humble sausage.

Andouillettes are either split and grilled or served *nature* – cut in slices and then seasoned with a trickle of olive oil mixed with aromatic herbs. They can be accompanied with fried onion rings: onions cut in rounds, dunked in beer or milk and then rolled in flour before being fried in deep oil.

Or serve them *à la poêle*: fry the *andouillettes* gently in a little lard until nicely browned. Push them aside and add a heaped tablespoon of chopped fresh herbs and 2-3 chopped cloves of garlic. Fry until the garlic is soft.

To bake *andouillettes*, put them in a casserole which will just accommodate them. Pour a glass of wine and a small carton of cream over them. Lid tightly and put to cook in a moderate oven 350°F/180°C/Gas 4 for 30 minutes. Baste the sausages every now and then. Serve with fluffy mashed potato, or a mixture of celeriac and potato, well mashed with cream and seasoned with grated nutmeg.

Good pork sausages take well to the same treatment.

Sausages with Onion Sauce
Geschmorte bratwurst

The Germans are the sausage experts of Europe. A British sausage can be prepared in the same way with excellent results.

QUANTITY
Serves 2-3

TIME
Preparation: 10 minutes
Cooking: 30 minutes

1 lb/500g bratwurst *or*
  fresh pork
2 tablespoons lard
  sausages
½ pint/300ml red wine
  or beer
1 tablespoon flour
½ pint/300ml stock
1 lb/500g onions
salt and pepper

UTENSILS
A roomy frying pan

Roll the sausages in flour. Peel and chop the onions. Fry the onions in the lard until they are golden brown. Push them aside and put in the sausages. Brown the sausages. Pour in the wine and stock, turn up the heat and allow the liquid to bubble up fiercely for 5 minutes to evaporate the alcohol. When the gravy has thickened a little and you have scraped all the brown bits into the sauce, taste and add salt and pepper, and a pinch of sugar if the wine is a little sharp.

Serve with plain-boiled potatoes to soak up the gravy, and a side salad of sauerkraut or raw shredded cabbage. German beer and pickled cucumbers to accompany.

Sausages with Raisins and Apples
Bratwurst mit Rosinen und Äpfeln

This German sausage dish is a sturdy supper from the fertile valleys of Thuringia. It is simple, easily prepared and delicious – raisins and apples are a particularly happy combination with sausages.

QUANTITY
Serves 4

TIME
Preparation: 15 minutes
Cooking: 15 minutes

1 lb/500g fresh all-meat
  pork sausages
1 glass water *or* cider *or*
  white wine
2 oz/50g butter
4 oz/100g raisins
1 lb/500g apples

UTENSILS
A frying pan and small
  saucepan

Put the sausages to cook gently in a frying pan greased with a tiny knob of the butter.

Peel, quarter and core the apples. Put them to simmer with the water, cider or wine, the raisins and the butter, for 15 minutes in a small saucepan with a lid.

Serve all together with plain boiled potatoes, dark rye bread, radishes with salt and a stein of good German beer.

Sausage and Potato Gratin
Gratin Vaudois

Gratins and *garbures* are the pride of the Swiss kitchen. In the absence of an oven, this *gratin vaudois* would cook on top of the stove, with hot coals in the inverted lid of the casserole to melt the cheese hat.

QUANTITY
Serves 4

TIME
Preparation: 30 minutes
Cooking: 1 hour 15
  minutes

1 *saucisson vaudois*
  weighing 1 lb/500g
  (any all-meat fresh
  sausage will do)
2-3 onions
2-3 cloves garlic
2 oz/50g butter
1½ lb/750g potatoes
2 glasses dry white wine
4 oz/100g grated cheese
  (best is Gruyère *or* Jura,
  but Cheddar will do)
pepper

UTENSILS
A large saucepan, a small
  saucepan and a deep
  gratin dish

Boil the potatoes in their skins in plenty of salted water for 10-15 minutes, depending on their size. Add the sausage, well pricked, for the last 5 minutes' boiling time. Drain. Peel the potatoes as soon as they are cool enough (or leave the skins on, if you prefer) and cut them into thick slices.

Meanwhile, peel the onions and the garlic cloves and slice them finely.

Butter a deep gratin dish. Lay a thick layer of potatoes in the base and sprinkle with some of the grated cheese. Cover with a layer of onions, dot with butter and season with freshly ground pepper (no salt – the cheese and sausage take care of that). Settle the sausage on this bed. Arrange the rest of the potatoes and cheese, onions, garlic and butter in layers (not forgetting to season with pepper) until the sausage is buried under a layer at least an inch/2.5cm deep. Finish with a layer of potatoes, cheese and dot with butter.

Preheat the oven to 475°F/240°C/Gas 9.

Heat the wine and pour it over the potatoes. Cover with a lid or foil, and put the gratin to bake in the hot oven for 15 minutes, by which time the wine should be bubbling. Turn the oven right down to 400°F/200°C/ Gas 6 and leave to bake gently for another hour. Take off the cover 15 minutes before the end of cooking. By this time the potatoes will have drunk all the wine and the meat juices, and the gratin will be beautifully golden and fragrant.

Slip the sausage from under the crust so that you can cut it in slices and slide them back before you take the dish to the table. Serve with a well-chilled bottle of the wine you used in the cooking. Follow with a green salad, dressed perhaps with hazelnut oil from the Swiss valleys. Nut bread (page 252) and a prune compote (page 140) complete the meal.

Toad-in-the-hole

This is a lovely nursery dish – quick, cheap and easy to prepare. Make it with the best pork sausages and serve it with mustard. Include a grated apple in the batter for a delicious change.

QUANTITY
Serves 4

TIME
Start ½ hour ahead
Preparation: 10 minutes
Cooking: 40-45 minutes

8 oz/250g plain flour
1 pint/600ml milk
1 level teaspoon salt
1 oz/25g lard *or* dripping
2 eggs
1 lb/500g best pork
    sausages

UTENSILS
A sieve, a bowl, a
    wooden spoon, a whisk
    and a roasting tin (and
    a liquidizer would
    speed things up)

Sieve the flour and the salt into the bowl. Make a well in the middle. Beat the eggs together with some of the milk. Stir the liquid into the well in the flour, drawing in dry flour slowly and beating to avoid lumps. Add milk gradually until you have a creamy batter. Beat it some more and watch the bubbles rise. Put it aside to rest for 20 minutes or so. You can do all this in the liquidizer if you have one.

Preheat the oven to 425°F/220°C/Gas 7. Melt the lard in the roasting tin in the oven – it is important that both should be very hot when the batter is poured in.

Separate the links of sausages and prick them. When the lard is good and hot, pour in the pudding batter. Arrange the sausages in the batter, well separated from each other but not submerged.

Bake for 40-50 minutes, until the pudding is puffy and well-browned – the cooking time depends on the size of the roasting tin and therefore the thickness of the layer of batter. The batter depends on the air you have incorporated to let it rise, so don't open and shut the oven or it will collapse – not the worst of fates, as it will still taste delicious.

SUGGESTIONS

If you have not included a grated apple in the batter, complete the meal with baked apples: core 4 cooking apples, and stuff the holes with a few raisins, brown sugar and a knob of butter. Put the apples to bake in a foil-covered dish, at the same time as the toad-in-the-hole, but in a cooler part of the oven.

Bean Suppers

Very few of the dried bean tribe can be reckoned fast-food for supper: chickpeas, butter beans, large and small haricot beans, borlotti, kidney and fava beans all need 2 hours soaking before they are ready to be prepared. The only way to avoid this problem is either to bottle your own according to the instructions on page 86, or buy them ready prepared and tinned.

The exceptions – those which do not need preliminary soaking – split peas and lentils, are an excellent storecupboard staple. Keep a store in your larder as the basic ingredient for quickly made soups and stews. Pulse vegetables are enjoyed by an interesting menagerie of small insects, so check your stores regularly, and examine newly bought supplies with an interested eye. They may have brought their own wildlife with them and it is wise to check. If you do find any strangers, keep the beans well away from your storecupboard and cook them at once. Any insects will float to the surface of the water when you soak the beans, and you can scoop them off before cooking. You will come to no harm.

The bean-eating populations of Europe – largely those around the Mediterranean – circumvent the soaking problem by milling their beans exactly as flour is milled. The fine-ground flour is then used in soups, purées and in more sophisticated dishes like the *panisses* of Provence. These flours are now factory-prepared but remain quite localized: one district prefers chickpeas alone, another mixes in a proportion of haricot, others only like lentil or dried chestnut flour – these last, with the chickpea and the fava bean, are the original pulse vegetables of all Europe's beans-and-bones stews. Buy a pound or two of such flours when you see them in local markets, and use a tablespoonful or two, slaked in water first, to add body to your favourite soups.

Chickpea-flour Soup
Potage de garbanzos

I make this Mediterranean soup with a chickpea and haricot bean flour mix. It works perfectly with any other pulse-vegetable flour. The final flavouring is a *sofrito*, a little fried paste of aromatic ingredients added at the end of cooking. This last is an alternative to the preliminary frying of onions and meat, which is the common method of adding flavour to soups and stews. To make a purée, halve the volume of water and take care with the stirring.

QUANTITY
Serves 4

TIME
Preparation: 10 minutes
Cooking: 30 minutes

8 heaped tablespoons
    chickpea flour
2 pints/1.2 litres
    fresh water *or* good
    homemade stock
salt and pepper
1 sprig thyme and a bay
    leaf

To finish
2-3 tablespoons olive oil
2 oz/50g finely chopped
    raw salt ham *or* bacon
2 slices day-old bread,
    cubed small
1 hard-boiled egg,
    chopped

UTENSILS
A large saucepan and a
    small frying pan

Mix the chickpea flour to a smooth paste with a cupful of the water, beating to avoid lumps. Bring the rest of the water to the boil in a roomy saucepan, and stir in the flour paste – keep beating so that the soup remains smooth. Add a teaspoon of salt and freshly milled black pepper, and the herbs tied in a little bunch. Bring the soup back to the boil, turn down the heat, cover loosely and simmer for 20 minutes. Give it a stir now and then to make sure it doesn't stick. When it is ready, remove the herbs.

Meanwhile make the *sofrito*: Warm the oil in a small frying pan and stir in the ham or bacon and the bread cubes. Fry gently until the bread is golden. Stir in the chopped hard-boiled eggs. Stir the *sofrito* into the soup just before serving. Accompany with bread and wine and a salad of chopped cos lettuce, tomatoes and onions dressed with olive oil, lemon juice and salt.

Split Peas and Salt Pork
Eisbein mit Erbspuree

Berliners love this winter dish. You can use all salt pork, or a piece of gammon if you prefer. All northern Europe has its own variations of bacon-and-peas.

QUANTITY
Serves 4

TIME
Preparation: 15 minutes
Cooking: 1¼ hours

1 lb/500g yellow split
   peas
1 bay leaf
1 lb/500g salt leg of pork
   or gammon
2 pints/1.2 litres water
6 allspice berries
1 onion
3 cloves

To finish
4 oz/100g sliced streaky
   bacon
2 medium onions

UTENSILS
A large stewpot, serving
   dish and small frying
   pan

Put the split peas and the pork or gammon into a large stewpot with the onion stuck with the cloves, the allspice and the bay leaf. Cover with cold water – no salt, as there will be enough salt in the meat. Bring to the boil, turn down the heat and leave to simmer for 1¼ hours – do not leave it too long as the meat should be tender but not overcooked.

Remove the meat. Purée the remaining peas and vegetables. Bubble on a high heat to evaporate the liquid if the purée is too runny. Taste and add salt.

Slice the meat thickly. Arrange the sliced meat and the purée on a heated serving dish and keep all warm.

To finish: chop the bacon and peel and chop the onions. Fry the bacon until the fat runs, then add the chopped onions. Fry all together until golden. Tip the mixture over the pea purée.

Beer with a chaser of schnapps to accompany.

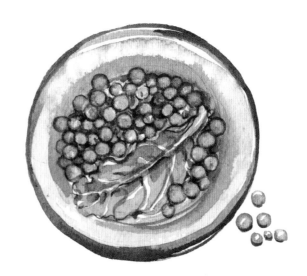

Lentils with Bacon

Linsen mit Speck

Make the German *linsen mit speck* with the little green lentils which are reckoned the best of their tribe. Lentils are indigenous to the Mediterranean, and are one of Europe's oldest available pulse vegetables. Esau sold his birthright for a mess of it; the Greeks thought them poor man's fare; the Romans imported quantities of the red ones from Cleopatra's Egypt; Charlemagne ordered them planted in his kingdom's vegetable patches. Louis XV's queen, Marie Leszczynska, popularized them at the court of Versailles – some consolation, perhaps, for her husband's dalliance with Madame de Pompadour. You will keep royal company with your lentil stew.

QUANTITY

Serves 4

TIME

Cooking: intermittent attention for 1¼ hours

1 lb/500g lentils
parsley
1¾ pints/1 litre water
4 anchovy fillets
4 oz/100g streaky bacon in a piece
1 teaspoon capers
bay leaf and thyme
1 tablespoon vinegar
1 onion
salt and pepper
1 clove garlic

UTENSILS

A large saucepan

Bring the lentils and water, with the rind of the bacon, bay leaf and thyme, to the boil in the saucepan. Turn down the heat, lid and simmer for 1 hour until the lentils are soft.

Meanwhile, peel and chop the onion and garlic. Chop the parsley, anchovies and capers finely. Chop the bacon and fry it crisp in its own fat. Take out the bacon pieces and replace them with the onion and garlic. Cook them until they soften, and then stir in the remaining chopped ingredients. Cook the mixture gently for 10 minutes, then stir it into the lentils when they are quite ready. Stir in the vinegar. Taste and add salt and pepper as required.

Add a slice of boiling sausage to each serving, if you please. Sprinkle the crisp bacon pieces over all, and serve in deep soup dishes.

Add a plate of white radishes with salt, pickled cucumbers and beer to complete the supper.

Lentil and Tongue Salad

Linsensalat

This is a favourite Viennese combination. Lentils, native to Syria and our oldest cultivated legume (since 7000 B.C.), probably arrived in Austria with the Ottoman Turks, along with Vienna's beloved coffee.

QUANTITY
Serves 4

TIME
Preparation: 20 minutes

1 lb/500g cooked lentils
2 tablespoons vinegar
4 oz/100g cooked tongue
5-6 tablespoons oil
1 small onion
pepper, salt and sugar
2 hard-boiled eggs
1 small bunch parsley

UTENSILS
A large and a small
   mixing bowl

Drain the lentils thoroughly. Chop the tongue. Peel and chop the onion finely. Mix the tongue and the onion with the lentils.

Make a salad dressing by pounding the yolks of the hard-boiled eggs with the vinegar, oil and seasonings. Dress the lentils with the mixture.

Leave for half an hour or so to infuse. Chop the egg whites and parsley and sprinkle over the top. Accompany with beer.

You could consider a Viennese Coffee (sweetened black coffee topped with plenty of whipped cream) to follow.

Broad Bean Soup with Bacon

Habas con jamon

Habas con jamon is Andalusia's version of one of the most ancient pottages of Europe. Serve it on a cold winter's evening – such a dish probably kept our ancestors warm when they first abandoned the warm valleys of the Mediterranean, and moved up into the icy northern mountains and plains.

QUANTITY

Serves 6

TIME

Preparation: 15 minutes
Cooking: 1 hour

1 lb/500g hulled broad
   beans (fresh *or* pre-
   soaked dried)
fresh marjoram and
   thyme
1 oz/25g lard *or* 3
   tablespoons oil
3 pints/1.5 litres water
1 bacon hock, bone in
2 carrots
salt and pepper
2 onions
2 cloves garlic
2-3 sticks celery

To finish
1 chorizo *or* paprika
   sausage (*optional*)
3 slices of bread, diced

UTENSILS

1 large saucepan with a
   lid, a small frying pan

Put the beans in the saucepan with the water. Wash, peel as necessary, and chop the vegetables and add them to the beans with the oil, bacon hock and the herbs.

Bring all to the boil, turn down the heat and simmer for an hour, until the beans are quite soft. Take out the bacon hock and strip it of its meat – discard the skin and the bone, but keep the meat and fat.

Dice the bacon and put it to fry gently in its own fat, with a little extra oil. Meanwhile slice the (optional) sausage. Add it to the bacon and fry for a moment. Push the meats to one side and fry the bread cubes in the aromatic oil. When the bread cubes are golden, transfer all to a small serving bowl.

Mash the soup to thicken it (you can liquidise it if you prefer). Taste and add salt and pepper. Serve the soup from a deep tureen and hand round the fried bread and bacon separately.

Accompany with good country bread and rough red wine.

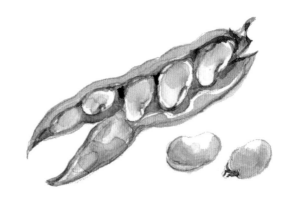

Bean and Bacon Casserole
Olleta

Olleta takes its name from the earthenware casserole in which it is cooked. It is one of the beans-and-bones soup-stews of which Spain has a huge repertoire. These depend largely on the inspiration of the cook and the range of local ingredients available. Adapt it as you will.

QUANTITY

Serves 4-6

TIME

Preparation: 15 minutes

Cooking: intermittent attention, 40-50 minutes

2 lb/1kg ready-prepared haricot beans (drained weight)

4 oz/100g green (unsmoked) streaky bacon

2 turnips

2 carrots

1 lb/500g cardoons (artichokes can replace the flavour, Swiss chard stalks replace the visual effect)

salt and pepper

To finish

1 onion

2 tablespoons olive oil

1 tablespoon chopped oregano *or* marjoram

1 short length black pudding (*optional*)

Peel and cube the turnips and carrots. Cube the bacon. Trim and chop the cardoon into short lengths – if you use fresh artichokes and chard, trim the hard tips of the leaves, remove the hairy choke and cut the artichoke into slices. Chard should be cut into short lengths. Put these ingredients in the casserole with the beans and enough water to cover. Bring to the boil and lid. Turn down the heat and cook gently on the top of the stove for ½ hour until the vegetables are quite soft. Taste and add salt and pepper.

1 tablespoon paprika (in
  Spain, this would be a
  crumbled *ñora*, a dried
  red pepper)

UTENSILS

An earthenware casserole
  which can withstand
  direct heat (otherwise
  you will have to cook
  the stew in the oven
  and it will take 10
  minutes longer), and a
  small frying pan

Make a *sofrito* to finish: peel and chop the onion. Warm the oil in a small frying pan and gently fry the onion. Sprinkle in the oregano or marjoram. Add the (optional) black pudding cut into slices. Fry gently. Add the paprika, but don't let it burn. Stir the *sofrito* into the stew. Serve with bread and wine.

Pasta Suppers

The Italians, the Chinese, the Persians, Egyptians, Romans, Turks – half the world has a claim to being the first to roll out a flour-and-water dough, cut it into fine strips, and throw the result into a pan of boiling water.

The basic paste is simplicity itself: a logical step as obvious (with hindsight) as attaching the first wheels to the first cart. Milled grain worked with water makes dough. Here is child's play, the most primitive of fuel-food, the easiest way of making farinaceous food palatable.

Just such an unsophisticated lump of dough (give or take a little salt, a little shortening), tied in a cloth and cooked in the cauldron with a savoury broth, gave Central Europe its dumpling. Patted out flat and baked on a heated hearthstone the same preparation supplied Northern Europe with its unleavened breads – the crisp flat-breads of Scandinavia, the soft griddle-scones of the Celts. The cooks of Italy had reduced the size of their pot-dumplings to gnocchi long before Marco Polo set out on his travels. The same dough (sometimes mixed with egg or milk or yoghurt for added protein) remains a staple preparation throughout Mediterranean and Eastern Europe. It is shaved into soup to give substance, or grated onto a cloth and dried and stored, to be cooked like rice porridge – a winter feast for Greeks and Bulgarians, Hungarians, Poles, Croatians and Serbs.

There is no name or date for that first enlightened cook who picked up a broom-handle to roll out the lump of dough into a thin sheet, and then sliced the sheet into fine ribbons. That first pasta-maker laid down the game-plan for the *maccheronaros* of eighteenth century Naples. It was their machines which gave us our modern repertoire of storecupboard pasta: shells and shoelaces, corkscrews and pen-nibs, butterflies and wedding-rings, each of whose curves are perfect for one of a thousand different saucings.

Good-quality dried pasta is by no means a poor relation of fresh pasta. Italian housewives sometimes make their own fresh egg pasta – delicate ravioli or little stuffed tortellini, ribbon or sheet pasta for a special occasion, but they do not usually expect to get their shop-bought pasta fresh. Instead, stores of dried pasta are kept in the larder for the family's favourite meals – fast food for busy housewives and farmers. Made with hard durum wheat and semolina to a quality strictly (in Italy) controlled by law, the best dried pasta should be pale beige, the colour of ripe wheat kernels, with a few dark freckles and a slight surface polish. If the pasta has been made with eggs, it will be yellower (and will probably proclaim on the packet the proportions of eggs to flour). The different pasta shapes dictate their own dressings – a diversity of colour, shape and flavour which at least gives the illusion of a varied daily menu, whatever the means and stores of the cook.

A well-stocked Italian larder will contain half a dozen or so varieties of dried pasta. Spaghetti remains the staple – its round smooth coils are at their best dressed lightly with an olive oil and herb-based sauce, or turned in a plain tomato *sugo*. The sauce most easily associated with spaghetti, the tomato and meat-enriched *ragù* which is the original Bolognaise sauce, is definitely not fast food: the sauce is left to simmer all day on the back of the stove. Since in many Italian households the *ragù* is made once or twice a week for daily use, the midday pasta can be sauced simply and quickly direct from the *ragù*-pan – but this is fast food only in a household which already has its pot simmering.

Small pasta shapes, including stuffed cappelleti, tiny thread-like vermicelli, and the children's favourite alphabet letters, come in useful to add body to the supper-time chicken or beef broth.

Flat noodles such as tagliatelle, and medium-sized shapes – bows, spirals, shells, quills, hats – take happily to saucing with whatever is in season and fresh: vegetables, mushrooms, chopped ham, chicken livers, squid and shellfish, nuts and pine nuts, raisins – an infinite and ever-changing range of possibilities for the imaginative and innovative cook. I find Chinese habits (chopped spring onions, stir-fried vegetables) have lately been creeping into my own combinations: Marco Polo would have been delighted.

The larger sheets and tubes of pasta (lasagne, cannelloni, maccheroni, rigatoni), are designed to stand up to the longer cooking needed for dishes which are sauced and finished in the oven. Make up your own combinations: pasta layered with a fresh, sweet tomato sauce and finished with a crisp hat of grated cheese; slices of fried aubergine inter-leaved with lasagne and a meat sauce; cannelloni stuffed with riccotta cream cheese and chopped spinach, finished *au gratin* with a cheese sauce. There is no better way to feed a large number of people cheaply and well.

I try to keep at least one pasta from each of the four groups on my larder shelves, to give me the basic ingredients for a wide variety of quickly prepared supper dishes.

Spaghetti with Anchovies and Olives
Spaghetti alla syracusana

Spaghetti takes kindly to rough and simple saucing. A clove or two of garlic crushed into fresh green olive oil (*ajo e ojo*), salted anchovies with plenty of black pepper (*con acciughe*), a slick of olive oil and a sprinkling of fried sage leaves (*con olio e salvia*), a handful of chopped marjoram and a panful of crisp-fried bacon (*con pancetta*), a spicing of garlic, oil and red chilli (*all'arrabbiata*), all make delicious dressings for plain-cooked pasta.

This pungent little sauce is popular in Sicily. When you have made it once, work out your own variations: try different herbs, green olives, more chilli, a few roughly chopped walnuts: whatever your larder dictates.

Put on at least 5 pints/3 litres of salted water to boil for the spaghetti.

Meanwhile skin and finely chop the garlic. Pit and chop the olives. De-bone the anchovies if they are whiskery.

Warm the oil in a small saucepan and put in the garlic to soften for a moment before you add the olives, anchovies and chilli powder. Let the mixture stew gently (a *sofrito* – one of the commonest words in Italian cookbooks, it sounds as it is, a soft-fry). Squash the ingredients with the wooden spoon so that they melt into a sauce. Stir in the parsley and the breadcrumbs.

Slide the spaghetti into the boiling water – push it gently down in a bunch – the bottom strands soften instantly to allow you to feed it all in without breaking. Give a good stir with the draining spoon as the water comes back to the boil to keep the strands separate. 8 minutes or so should see it *al dente* – firm to the tooth.

Drain immediately and transfer to a warm dish. If the spaghetti has to wait at all, turn it in a little oil so that the strands do not stick together – this is near-enough the basic mix for wallpaper paste, so you can't be too careful.

Toss the spaghetti with the sauce before you serve it. Hand a bowl of grated cheese separately.

An artichoke would make a good *antipasto* – it takes about as long to eat as the spaghetti to cook.

UTENSILS

A large deep saucepan
(one with two
handles is easiest to
manoeuvre) and a
draining spoon, a small
saucepan and a wooden
spoon, and a large
colander (preferably
one of the Italian ones
with little feet which
can stand in the sink)

Complete the light meal with fruit – a bunch of sweet grapes or a peach perhaps, to keep the mood Italian. The best and sweetest table grapes are reckoned the *uva regina*, ripened in the sunshine of Sicily.

Spaghetti with Sweet Pepper Sauce
Spaghetti con peperonata

This is the simplest of vegetable sauces, at its best on spaghetti, the simplest of pastas. The Italians do not like to drown their pasta, preferring instead a well-concentrated ladleful of sauce which enhances rather than disguises the nutty flavour of good wheat.

The red pepper paste on page 27 is delicious as a replacement for the fresh peppers in this recipe. Those who like it hot can include a chopped chilli.

QUANTITY
Serves 4

TIME
Preparation: 15 minutes
Cooking: 20 minutes

10 oz/275g spaghetti
1 small bunch basil
1 large ripe red pepper
6 tablespoons olive oil
1 large onion
Salt and freshly milled
    black pepper
1 clove garlic

Put on a large pan of salted water to boil – spaghetti needs plenty of room.

Roast the peppers on the gas flame or in the oven till they blister black – I do this on an electric ring if necessary. The scent of roasting peppers is one of the pleasures of this dish. Strip off the fine skin, hull and de-seed the peppers, slice and chop them.

Peel and chop the onion and garlic finely. Scald, peel and chop the tomatoes if you are using fresh ones. Chop the basil (or tear it, if you don't want the witches after you).

Heat the oil gently in a small saucepan. Stir in the onions and garlic and let them soften without taking colour. Add the peppers and soften them. Stir in the tomatoes. Heat until the mixture bubbles up, and then turn down the flame. Stir in the basil.

1 lb/500g tomatoes (*or* 1
tin chopped tomatoes)

To finish
grated Parmesan *or* any
other hard strong
cheese

UTENSILS
A large saucepan and a
draining spoon, a small
saucepan and a wooden
spoon, and a large
colander

Leave the sauce to simmer gently, unlidded, for 15-20 minutes.

Follow the instructions on the packet for cooking the spaghetti – this will take 8-10 minutes. Drain it as soon as it is soft but still has a nutty little bite to the teeth. Toss it in a little oil to keep the strands separate.

Taste the sauce and add salt and pepper – and maybe a little sugar if the tomatoes were not really sun-ripened.

Turn the spaghetti in the sauce. Hand a bowl of grated cheese round separately, and accompany with a bowl of quartered lettuce hearts.

Complete the simple meal with a delicious creamy *tira mi su* (page 319).

SUGGESTIONS

Any spaghetti-and-sauce leftovers can be roughly chopped and stirred into lightly beaten egg. Fry a pancake of the mixture in olive oil, turned once, as a *frittata*. My family likes it fried as small patties, served with more tomato sauce spiked with chilli and chopped marjoram.

Pasta Ribbons and Wild Mushrooms
Tagliatelle con porcini

Fresh *porcini* (the English call them penny buns, the French *ceps*) are on sale throughout the markets of Italy from May through to the autumn – in Italy they are the commonest mushroom available.

In Britain *porcini* are harder to come by in the shops, and can usually only be found dried and packed in little cellophane envelopes in Italian delicatessens. In Italy, they are sold loose from large glass jars. In spite of the harvest freely available in our woods and fields every year, the British do not easily see their penny buns as an edible mushroom. This seems an excellent reason to go looking for your own *boletus edulis* – particularly since the boletus are the safest group of all the edible funghi.

Nothing else looks like a *porcini*. All members of this large family have *spongy* under-parts rather than gills, and their caps are domed and in many species cheerfully shiny – particularly after rain when they look like the eponymous sticky brown buns. Slugs love them, wet or dry.

Take a good identification manual when you go gathering in Britain, and, the first time, go with someone who knows both fungi and area well. Learn one new species each season, and then you will be sure of your gathering. Best of all, make friends with a knowledgeable Italian, Polish or Swiss mushroom-fancier who can advise you on which of the wild crop is suitable to dry for your own larder.

Pick the boletus on a fine day, whether for use fresh or for drying: they will not last long if they start off water-logged. Wipe and slice the caps not too thin, and don't, as some manuals advise, strip off the sponge – it's a terrible waste of good food. I find its peculiar gluey texture absolutely addictive – the Japanese, connoisseurs of such joys, would love it.

Any of the ribbon pastas will do for this dish – pick one which is long enough to wrap round your fork – one slippery article at a time is plenty.

QUANTITY
Serves 4

TIME
Preparation: 30
  minutes if using
  dried mushrooms, 15
  minutes if using fresh

Put a large pan of salted water on to boil for the tagliatelle.

If you are using dried *porcini*, you will have put them to soak in a little warm water half an hour ago. If using fresh mushrooms, wipe and slice them. Peel and chop the garlic very finely with the parsley.

Bring the cream gently to the boil in the small saucepan and stir in the mushrooms (with their soaking liquor if they were dried), the garlic and the parsley. Bring all back to the boil, turn the heat down and simmer gently to thicken and reduce – particularly if you are including soaking liquid from dried

Cooking: 10 minutes

8 oz/250g tagliatelle
½ pint/300ml double
  cream
1 oz/25g dried *porcini or*
  8 oz/250g fresh wild *or*
  cultivated mushrooms
salt and pepper
1-2 cloves garlic

To finish
1 small bunch parsley
grated Parmesan *or* any
  other hard strong
  cheese

A large saucepan and a
  draining spoon, a small
  saucepan and a wooden
  spoon, and a large
  colander

mushrooms. After 6-7 minutes, taste and add salt and plenty of freshly-milled black pepper.

Meanwhile, cook the tagliatelle according to the instructions on the packet. It will need 4-6 minutes to be soft but still slightly firm.

Drain the pasta immediately, pile it in a pretty serving dish, and turn it with the sauce.

Hand a bowl of grated Parmesan separately.

Finish the meal with an almond biscuit, to be nibbled with a little glass of butter-cup yellow *strega*, my favourite honey-sweet herb-scented liquor which was, I am told, named for the witches of Benevento.

SUGGESTIONS

Layer the sauced pasta into a shallow oven-proof dish with fried aubergines or courgettes, top with grated cheese and bake in a medium oven 375°F/190°C/Gas 5 for 20 minutes until golden and bubbling.

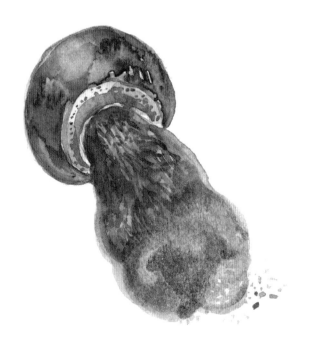

Pasta Butterflies with Green Vegetables
Farfalle al verde

Any combination of green vegetables can be used for this simple dish (small artichokes and broad beans make a happy couple, as do green peppers and swiss chard). It is, however, important to trim and slice the vegetables to roughly the same size and shape as the farfalle. The excitement and delight of these combinations lies in a chosen confusion of flavour and texture.

QUANTITY
Serves 4

TIME
Preparation: 15-20 minutes
Cooking: 15 minutes

10 oz/275g green farfalle pasta
1 tablespoon chopped oregano *or* marjoram
1 bulb fennel (with its feathery leaves)
8 oz/250g green beans
black pepper and salt
1-2 cloves garlic
4-5 tablespoons olive oil
2 oz/50g diced bacon or ham
To finish
3-4 chopped spring onions

UTENSILS
A large saucepan and a draining spoon, a wide frying pan, and a large colander

Put on a large pan of salted water to boil for the farfalle – at least 5 pints/3 litres. Butterflies like plenty of space.

Meanwhile prepare the rest of the ingredients. Slice the fennel thinly across its width, feathery leaves and all, halving the larger pieces. Trim the green beans and cut them on the diagonal, like a butterfly's wing. Peel and chop the garlic.

Cook the farfalle according to the instructions on the packet. Give them a stir as they come back to boil to keep them separated. When the pasta is soft but still firm – 4-6 minutes, so you need to keep an eye on it – drain it immediately, and transfer to a warm serving dish. Toss it quickly with a tablespoon of olive oil to stop the butterfly wings sticking while you finish the vegetables.

Heat the rest of the oil in the frying pan. Fry the bacon or ham and the garlic for a few moments. Add the fennel and the beans and turn them in the hot oil. Cook the vegetables for a few minutes to soften them but still leave them with a slight bite. Stir in the oregano or marjoram. Taste and add plenty of black pepper and plenty of salt, then toss in the farfalle. Remove from the heat and stir in the chopped spring onions.

Serve the green butterflies immediately.

Finish the meal with fruit and a handful of almonds and walnuts. Ripe figs would be delicious and very Italian – the huge sweet figs of Terra di Bari in Puglia are particularly famous.

SUGGESTIONS

Make a little farfalle salad with the leftovers. Dress the pasta with extra oil and a little vinegar, and toss it with more chopped spring onion and a chopped green pepper.

Pasta Quills with Tuna
Penne al tonno

The shape of this slant-cut macaroni takes well to flakes of tuna fish conserved in oil – sold by weight from industrial-sized tins or big barrels in every market throughout Italy.

Tuna has been harvested in the Mediterranean since Neolithic times. When the gun-metal-backed shoals of the largest of the tuna family, the blue-fin, are spotted on their twice-yearly migration, fishermen from the Golden Horn to the Pillars of Hercules form gangs for the netting. The ritual is as ancient as the olive harvest: Romans and Greeks, Persians and Egyptians have all left visual and verbal accounts of the bloody marine battlefields where the great fish were herded through the knotted corridors of the tuna trap.

These days, most of Europe's tinned tuna comes from the South Pacific, although a few of the Mediterranean's tuna-fisheries are still active – mainly those of Sicily, Greece and the east coast of Spain.

QUANTITY
Serves 4

TIME
Preparation: 20 minutes
Cooking: 15 minutes

10 oz/275g penne pasta
   (*or* any medium-sized
   macaroni)
6 tablespoons olive oil
1 tablespoon capers
1 small tin tunny fish in
   brine
1 chopped hard-boiled
   egg
1 onion
1 heaped tablespoon
   chopped parsley
1-2 cloves garlic
Salt and cayenne pepper
1 large red pepper

Put on a large pan of salted water to boil for the penne.

Meanwhile prepare the rest of the ingredients. Drain the tunny fish. Peel and chop the onion and garlic. Hull, de-seed and chop the red pepper.

Warm the oil in the frying pan. Fry the chopped onion, garlic and pepper gently in the oil until soft.

Cook the penne according to the instructions on the packet. Give them a stir as they come back to the boil and keep giving the occasional stir as they cook. When the pasta is soft but still retains a little bite – it will need about 10 minutes – drain it immediately and transfer it to a warm serving bowl.

A large saucepan and a
draining spoon, a small
frying pan, and a large
colander

Tip in the contents of the frying pan and turn all thoroughly until the quills are well coated with the aromatic oil. Sprinkle with salt and cayenne pepper (this pasta should be as pink as possible, to echo the tuna flesh). Toss in the tuna flakes, capers, egg and parsley and serve the penne immediately.

The dish is equally good hot or cold.

If serving the pasta cold, season it with a little good wine vinegar, perhaps with a teaspoon or two of *aceto balsamico* from Modena in Emilia Romagna. This is the most prized vinegar of all, precious enough, in the old days, to form part of a girl's dowry. The nectar has to be in the cask for half a century before it earns its release. Dark as old honey, with a strong nutty flavour – a kind of vinegar equivalent of the aromatic *crianza* mother-sherries of the bodegas of Jerez – only a few drops are needed to perfume a dish.

Finish the meal with a salad of oranges dressed with their own finely-pared rind simmered till soft in a little syrup.

Pasta Shells with Clams or Cockles
Conchiglie alle vongole

Pasta alle vongole is the classic Neapolitan dish. Most varieties of clam, mussels, shrimps, or squid can replace the *vongole* in the recipe. Italian delicatessens stock little tins of *vongole* in brine, and every British fishmonger offers shelled ready-cooked cockles, which, give or take the marine biologist's strictures, are indistinguishable. *Vongole* (the *palourdes* of France) are larger than our cockles.

QUANTITY
Serves 4

TIME
Preparation: 15 minutes
Cooking: 15 minutes

10 oz/275g conchiglie
   pasta
4-5 tablespoons olive oil
4 oz/100g *vongole*
   or clams (weighed
   without shells –
   unshelled about
   2 1b/800g)
2 tablespoons chopped
   parsley
2 tablespoons chopped
   fennel fronds *or* 1
   teaspoon fennel seeds
1-2 cloves garlic
1 small onion
1 glass dry white wine

UTENSILS
A large saucepan and a
   draining spoon, a frying
   pan (with a lid if you
   are using fresh shellfish)
   and a large colander

Put on a large pan of salted water to boil for the pasta.

Meanwhile prepare the rest of the ingredients. Drain the *vongole* (if you are using fresh ones, see below). Peel and chop small the garlic and onion.

Cook the conchiglie according to the instructions on the packet – they will need 6-10 minutes. Stir them from time to time, particularly as they come back to the boil. Drain the pasta immediately and transfer it to a warm serving dish. Toss in a spoonful of olive oil so that the pasta does not glue up while you finish the sauce.

Heat the oil gently in the frying pan. Put in the garlic and onion and cook it until it is soft but not caramelized. Sprinkle in the herbs and add the wine. Turn up the heat and allow all to bubble up fiercely for a moment or two until you can no longer smell raw alcohol. Add the *vongole* and the herbs and heat very briefly (all shellfish quickly becomes rubbery if overcooked). Taste and add salt and freshly-milled pepper.

To make the dish with fresh live clams, cockles or mussels, leave 2 lb/800 g (unshelled weight) shellfish in a bucket of salted water for a few hours to allow them to spit out their sand. Discard any which do not open and shut, or feel heavy and full of sand. When you are ready to serve, cook the shellfish briefly in the hot sauce, just long enough for them to open (a lidded wok is perfect for the job). If you are worried about sand in the pasta, cook the shellfish separately in a little water, and boil down and sieve the juices before adding them to the sauce. You can shell the molluscs before you toss them with the cooked pasta. I rather like them left in their shells, if only for the fun of chasing the slippery conchiglie through the parsley-sprinkled shells, and sucking out the juicy little morsels of fish.

Pour the contents of the frying pan into the pasta. Toss all together and serve.

Grated cheese is not usually handed with fishy pasta in Italy. Do as you please: I like it with shrimps but not with shellfish.

SUGGESTIONS

This is delicious cold, dressed with extra oil and a little vinegar, mixed with sliced raw bulb fennel and chopped green peppers or cucumber.

Stuffed Pasta with Courgettes
Tortellini con zucchini

Tortellini are little stuffed half-moons of pasta, twisted into a crescent shape. They are an Italian favourite for a special occasion, when it is made at home fresh, often filled with the most delicate of mousses – cream and chicken, curd cheese and spinach, minced pork and mushrooms – whatever the cook's pleasure and the season dictates.

Factory-made dried tortellini is made of sterner stuff – the filling is a paste of dried ham and cheese which can stand up to long storage. They make a useful standby for poaching in a strong home-made chicken or beef stock as the mainstay of the evening meal. Stuffed pastas are also excellent served 'dry'. I like them tossed with a dressing of crisp vegetables in their own herb-scented oil. The green discs of courgette look like the lucky coins in the lovers' fountain in Rome – perfectly appropriate for a pasta whose curves, say the romantic Italians, were inspired by the navel of the goddess of love.

QUANTITY

Serves 4

TIME

Preparation: 10 minutes
Cooking: 20 minutes

8 oz/225g tortellini
  stuffed pasta

Put on a large pan of salted water to boil for the tortellini.

Meanwhile prepare the rest of the ingredients. Slice the courgettes into fine rings. Peel and chop the garlic.

Cook the tortellini according to the instructions on the packet. Give them a stir as they come back to the boil, and stir them every now and then as they poach – don't let the water boil too fiercely or the tortellini trail edges of pasta like battered goldfish. Depending on the size, 16-18 minutes will find the little morsels tender but still firm. Tortellini takes longer to

2 heaped tablespoons
    chopped parsley

2-3 medium courgettes

1 heaped tablespoon
    chopped mint

2 cloves garlic

salt and pepper

8 tablespoons olive oil

UTENSILS

A large saucepan and
    a draining spoon, a
    frying pan and a large
    colander

cook than most pasta since the stuffing has to plump out as well as the dough. Taste to make sure.

When they are ready, lift them out gently with the draining spoon and transfer to a warm lightly oiled serving dish. Turn them in the oil and keep them covered while you finish the dressing.

Heat the oil in a frying pan. When it is hot, throw in the sliced courgettes. Fry them quickly so that they brown a little as they cook. Sprinkle in the garlic – it should soften immediately in the hot oil. Add the parsley and the mint, salt and pepper.

Tip the contents of the pan over the tortellini. Toss, taste to check the seasoning, and serve immediately. Hand a bowl of grated cheese separately.

Follow with a salad of sliced tomatoes sprinkled with freshly torn basil leaves and freshly milled black pepper, accompanied by a flask of good olive oil. (Mediterranean housewives find other uses for basil. A potted basil plant is often placed on the kitchen windowsill to discourage flies – only the small-leaved near-wild plant will do for this chore.)

Finish the meal Sicilian-style with a glass of sweet Marsala (there is a dry and medium version as well), a piece of marzipan and an orange.

Chicken Broth with Ravioli
Ravioli in brodo

This dish should be made much more grandly (and expensively) with a boiling hen, beef bones and the full complement of pot herbs. But this version has a well-rounded domestic thrift to it, and the broth still has a fine flavour. I have to admit that this is my family's Sunday supper dish when we have had roast chicken for lunch.

QUANTITY
Serves 4

TIME
Preparation: 5 minutes
Cooking: 1½ hours

1 roast-chicken carcass
(include skin and
trimmings and the
onion and herbs with
which it was stuffed for
roasting)
sprig parsley and thyme
6 black peppercorns, salt
6 oz/175g ravioli (*or* any
small stuffed pasta)
1 large onion (skin left
on to colour the broth)
1-2 large carrots
1 bay leaf
1 branch celery *or* lovage

To finish
2-3 tablespoons peas
(fresh *or* frozen)
2-3 spring onions

UTENSILS
A large stewpan with a lid

Put the chicken carcass, whole onion, carrots, celery or lovage, herbs and peppercorns in the stewpan and cover all with 3 pints/1.8 litres water. Add a teaspoon of salt. Bring all to the boil. Turn down the heat and leave the broth to simmer gently for at least an hour – it should reduce by ⅓.

When the chicken carcass has fallen to pieces and the broth tastes good and strong, strain out all the solids and return the soup to the pan. If you had a household pig, he would be grateful for the rejects; if not, they must be thrown out. Taste and add salt and pepper.

Bring the broth back to the boil and drop in the ravioli. Poach them for 15-20 minutes, as indicated on the packet.

When you are ready to serve the soup, stir in the peas and the spring onions and bring all back to the boil. Plain pasta can be used instead of the stuffed ravioli.

Bread and cheese and your favourite *gelato* will round off the meal perfectly.

Little Diamonds with Pine Nuts and Raisins

Diamantini alla Veneziana

Both Marseilles and Venice built their riches on the Crusader trade, providing ships and provisions to transport soldiers and pilgrims, and filling their coffers with the spoils of the east-west traffic. The spices, oranges and sugar which ballasted the returning transport ships were particularly profitable. By the thirteenth century the merchants of the Most Serene Republic of Venice had established trading posts from Cairo to Constantinople, Trebizond to Tripoli. The exotic flavours of the east remained in Venetian kitchens long after the trade routes withered. Pine nuts are now easier to obtain in Britain – look for them in health-food shops as well as the delicatessen. Use any small pasta shape which is roughly the same dimension as the pine nuts.

QUANTITY
Serves 4

TIME
Start 1-2 hours ahead
Preparation: 15 minutes
Cooking: 10 minutes

10 oz/275g diamantini (*or* any similar small pasta shape such as ditallini, gnocchetti, farfallini)
1 small onion
6 tablespoons olive oil
3 oz/75g pine nuts (*or* slivered almonds)
3 oz/75g raisins
1 teaspoon chopped thyme
juice and finely-pared rind of 1 orange
salt and pepper
1 clove garlic

Put the raisins to plump up on the orange juice an hour or two before you are ready to start cooking.

Put on a large pan of salted water to boil for the diamantini.

Meanwhile prepare the rest of the ingredients. Peel and chop finely the onion and the garlic.

Heat the oil in the frying pan. Stir in the pine nuts and let them fry golden. Push them to one side and fry the onion and garlic. Add the thyme, the raisins and their juices, the orange rind and bubble all up for a moment or two.

Stir the pasta into the boiling salted water and cook it according to the directions on the packet – it will only take 2-3 minutes as the pasta is tiny. Drain and toss the contents of the frying pan. Taste and add salt and pepper.

A glass of light dry Tokai wine from the Veneto might accompany the meal. To finish, cheese (the hard Italian *Gratia* and *Pecorino* cheeses are delicious) and a salad of bitter red radicchio – a chicory grown all around Venice – dressed with orange juice and nut oil, to complete it.

UTENSILS

A large saucepan and a draining spoon, a small frying pan and a large colander

Baked Pasta in Truffled Cream
Lasagne incassettata

The inhabitants of Le Marche on the Adriatic coast of Italy like their pasta substantial and richly sauced, to go with their excellent strong wines. The local black truffles, wrested from beneath the foraging noses of the black pigs which are the other speciality of the region, are used generously when in season. Peasant housewives throughout Europe with easy access to the wild crop have long found the aromatic flesh of the freshly-dug tuber an excellent meat substitute.

This version of the Marchigianas' favourite *pasta al forno* was given to me by a young American friend who studied at the university of Perugia. A botanist by training, he had the recipe from his landlady as a parting gift in gratitude for a few successful forays into the local undergrowth in search of the fragrant main ingredient.

The dish is quite delicious. It is also very filling – a priority in the life of a poor and hungry student.

QUANTITY
Serves 4

TIME
Preparation: 30-40
  minutes
Cooking: 30 minutes

6 oz/175g lasagne
2 oz/50g flour
1 fine fresh black truffle
  (if not, 8 oz/250g
  button mushrooms will
  have to do)
2 oz/50g butter
1 pint/600ml milk
¼ pint/150ml thick
  double cream *or* 4
  oz/100g Mascarpone
  (fresh white cheese)
3 oz/75g ham *or* lean
  bacon

Put on a large pan of salted water to boil for the lasagne. Meanwhile prepare the rest of the ingredients. Dice the ham or bacon. Clean the truffle carefully without peeling it. Slice it, but not too neatly as this is a rough country dish.

Melt the butter in the small saucepan. If you are using fresh mushrooms, chop them and fry them gently in the butter. Stir in the flour and cook it until sandy but not brown. Add the milk slowly, whisking to avoid lumps. Bring back to the boil, turn down the heat and simmer until smooth and thick – about 8-10 minutes. Whisk in the cream or Mascarpone. Taste and add nutmeg, salt and plenty of freshly milled pepper and the chopped ham or bacon.

Cook the lasagne according to the instructions on the packet. Flip the sheets apart with the draining spoon as the water comes back to the boil. Cook the pasta for about 6 minutes – it should still be quite firm as it is to be finished in the oven. Lift the sheets out carefully with the draining spoon and pass them immediately through cold water to stop them sticking.

Preheat the oven to 375°F/180°C/Gas 5.

Pour a layer of the white sauce to cover the base of the gratin dish. Lay on a layer of lasagne. Pour on another layer of sauce and sprinkle with cheese and chopped truffles. Continue until

½ teaspoon grated
  nutmeg
4 oz/100g grated
  Parmesan *or* any other
  hard strong cheese
Salt and pepper

UTENSILS

A large saucepan and
  a draining spoon, a
  medium saucepan
  and a whisk, an
  earthenware gratin
  dish

all is finished up – the last layer should be sauce sprinkled with cheese.

Bake for 20-30 minutes until bubbling hot and golden.

Follow with a bowl of whole ripe tomatoes and quartered short cucumbers. Provide little bottles of oil and vinegar, in the Italian manner, for each trencherman to dress his own salad.

Finish the meal with a bowl of strawberries sprinkled with orange juice, or a handful of grapes and a little *digestif* of *grappa* – another small pleasure of Le Marche.

Baked Pasta with Tomato Sauce
Timbale di pappardelle

Pappardelle, a kind of thin-rolled, wide-cut tagliatelle, are my favourite egg-pasta. Any of the ribbon pastas are good in this recipe – tagliatelle, tagliarini or the ruffle-edged lasagnette.

A *timballo* is a fancy mould – although a plain earthenware gratin dish would be fine. There are plenty of these recipes for baked, layered pasta, particularly in the repertoire of southern Italy. Like the Greek/Turkish *moussaka*, the dish could be prepared in advance and taken to be finished off in the baker's oven after the day's bread had been baked.

QUANTITY
Serves 4

TIME

Preparation: 25 minutes
Cooking: 30-40 minutes

8 oz/250g pappardelle (*or*
  any flat ribbon pasta)
2 oz/50g pitted and
  chopped black olives

Cook the pappardelle in plenty of boiling salted water – drain it before it is quite soft.

Butter a mould or pudding basin.

Preheat the oven to 350°F/180°C/Gas 4.

Fry the mushrooms and aubergines gently in the oil. Stir in the flour and fry for a moment. Whisk in the stock or milk gradually, beating as you do so. Bring all back to the boil and simmer for 5 minutes. Stir in the ham, olives and cheese. Taste and adjust the seasoning. Beat in the egg.

Stir in the pappardelle and pour the mixture into the mould. Cover with foil and bake for 35-40 minutes.

1 aubergine, diced
1 tablespoon chopped
   marjoram *or* oregano
4 tablespoons olive oil
2 oz/50g button
   mushrooms, sliced
2 oz/50g grated
   Parmesan *or* Cheddar
2 heaped tablespoons
   flour

Tomato sauce
¾ pint/450ml good stock
   or milk
1 lb/500g tomatoes
   (*or* 1 lb tin chopped
   tomatoes)
¼ pint/150ml double
   cream *or* fresh white
   cheese
1 tablespoon tomato
   purée
1 egg
1 clove garlic
salt and pepper
2 tablespoons olive oil
3 oz/75g chopped raw
   ham *or* gammon

UTENSILS
A large saucepan and a
   draining spoon, a small
   saucepan and a wooden
   spoon, and a large
   colander

Meanwhile, make the sauce.

Scald and skin the tomatoes if they are fresh. Peel and chop the garlic. If you are using a food processor, put in all the ingredients and liquidize them. Transfer the mixture to a small saucepan and leave it to simmer gently while the *timbale* finishes cooking.

Otherwise, fry the garlic lightly in the oil in a small saucepan, and then stir in the tomatoes and the purée. Simmer as above.

Turn the pie out of its *timballo* on to a warm serving dish, and pour the tomato sauce round it. Hand a bowl of grated cheese separately.

Round off the rich meal with a coffee *granita* – crushed ice with chilled strong sweet coffee poured on it, the liquid to be sucked through a straw as the ice melts.

9. Biscuits

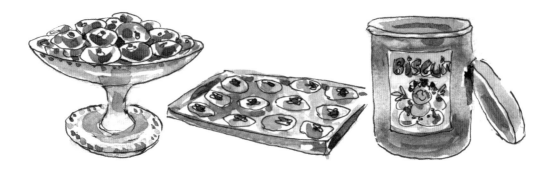

Salt Biscuits

Biscuits, one of the earliest fast-foods, evolved from those primitive preparations of unleavened bread designed to conserve grain in a readily available and palatable form. East European noodles, Italian pasta, Scandinavian crispbreads and Scottish oatcakes all belong to the same group. Breads made with yeast had a relatively short shelf life, but the hard-baked biscuit, needing the minimum of preparation, was the ideal traveller's food. Napoleon's army marched on army biscuits. The British navy sailed on ship's biscuits, the notoriously weevil-bored sea-soaked provender which was the last resort of the storm-tossed crew.

Biscuits were still important ship's stores in Edwardian times. These were made of wholemeal wheat flour from which only the coarsest bran had been separated, worked into a stiff dough, rolled and baked, then stored in lofts over the baking ovens until they were quite dry – giving them the French name of *bis-cuit*, 'twice-cooked'. The Captain's biscuits were made of finer refined flour – less healthy by modern standards.

Plain Biscuits

Here is Mrs Beeton's recipe for 'Simple Hard Biscuits'. She says they are very nice for the cheese course. Add paprika pepper, dried herbs, caraway or celery seeds as you please.

QUANTITY
Makes about 30 biscuits

TIME
Preparation: 20 minutes
Cooking: 6-10 minutes

1 lb/500g flour
about ½ pint/300ml
   skimmed milk
1 teaspoon salt
2 oz/50g butter

UTENSILS
A sieve, a pastry board
   and rolling pin, a
   3-in/8-cm diameter
   plain round cutter, a
   baking tray and rack

Preheat the oven to 375°F/190°C/Gas 5.

Sift the flour with the salt onto a pastry board. Warm the milk with the butter until it melts. Pour the warm mixture into a well in the flour. Work it with one hand into a very stiff dough.

Beat the dough with a rolling pin until it looks perfectly smooth (very therapeutic). Roll the dough out *very* thin – or you'll break your jaws on the finished product.

Cut the paste into rounds and transfer them to a greased baking tray. Prick the rounds well with a fork, and bake for 10-15 minutes in the preheated moderate oven – they should remain quite pale. Transfer them to a rack to dry. Store when quite cool in an airtight tin.

Water Biscuits

This recipe was supplied by Mrs Dorothy Allheusen to Florence White, author of *Good Things in England*, in 1932. Mrs Allheusen had it from the aristocracy – Lady Congreve, of Crofton House, Titchfield.

QUANTITY
Makes about 30 biscuits

TIME
Preparation: 15 minutes
Cooking: 8-10 minutes

Preheat the oven to 450°F/230°C/Gas 8.

Sift the flour with the salt into a bowl. Cut the butter into the flour with a knife, and then rub in with your fingertips.

Knead in enough water to make a fairly stiff dough. Work the dough for a few minutes until it is smooth.

On a floured board, roll the dough out as thin as a wafer. Transfer to a buttered and floured baking sheet and prick it into

8 oz/250g self-raising
   flour
2 oz/50g butter
½ teaspoon salt
about 1 glass cold water

UTENSILS
A sieve, a bowl, rolling
   pin and pastry board,
   baking sheet and rack

squares (or you can, of course, cut the dough into rounds). Bake in the preheated oven for 8-10 minutes. The biscuits should blister and bubble brown – keep an eye on them and take them out when they are done. Put them to dry on a rack and store them in an airtight tin.

Digestive Biscuits

I think these must be a commercial invention, offspring of the oatcake. Cookery collections from the first half of the last century give similar sweetened oatmeal/flour recipes as 'oatmeal biscuits'. Whatever the origin, they are very good with potted cheese or a fine ripe Stilton.

QUANTITY
Makes about 20 biscuits

TIME
Preparation: 20 minutes
Cooking: 25-30 minutes

4 oz/100g wholemeal
   flour
2 tablespoons sugar
½ teaspoon salt
4 oz/100g lard *or* butter
1 level teaspoon baking
   powder
2-3 tablespoons water
4 oz/100g medium
   oatmeal

Preheat the oven to 325°F/170°C/Gas 3.

Sift the flour with the salt and baking powder into a bowl. Stir in the oatmeal and the sugar. Rub in the lard or butter with the tips of the fingers until you have a mix like fine breadcrumbs. Knead in just enough water to give a firm dough (the less the water, the lighter the biscuit).

Roll out the dough to the thickness of a pound coin, and cut into rounds with the 2 ½-in/6-cm biscuit cutter or a sharp-edged wine glass. A blunt instrument would seal the edges and the biscuit would not rise lightly.

Transfer to a greased baking tray and prick the biscuits with a fork. Bake them in the preheated low oven for 25-30 minutes, until crisp and well browned.

UTENSILS

A sieve, a bowl, pastry board and rolling pin, a 2½-in/6-cm biscuit cutter, baking sheet and rack

Cheese Biscuits

This must be the most perfectly simple of recipes – make it once and you will never need to check the quantities in the book again.

QUANTITY
Makes about 30 biscuits

TIME
Preparation: 20 minutes
Cooking: 20 minutes

8 oz/250g flour
8 oz/250g hard cheese
  (mature Cheddar for
  preference)
½ teaspoon salt
8 oz/250g cold butter

UTENSILS
A sieve, a bowl, a grater,
  a rolling pin and pastry
  board, a 2-in/5-cm
  biscuit cutter, a baking
  tray and a rack

Preheat the oven to 350°F/180°C/Gas 4.

Sieve the flour with the salt into a bowl. Finely grate the cheese into the flour. Grate the butter through the larger holes into the flour. Mix all together with a knife, and press into a ball with the tips of your fingers. You may need a little water to make the dough stick – cheese and butter vary in their water content.

Roll the dough out very thinly on a floured board. Cut it into rounds. Lay the rounds on a baking tray (no need to butter it). Bake in the preheated oven for 20 minutes, until the biscuits are pale gold – don't let them overcook. Cool them on a rack and store them in an airtight tin.

Greek Cheese Biscuits

Tyropita Trifti

These crisp little biscuits, *tyropita trifti*, are a speciality of the Thracian storecupboard and are served as an accompaniment to the evening glass of ouzo or wine. Mediterranean housewives have a repertoire of these biscuits and cakes made with olive oil, the locally-grown shortening which replaces the butter in our northern recipes. Olive oil and cheese is a particularly happy combination.

QUANTITY

Makes about 30 biscuits

TIME

Preparation: 20 minutes
Cooking: 20-25 minutes

8 oz/250g self-raising
    flour
scant ¼ pint/150ml milk
½ teaspoon salt
    (unless the cheese is
    particularly salty)
4 oz/100g grated
    Kefalotiri or *Kasseri*
    cheese – *or* any hard,
    well-flavoured cheese
    (Cheddar, Gruyère)
4 oz/100g butter
¼ pint/150ml olive oil

UTENSILS

A sieve, a bowl, a food
    processor would be
    useful, a rolling pin
    and a baking sheet and
    rack

Preheat the oven to 350°F/180°C/Gas 4.

Sieve the flour and salt.

Soften the butter and beat it until light and fluffy (an electric mixer will do the job quickly – the old way would have been with a warm hand). Beat in the olive oil. When it is all incorporated, beat in the milk and grated cheese. You may have to beat in a little of the flour to keep the mixture homogenized.

Work in the rest of the flour and the salt by hand – only enough to give you a soft dough. Too much flour will make your biscuits less crisp than they should be. Knead the dough lightly and press it out into a ¼-in/½-cm thick sheet directly onto a baking tray. Smooth the surface with a rolling pin. Cut the dough into small squares – no more than 1 in/2.5 cm as this is a very rich mixture. Bake in the preheated oven for 15 minutes. Raise the temperature to 375°F/190°C/Gas 5 to crisp and brown the biscuits for another 5-10 minutes. Total baking time is 20-25 minutes, less if you cut the mixture into little fingers for cheese straws.

Transfer to a baking rack to cool. Store in an airtight tin.

Serve them as an appetizer with a glass of ouzo. Or with a little pickled fish and a salad as a light meal.

Salt Sticks

Grissini

Grissini are those crisp little breadsticks which the Italians play with when they are waiting for the serious business of eating to begin. *Grissini* store well – the original purpose of their baking – and make excellent dip-sticks for potted cheeses. Serve them as part of a selection of Mediterranean appetizers.

QUANTITY

Makes about 20-50
  sticks, depending on
  the length chosen

TIME

Preparation: 20 minutes
Cooking: 10 minutes

8 oz/250g self-raising
  flour
2 oz/50g butter
½ teaspoon fine salt
2-3 tablespoons milk
2 eggs
2-3 tablespoons coarse
  salt crystals

UTENSILS

A sieve, pastry board,
  rolling pin, baking
  sheet and rack

Preheat the oven to 425°F/220°C/Gas 7.

Sieve the flour with the salt onto the pastry board or straight onto the table. Separate the eggs – you will only need one of the yolks. Whisk the whites until stiff. Soften the butter and work it and the egg yolk and the whisked whites into the flour until you have a soft smooth dough. Roll out 1 in/2.5 cm thick. Cut the dough into sticks ½ in/1 cm wide by 2-6 in/5-15 cm long, depending on your preference. Roll the sticks between your hands to round them. Paint the sticks with milk and sprinkle them with the coarse salt. Arrange them on a greased baking tray.

Bake for about 10 minutes, until crisp and golden. Let them cool on a rack and store in an airtight tin.

Rye Rusks

Krydskorpor

Unleavened breads such as these Swedish *krydskorpor* keep very well in the cold dry air of Scandinavia. The Swedes, who like leavened bread (the Norwegians traditionally make unleavened doughs), bake yeast-raised breads especially for drying into rusks. These are excellent with a soup for supper, with pickled herrings, with a slice of liver sausage and a pickled cucumber.

QUANTITY
Makes 2 dozen rusks

TIME
Start 3 hours ahead
Preparation: 20 minutes
Cooking: 35-40 minutes

1½ lb/750g strong white
   flour
1 oz/25g fresh yeast *or*
   ½ oz/12g dried
1 teaspoon salt
2 oz/50g lard
8 oz/250g rye flour
2 oz/50g butter
1 pint/600ml warm milk
4 tablespoons molasses

UTENSILS
A sieve, a large and small
   bowl, clean cloth,
   small saucepan, large
   baking tray and rack

Sieve the white flour with the salt into a large warm bowl. Mix in the rye flour. Dissolve the yeast in a little of the warm milk and pour it into a well in the flour. Sprinkle a dusting of flour over the liquid, cover with a clean cloth and leave it aside.

Melt the lard, butter and molasses with the remaining milk in a small saucepan over a gentle heat. Let the liquid cool to blood temperature, and work the mixture into the flour until you have a soft smooth dough which no longer sticks to your fingers (you may need more milk – this dough should be on the wet side).

Knead the dough into a ball, cover and leave aside in a warm damp place (covered with a damp cloth, near the stove) for 1½-2 hours to prove. Knock it down when well-risen and knead the dough into a long sausage. Cut the sausage into 4 pieces and roll each into a long thin stick, as for a long baguette. Grease and lightly flour a flat baking tray and transfer the bread sticks, leaving plenty of room. Put to rise again until they have again doubled their volume – about an hour, rye is sluggish.

Preheat the oven to 375°F/190°C/Gas 5.

Put the loaves in to bake for 35-40 minutes, until light and golden (they should not be dark). Take them out and put them on a wire rack to cool. When they are cool, split them lengthwise and cut the pieces into fingers. Put in the oven on the lowest possible heat to dry and crisp.

When the rusks are quite cold, store them in an airtight tin. This precaution would not have been necessary in a cold northern larder, where the air in the winter can freeze-dry a fish as fast as any mechanical deep-freeze.

Milk Rusks

Mjölkskorpor

Mjölkskorpor, Swedish rusks, make a crisp accompaniment to cheese and ham. Or have them for tea with sweet fresh butter and your best home-made jam or crumble them into your breakfast bowl, then pour over them plenty of soured milk or soured cream (the Scandinavian speciality, not the same thing as yoghurt since it has no bacteria starter) and a spoonful of preserved or fresh berries.

....

QUANTITY

Makes about 50 rusks

TIME

Start 3 hours ahead
Preparation: 20 minutes
Cooking: 15-20 minutes
  plus 30 minutes

2 lb/1kg flour
2 oz/50g lard
1 teaspoon salt
2 oz/50g butter
1 oz/25g fresh yeast *or*
  ½ oz/12g dried
2 oz/50g sugar
1 pint/600ml warm milk

UTENSILS

A sieve and bowl, a small
  saucepan, a baking tray
  and a rack

Sieve the flour into a warm bowl with the salt. Warm the milk to blood temperature (test with your finger). Dissolve the yeast in a little of the warm milk and pour the mixture into a well in the flour. Sprinkle a dusting of flour over the liquid and put it aside to bubble – this is 'setting the sponge', a convenient little ritual which just gives you time to prepare the rest of the ingredients.

Add the lard and the butter to the milk in the saucepan and heat gently until the fats melt. Leave to cool until the liquid is again finger-warm, then pour it into the well in the flour. Sprinkle in the sugar.

Knead the liquids into the flour until you have a soft smooth dough (you may need extra flour or a little warm water). Form the dough into a ball, cover the bowl with a damp cloth and put it aside in a warm place to rise for an hour.

When the dough has doubled its bulk, knuckle it down with your fists and then cut it into 6 pieces. Cut each piece into 10 nuggets. Roll each nugget into a little bun, all folds tucked neatly underneath.

Preheat the oven to 425°F/220°C/Gas 7.

Grease 2 baking sheets and arrange on it the little buns, allowing them plenty of elbow room. Put them to rise again in a warm damp place. It will take about 30 minutes for them to double in bulk.

Transfer the rusks to the preheated oven to bake for 15-20 minutes. Remove them when they are firm and perfectly light and golden. Put them on a wire rack to cool.

Keep some fresh buns by for tea, and pull the rest in half with a fork. Put the halves directly on the grid in the lowest possible oven, and leave them to dry and crisp – they will be ready in about half an hour.

Stored in an airtight tin, the buns will keep for a long time.

SUGGESTIONS

Try them as part of a Dutch farmhouse breakfast: black coffee, a glass of fresh milk or buttermilk and a plate of buttered rusks accompanied by a slice of ham or a slice of grilled bacon, a piece of cheese, or, for a special treat, fresh strawberries in season.

Sweet Biscuits

Biscuit-making remains an essential item in the housewife's repertoire throughout Europe. In Britain we usually buy ours ready-made, and have a thriving export business in the products of our commercial biscuit-makers. These manufacturers were already well established at the beginning of the last century. My 1912 edition of Mrs Beeton lists and illustrates 66 varieties of shop-bought biscuits, including quite a few which seem to have dropped out of the repertoire: Roseberies, Pat-a-cakes, Jamaicas, Monarchs, Acorns and Cinderellas no longer grace our supermarket shelves. Those still easily found include the familiar digestives. Nice biscuits, gingernuts, cream crackers, Marie biscuits and petit buerre looked much the same then as now.

Flaky Biscuits
Fines salées

This recipe for *fines salées* comes from Corcelles in the Swiss Vaud – there are variations on it in every canton, and on the French side of the border too. No nation is so fiercely regional as the Swiss – and this extends far beyond the obvious distinctions between the German-, French- and Italian-speaking areas. Dialects can vary from one side of the mountain to the other, and a housewife going to market in her own village may have difficulty striking a bargain with a travelling salesman from the neighbouring valley. The Swiss themselves take pride in this individuality, which is reflected in their virtually self-governing cantons. However, all warring factions arguing the toss in the local hostelry will unite instantly against a true foreigner, even one who shares a mother-tongue.

QUANTITY
Makes 4 large squares

TIME
Start a day ahead
Preparation: 20 minutes
Cooking: 15 minutes

1 lb/500g flour
2 medium-sized eggs
   plus 2 yolks
4 oz/100g caster sugar
½ pint/300ml cream
4 oz/100g lard
3 oz/75g butter

To finish
2 oz/50g butter
2 oz/50g caster sugar
1 teaspoon powdered
   cinnamon
½ teaspoon salt (*optional*)

Sieve the flour into a bowl.

Break the eggs and the extra yolks into a medium bowl and beat them thoroughly with the sugar, the cream and the salt.

Beat the lard and butter together in a large mixing bowl with a wooden spoon until they are soft and thoroughly mixed. Reserve a quarter of these fats – you are going to add them later.

Gradually beat the egg mixture into the remaining butter and lard. Work in the flour, first with the spoon, then using your hands – if the eggs are large, you may have to use extra flour to give you a soft smooth dough. As you knead lightly with tips of your fingers, incorporate the remaining butter and lard. Form the dough into a ball, cover it with a damp cloth, and leave it to rest overnight in a cool place.

The next day, preheat the oven to 425°F/200°C/Gas 7.

Cut the dough into four pieces. Butter a large flat baking tray. With a well-floured rolling pin, roll out each doughball into a large square, as thick as a penny. Sprinkle with sugar and powdered cinnamon, and dot with flecks of butter. Transfer to a baking tray.

Bake the biscuits in the preheated hot oven for 12-15 minutes. They should be flaky, golden and prettily blistered when you take them out of the hot oven. Break it into convenient pieces and put these to cool on a wire rack. If you like neat biscuits, use a biscuit cutter before baking.

A sieve and bowl, a
medium and a large
mixing bowl and
wooden spoon, a clean
cloth, a rolling pin and
pastry board, baking
tray and rack

Repeat with the other three pieces.
Store when cool in an airtight tin.

SUGGESTIONS

To make a quick *mille-feuille*: Spread a layer of homemade
raspberry jam (see page 128) on a single layer of biscuits,
follow with whipped cream and top with more biscuits
(make a double-decker if you prefer).

Vanilla Rings
Vaniljekranser

These biscuits are now familiar in Britain from those tins of Danish Butter Cookies which
appear on our supermarket shelves. They are very easy to make and store well. Serve them
with a glass of sweet wine instead of a dessert.

QUANTITY
Makes 20-30 biscuits

TIME
Start an hour ahead
Preparation: 20-25
minutes
Cooking: 15-20 minutes

8 oz/250g flour
6 oz/175g butter
4 oz/100g ground
almonds *or* hazelnuts
4 oz/100g caster sugar
1 in/2.5cm piece vanilla
pod *or* 2-3 drops
vanilla essence
1 large egg

Sieve the flour into the almonds. Add the contents of the piece
of vanilla pod, if you have it – lovely sticky little black seeds
with a heavenly scent – otherwise add the essence.

Using a wooden spoon, beat the butter with the caster sugar
until the mixture is light and fluffy. Beat in the egg. Work in
the flour and nut mixture until you have a ball of soft dough.

Cover with a clean cloth, and leave the dough to rest for an
hour to firm up.

Heat the oven to 375°F/190°C/Gas 5.

Roll the dough out to three times the thickness of a pound
coin. Cut thin strips as long as a watch-strap, and join each
with the tip of a damp finger to make a ring.

Put the rings on a well-buttered baking sheet, and bake for
15-20 minutes until they are well risen and tipped with gold.

Transfer to a rack when cool and store in an airtight tin.

UTENSILS

A sieve, a bowl and a large mixing bowl, a clean cloth, a
rolling pin and pastry board, a baking sheet and rack

Spiced Almond Biscuits
Mandelflarn

Serve these Swedish biscuits with *zabaglione*, ice cream or a creamy fool. They include no butter so they can accompany rich desserts perfectly.

. . . .

QUANTITY
Makes 30-40 biscuits

TIME
Start 1 hour before
Preparation: 20 minutes
Cooking: 15-20 minutes

8 oz/250g self-raising
   flour
2 medium eggs
4 oz/100g ground
   almonds
5 oz/125g caster sugar
1 lemon
1 level teaspoon
   cardamom seeds
1 level teaspoon
   powdered ginger

To finish
blanched split almonds

UTENSILS
A sieve and mixing
   bowl, grater and
   juice-squeezer, whisk
   and bowl (*or* a food
   processor), pestle and
   mortar, baking tray
   and rack

Sieve the flour into a bowl and mix in the ground almonds.

Grate the rind of the lemon and squeeze the juice. Hull and pound up the cardamom seeds – they have a gloriously powerful scent. Sprinkle the crushed cardamom, the ginger and the grated rind of the lemon into the flour.

Whisk the whole eggs with the caster sugar until they are pale and fluffy – this always takes longer than you think, even with an electric beater. Fold in the flour mixture. Add lemon juice until you have a soft, workable dough.

Heat the oven to 400°F/200°C/Gas 6.

Pinch off marble-sized nuggets of dough, and roll them into marble-sized balls. Put the little balls on a buttered baking tray, allowing them enough room to expand as they cook. Press a sliver of almond into the top of each ball.

Bake the biscuits for 15-20 minutes, until they are pale gold. Transfer them to a wire rack to cool. Store in an airtight tin.

Danish Gingernut Fingers

Brune kager

These crisp little biscuits are delicious served with mulled wine instead of a dessert on a cold evening.

QUANTITY
Makes about 50 little
  biscuits

TIME
Start a day ahead
Preparation: 20-30
  minutes
Cooking: 8-10 minutes

12 oz/350g self-raising
  flour
½ teaspoon powdered
  cloves
1 small orange
1 teaspoon powdered
  cinnamon
8 oz/250g molasses *or*
  golden syrup
1 teaspoon powdered
  ginger
4 oz/100g soft dark
  brown sugar
icing sugar
2 oz/50g butter

UTENSILS
A sieve and a bowl, a
  rolling pin and pastry
  board, a crinkle-edged
  pastry cutter, a baking
  sheet and rack

These are crisp plain little biscuits rather like nutty sponge fingers. They are delicious with a creamy pudding.

Sieve the flour into a bowl. Grate the peel from the orange and squeeze out the juice.

Put the molasses or syrup, sugar and butter into a heavy saucepan and melt all together. Take the pan off the heat and pour the hot liquid into a well in the flour. Beat vigorously until you have a smooth dark mixture. Beat in the spices, the grated orange and the orange juice. Leave the dough, covered, to rest overnight.

When you are ready to bake, preheat the oven to 425°F/220°C/Gas 7.

Dust a pastry board with sieved icing sugar. Roll the dough out with an icing-sugared rolling pin until it is very thin – the thinner the better. Cut the sheet into fingers about 1 in/2.5cm wide by 3 in/7.5cm long, preferably with a crinkled-edged cutter, and lay them on a well-buttered baking sheet.

Bake the gingernut fingers in the preheated oven. They will take no more than 8-10 minutes. They do not brown further, being already the colour of ripe chestnuts. Store in an airtight tin – they will keep fresh and crisp for a long time.

Hazelnut and Nutmeg Biscuits
Nötkakor

This Swedish biscuit is good for dipping into a steaming mug of hot chocolate or *café au lait* on a winter evening. In summer, have them with a bowl of strawberries or raspberries dressed with fresh orange juice.

QUANTITY
Makes 40-50 biscuits

TIME
Start an hour or so ahead
Preparation: 20 minutes
Cooking: 20 minutes

8 oz/250g flour
4 oz/100g caster sugar
4 oz/100g hazelnuts
1 large egg
½ teaspoon grated
   nutmeg
6 oz/175g butter

To finish
whole hazelnuts

UTENSILS
A sieve and a bowl, a
   liquidizer *or* pestle and
   mortar, a clean cloth, a
   baking tray and rack

Sieve the flour into a bowl. Grind the hazelnuts to a fine flour in the liquidizer – or crush them in a mortar. Add them to the flour and grate in the nutmeg.

Soften the butter and then beat it with the sugar until light and fluffy. Beat in the egg. Stir in the flour and nut mixture with a wooden spoon, and work all well into a soft dough. Cover it and leave to rest for an hour or two.

Pre-heat the oven to 450°F/230°C/Gas 8.

Break off small pieces of the dough and roll them into little balls the size of a sparrow's egg. Arrange the balls on a baking tray in rows – they can be quite close as they will not expand much. Flatten each ball with your thumb and press a hazelnut into the dip.

Put the biscuits in the hot oven to bake light brown and crisp. 20 minutes should be enough, but keep an eye on them in case they burn – ovens are so variable.

When the little biscuits are ready, transfer them to a wire rack to cool. They keep well in an airtight tin – children love them.

Danish Aniseed Biscuits

Jødekager

These make an excellent simple dessert with a glass of kummel or mulled wine. Or serve them with a Scandinavian berry soup or a creamy custard. They are known as Jewish cakes, *Jødekager*, in Denmark, but I cannot fathom why. It may have something to do with trade and spice-boxes.

QUANTITY
Makes 40-50 biscuits

TIME
Start an hour or two ahead
Preparation: 20-25 minutes
Cooking: 15-20 minutes

10 oz/275g self-raising flour
1 egg
1 teaspoon aniseeds
1 small glass aquavit *or* vodka
6 oz/175g butter
5 oz/125g caster sugar

To finish
3-4 tablespoons granulated sugar

UTENSILS
A sieve and a bowl, a mixing bowl, clean cloth, baking tray and wire rack

Sieve the flour into a bowl. Sprinkle in the aniseeds.

Soften the butter and beat it until light and fluffy with the sugar. Then beat in the egg and the aquavit or vodka, followed by the flour, a spoonful at a time.

When you have a soft smooth dough ball, cover it with a clean cloth and leave it to rest for an hour or two.

When you are ready to bake, preheat the oven to 425°F/220°C/Gas 7.

Roll the dough out to the thickness of a pound coin, and cut out little discs with a liqueur glass. Continue until all the dough is used up. Butter a baking tray and lay the biscuits on it – you do not need to leave them room to expand.

Sprinkle granulated sugar over each biscuit. Bake them in the pre-heated oven for 15-20 minutes, until they are golden and crisp.

Transfer them to a wire rack to cool. Store in an airtight tin.

Gingerbreads

Nonettes de Reims

Nonettes de Reims are little round gingerbreads now made commercially in Reims and Dijon. Make the honey and flour paste when you make your Christmas cake, so they will be ready for baking at Christmas. They are probably one of the most ancient of all sweet biscuits.

QUANTITY
Makes about 30 biscuits

TIME
Start 1 month ahead
Preparation: 20 minutes
Cooking: 30 minutes

8 oz/250g clear honey
¼ pint/150ml water
8 oz/250g flour
1 teaspoon baking
  powder
2-3 oz/50-75g icing
  sugar

To finish
2 eggs

UTENSILS
A bowl and a sieve, a
  mixing bowl, a baking
  sheet and a whisk

Warm the honey over hot water. When it is quite liquid, shower in the flour through a sieve, beating as you do so. Beat it some more, until you have a shiny thick paste. Beat it again. Cover with cling film and leave it for a month in a cool place – this used to be the larder, but in these days of central heating, the salad compartment of the refrigerator will have to do instead.

When you are ready to bake, bring the honey paste up to room temperature. Heat the oven to 325°F/170°C/Gas 3.

Separate the eggs and beat the yolks up with the water. Stir in the baking powder and work the liquid into the honey paste. Beat well until all is well amalgamated. Butter a 10 in x 6 in/25 x 15cm baking sheet and spread the mixture on it.

Bake the biscuit in the preheated gentle oven for 30 minutes.

Meanwhile whisk the egg whites with the icing sugar until light and fluffy.

When the biscuit is ready, take it out and cut it into diamonds with a sharp knife. You can cut out round biscuits with a biscuit-cutter if you like, but this is rather wasteful of precious biscuit. Spread each piece with icing, and return the biscuits to the oven for 5 minutes to glaze and set the icing.

Serve with a glass of Pineau, the herb-flavoured aperitif from Charentes.

Macaroons

Macarons

This recipe is from Champagne. They are made to be nibbled while enjoying a sparkling glassful of the most famous product of the area. Almond sweetmeats figure large in European larders. The almond itself is native to India, was cultivated by the Greeks, planted in Spain by the Moors, and soon became a valuable larder store throughout Europe.

These little biscuits are now winter treats throughout Europe, including Britain – Kenelm Digby has a recipe for them in his 1669 *Closet Open'd*. If you have no orange flower water, put the finely pared peel of an orange to infuse in a cupful of boiling water. Use it when cool.

QUANTITY
Makes 30-40 biscuits

TIME
Preparation: 20 minutes
Cooking: 30 minutes

1 lb/500g whole
    unpeeled almonds
    (*or* 1 lb/500g ground
    almonds)
1 lb/500g icing sugar
4 tablespoons orange
    flower water (*optional*)
4 egg whites
To finish
rice paper
4 oz/100g split blanched
    almonds

UTENSILS
A bowl, food processor *or*
    pestle and mortar for the
    almonds, small saucepan,
    a bowl and whisk, and a
    baking sheet

Put the whole almonds into a bowl and cover them with boiling water. When the skins are loosened, after a few moments, peel the nuts and then throw them into a bowl of cold water. When all are done, drain them and dry them well in a clean cloth. Pound them to a fine paste, dampening the mix with the orange flower water to stop it oiling. This can be done either with a pestle in a mortar, or in the food processor. If you are using ground almonds, mix them directly with the orange flower water, and work in the icing sugar.

Transfer the mixture to a small saucepan and cook it over a gentle heat, stirring constantly, until your nose tells you the almonds are lightly roasted.

Remove the pan from the heat and put it aside to cool the paste a little. Beat the egg whites to a snow. Fold them into the warm mixture, 'tiring' it thoroughly – that is, working all well together. Break off small pieces of paste the size of an acorn, and mould each into a round ball. Put it on its own little square of rice paper. Press an almond into the top of each or, if you are making plain ones, indent the top lightly with your finger.

Preheat the oven to 325°F/170°C/Gas 3.

Transfer the macaroons on their paper onto a baking sheet – they will need a little room to expand. Bake them for 30 minutes.

Macaroons are a great standby for trifles as well as being delicious to nibble. Crumbled, they make the best of all bases for cheesecake.

Almond Croquettes

Craqueto

The *craqueto* of Provence is a crisp biscuit to be taken with coffee or delicately dipped into an infusion. Or serve a plateful as a simple dessert, to be dipped into a glass of a flowery dessert wine – all the great wine-making nations produce these delicious wines, and they remain somewhat neglected except in their own home territory, where they seem often to be taken as an aperitif or a fortifier for invalids and elderly ladies.

QUANTITY
Makes 30-40 biscuits

TIME
Preparation: 10 minutes
Cooking: 10 minutes

8 oz/250g whole
   unpeeled almonds
8 oz/250g caster sugar
8 oz/250g flour
2 eggs
½ teaspoon salt
grated rind of 1 orange

UTENSILS
A bowl and a sieve,
   a small bowl and a
   whisk, and a baking
   tray

Pick over and rinse the almonds but do not peel them – these are sturdy country biscuits. Sieve the flour and salt into a bowl and add the sugar. Whisk the eggs lightly, reserving 2 tablespoonfuls of egg for gilding the top.

Work all the ingredients together to make a soft dough. Divide the dough into two pieces. On a well-floured table form each piece into a thin roll about 8 in/20cm long.

Heat the oven to 350°F/180°C/Gas 4.

Butter a baking tray and lay in the rolls. Brush the top of each biscuit roll with the reserved egg.

Bake for 15 minutes, until the biscuit is pale gold and crisp. As soon as you take them out of the oven, cut each biscuit roll into slices about ¼ in/0.5 cm thick. Dry them off in a low oven if necessary. Cool and store in an airtight tin.

Madeleines

These little French cakes were made irresistible by Proust in *Remembrance of Things Past*. The author describes his first taste when his Aunt Leonie took her lime-blossom *tisane*:

> Beyond all else the rosy, moony, tender glow which lit up the blossoms among the frail forest of stems from which they hung like little golden roses. . . . Presently my aunt was able to dip in the boiling infusion, in which she would relish the savour of dead or faded blossom, a little madeleine, of which she would hold out a piece to me when it was sufficiently soft.

QUANTITY

Makes about 24 cakes

TIME

Preparation: 20 minutes
Cooking: 25-30 minutes

3 large eggs (each
  weighing about
  2 oz/50g)
grated rind of 1 lemon
1-in/2.5-cm piece vanilla
  pod, *or* replace 1
  tablespoon sugar with
  vanilla sugar
6 oz/175g sugar
3 oz/75g unsalted butter
small glass rum
6 oz/175g flour

Beat the eggs with the sugar until they are pale and fluffy and the whisk when lifted leaves a trail on the surface. Melt the butter – but don't let it brown.

Butter the madeleine tins.

Preheat the oven to 350°F/180°C/Gas 4.

Sieve the flour and fold it into the egg and sugar mixture. Stir in the melted butter, lemon rind, contents of the vanilla pod and enough rum to give a soft mixture. Fill the tins three-quarters full. Refrigerate for an hour or two to produce the madeleine's characteristic bump in the middle when baked.

Preheat the oven to 350°F/180°C/Gas 4.

Bake the madeleines for 25-30 minutes. They are done when they feel firm to the finger. Transfer them to a wire rack to cool.

Delicious, with or without the assistance of Aunt Leonie and her *tisane* (see *lime blossom tea* on page 308). Best on the day they are made, but they keep for a week or two in a tin.

UTENSILS

A bowl, a whisk and some shell-shaped madeleine tins (there are special ones). Failing these – little shallow cake tins or scallop shells will do (butter these last very thoroughly)

Meringues

Meringues have been on the European menu since the early eighteenth century – the period when refined cane sugar first became widely available. There are a few points to remember when making them. The eggs should be at room temperature when you start the operation. A proportion of 2 oz/50g sugar to 1 white of egg gives a soft meringue; double the sugar for a crisp meringue. Fine-ground sugar gives a smooth meringue – grainy sugars remain granulated. The bowl and whisk must be absolutely grease-free, and there must not be even a speck of yolk in the whites. Be careful not to over-beat. Once the whites go grainy (they start leaking water) you will have to start again with another lot of whites. So stop beating just *before* you think you should. A copper bowl makes the foam less susceptible to overheating – see Howard McGee's *On Food And Cooking* for detailed science about this contentious matter.

QUANTITY
Makes 20-30 meringues

TIME
Preparation: 15 minutes
Cooking: from 15
    minutes to 2 hours

4 egg whites
7 oz/200g caster sugar

UTENSILS
A bowl and a whisk, a
    baking sheet and rack

When you separate the whites from the yolks to make meringues, make sure the bowl for the whites is absolutely free from grease and (as stated above) there is not even a speck of yolk in the whites – the presence of anything oily (and that includes yolk of egg) will prevent the whites rising.

Beat the whites until they form stiff peaks. Still beating, sprinkle in the sugar, spoonful by spoonful – if you add all the sugar at once the whites will fall.

Brush a clean baking sheet (meringues stick to things) with oil, and drop on spoonfuls of the mixture. The meringues will not expand much so they do not need a great deal of room.

Bake on the lowest oven setting 225°F/110°C/Gas ½ (or in the plate-warmer) for 1-2 hours. If the oven is too hot the meringues will turn out brown and soft. The application of heat is more of a drying-out than a cooking process – when I lived in Spain, I successfully put meringues out to cook in the heat of summer in a particularly sunny corner of the patio, and finished them in a low oven. The meringues must be quite dry and crisp if you intend to store them.

Pure white meringue is the *haute cuisine* ideal but some people, my children included, like their meringues slightly brown with sticky middles – this may happen anyway if the heat is a little high. For brown, sticky meringues, bake them at 350°F/180°C/Gas 4 for 15 minutes.

Either way, the meringues will be quite delicious sand-wiched in pairs with whipped cream. For a perfect summer treat accompany them with strawberries, raspberries, peeled sliced fresh peaches or nectarines. In winter, make double-deckers with whipped cream and either a chestnut purée or a chocolate, coffee or lemon cream filling.

Make meringues with the whites left over from making mayonnaise. Or use the leftover yolks to make lemon curd (see page 133).

To make almond or hazelnut meringues, replace 2 oz/50g of the sugar with 2 oz/50g flour, and fold in 4 oz/100g powdered nuts. Bake at 350°F/180°C/Gas 4 for 20 minutes.

Breton Wafer Biscuits

These are the little 'cigarettes' which are so good with ice cream, and are now rather hard to come by in the shops.

QUANTITY
Makes about 30 biscuits

TIME
Preparation: 20 minutes
Cooking: 10 minutes

4 oz/100g softened
    unsalted butter
whites of 4 large eggs
6 oz/175g icing sugar
4 tablespoons milk
5 oz/150g flour

UTENSILS
A bowl and a wooden
    spoon, a large bowl
    and a whisk, 1-2
    baking sheets

Beat the butter in a warm bowl with a wooden spoon until it is soft and light, and then beat in the sugar. Stir in the flour with a metal spoon.

Preheat the oven to 350°F/180°C/Gas 4.

Whisk the egg whites until stiff and fold them into the mixture. Stir in the milk. Blend all the ingredients together until smooth. The paste should be quite liquid.

Butter a baking sheet (2 sheets would be better – these biscuits need plenty of room). Using a teaspoon and a wet forefinger, drop little mounds of the mixture onto the baking sheets, spacing them quite widely apart.

Bake them in the preheated oven. The biscuits will take about 10 minutes for the edges to turn brown and lacy.

Take them out and roll each biscuit immediately round the handle of a wooden spoon, a pencil or a chopstick. Let them cool on a rack. They will dry deliciously crisp and keep well in an airtight tin.

SUGGESTIONS

TUILES AUX AMANDES___For these, add 2 oz/50g slivered almonds to the basic mix. They will need a slightly hotter oven to cope with the extra thickness. Roll the cooked *tuiles* round a rolling pin rather than a pencil – they are not as flexible as the cigarettes.

Brandy Snaps

If you have small children, this is an easy recipe for them to help you with, as the warm biscuits have to be curled round a wooden spoon handle. It's much more fun than sand-and-water play.

QUANTITY
Makes about 30 biscuits

TIME
Preparation: 25 minutes
Cooking: 10 minutes

8 oz/250g plain flour
8 oz/250g demerara
  sugar
1 heaped teaspoon
  powdered ginger
8 oz/250g golden syrup
8 oz/250g butter

UTENSILS
A bowl, small saucepan,
  2 large baking sheets,
  wooden spoon and a
  rack

Sieve the flour and powdered ginger into a bowl. Put the butter, sugar and syrup into a small pan and melt the mixture over a gentle heat. When everything has dissolved, take it off the heat and leave for a moment to cool. Beat in the flour.

Preheat the oven to 375°F/190°C/Gas 5.

Butter a couple of large baking sheets.

Put teaspoons of the mixture onto the buttered baking sheet – leave them plenty of room to spread. Bake for 10 minutes, when they will be bubbly and golden but still soft. Leave to cool for a minute or you will burn your fingers.

Butter the handle of a wooden spoon and wrap each biscuit round the handle to give the characteristic tube shape. Leave it for a moment to set brittle. Slip it off and continue until all the biscuits are curled. If they cool and harden before you can curl them, warm them up again and they will soften. Let them cool and store them in an airtight tin.

Brandy snaps are delicious stuffed with whipped cream.

German Shortcake Biscuits
Rheinischer Spekulatius

These *Rheinischer Spekulatius* are enjoyed at their best with a small glass of one of the late-picked Moselle wines – sweet and light.

QUANTITY
Makes 8 small rounds

TIME
Start ½ hour ahead
Preparation: 20 minutes
Cooking: 25 minutes

1 lb/500g flour
grated rind of 1 lemon
2 eggs
1 teaspoon powdered
  cinnamon
3-4 tablespoons milk
  (quantity depends on
  the size of the eggs)
1 teaspoon cardamom
  seeds
½ teaspoon powdered
  cloves
8 oz/250g sugar
1 teaspoon salt
4 oz/100g softened
  butter

UTENSILS
A bowl, a small wooden
  shortbread mould is
  optional, a baking tray
  and rack

Sieve the flour into a heap on the table. Beat the eggs lightly with the milk.

Make a well in the middle of the flour and put in all the ingredients, wet and dry. Work the flour into the liquid, using a circular movement of your hand and pushing the flour towards the middle, until you have a soft dough. Knead the dough lightly and then put it aside to rest for 20 minutes in a cool place.

Heat the oven to 375°F/190°C/Gas 5.

Cut the dough into egg-sized pieces and press each one at a time into a small well-floured shortbread mould – trim the edges with a knife. If you have no mould, roll the pieces into balls and flatten them with your hand. As it is done, tip each one out onto a cloth and then lay it on a buttered baking tray. If the dough sticks to the mould, you will need more flour either in the mix or in the mould.

Bake in the preheated oven for 25 minutes and transfer the biscuits to a rack to cool. Store in an airtight tin. They keep for months.

Clove

Greek Twice-Cooked Biscuits

Paximadia

Paximadia are crisp dry finger biscuits to be found in every Greek storecupboard. They are served with a drink – coffee, or a glass of wine or brandy. Delicious for dunking in a glass of one of the Greek sweet red wines, or a muscatel.

QUANTITY
Makes 40 biscuits

TIME
Preparation: 1 hour intermittent attention
Cooking: about 15 minutes

3 eggs
2 tablespoons aniseeds
8 oz/250g granulated sugar
8 tablespoons olive oil
1 lb/500g self-raising flour
juice of 1 lemon
pinch salt

UTENSILS
An electric mixer *or* a whisk and bowl, and 2 baking sheets

Beat the eggs and sugar together until light and fluffy – an electric mixer does the job quickly. Sieve in the flour and the salt with the aniseeds. Work all together, adding olive oil and lemon juice, until you have a soft dough. Knead well until smooth.

Heat the oven to 325°F/170°C/Gas 3.

Divide the dough into 4 pieces. Form each piece into a long thin rectangular loaf, about 3 in/8cm wide by 1½ in/4cm deep. The long sides should slope gently down to the base. Transfer the biscuit loaves to a lightly oiled baking sheet.

Bake them for 20 minutes to dry the dough out. Take the loaves out of the oven – the dough will not yet have taken colour. Let it cool.

Turn the oven up to a high temperature – 425°F/220°C/Gas 7.

Using a sharp knife cut the biscuit loaves diagonally, to give you long thin slices about 1 in/2.5cm thick. Lay the slices on the baking sheet, cut side up (you will need at least 2 oiled baking sheets to accommodate them).

Bake the biscuits for 5-7 minutes a side, turning once, until they are a warm golden brown.

Remove from the oven and transfer the biscuits to a rack to cool. Store in a tin. They keep for ever.

Serve them at the end of a meal with a dish of sweet figs or slices of ripe melon. Or use the biscuits as the base for a simple sweet: arrange one or two per person on a pretty, flat dish; pour a trickle of warmed honey over the biscuits and sprinkle with walnuts or toasted almonds; finish with a dollop of thick cream.

Greek Butter Biscuits

Koulourakia

Koulourakia were kept as a celebration treat, since the ingredients are extravagant. Always made in large quantities to satisfy large family gatherings, these biscuits are still often sent for baking to the communal baking oven. Children love the crisp, buttery flavour. Both the ingredients and the method of preparation are very similar to that used for the various Scandinavian Christmas biscuits which are now so popular marketed as Danish butter cookies. Perhaps those engaged in the ancient commerce in salt cod between Norway and the Mediterranean exchanged recipes as well as trade goods.

Greek butter, in common with most butter prepared for use in hot climates, is usually cooked to evaporate its moisture. Such clarified butter does not go rancid in warm weather and can be stored without refrigeration. The taste is noticeably 'cooked' if the butter is used northern-style to spread on bread.

. . . .

QUANTITY
Makes about 100 biscuits

TIME
Start 1-2 hours ahead
Preparation: 30 minutes
Cooking: 15-20 minutes

2 lb/1kg self-raising flour
6 oz/175g clarified butter
1 small glass brandy *or*
    ouzo
1 whole egg and 2 yolks
5 fl oz/150ml double
    cream
12 oz/350g sugar

Flavouring: grated rind
    of 1 orange *or* 1 lemon,
    or contents of short
    length of vanilla pod

Sieve the flour into a large bowl.

Cream the butter in a warm bowl and beat it until light and fluffy with the sugar. A mixer will save your muscles – the old way is with the bare hand, and many a housewife still says that makes a lighter biscuit.

Beat in the egg and the yolks. Beat in the cream and the brandy or ouzo. Make a well in the flour and pour in the egg mixture. Add your chosen flavouring.

Mix the liquid into the flour with your hand, working the dry flour in gradually. Knead until you have a soft shiny dough. Roll the dough into a ball and put it aside to rest for an hour or two in a cool place.

Heat the oven to 350°F/180°C/Gas 4.

Break off nut-sized pieces of dough and roll them into short ropes the thickness of your finger. To make the simplest shape for this biscuit, join the rope into a ring, pressing the ends together. Or you can make a snail-curl, or a butterfly-curl, or twist the rope before you join it into a ring, or bend the ring into a figure-of-eight. Invent your own trademark-curl as the Greeks do.

Lay the biscuits on a baking sheet. Finish, if you please, with a brush of beaten egg and a sprinkle of sesame seeds.

To finish
beaten egg and sesame
seeds (*optional*)

UTENSILS
A large bowl, another
bowl, an electric mixer
would be helpful, a
baking sheet

Bake the biscuits for 15-20 minutes until they are well gild-
ed. Transfer to a wire rack to cool. Store them in an airtight tin.

They are delicious with a fresh fruit salad or a compote of
dried fruits, or with ice cream.

Serve, to welcome friends, with a tiny cup of bitter-sweet
Turkish coffee (see page 311) and a glass of water.

Merveilles

Variations on this recipe are the celebration treat of all of dairy-farming Europe, from the
Italian Alps to the Norwegian fjords. They are made with the best the larder has to offer.
The cream can be replaced with an extra egg, or the butter omitted. These biscuits need no
oven for the baking – ovens were not standard equipment in the peasant kitchen.

Expatriate north Europeans often remember the scent of *merveilles* frying as the most
evocative culinary memory of the Christmases of their youth. The *merveilles* can be cut
into any shape – crescents, twisted bars, triangles – and the Scandinavians make them in
a rough shape of reindeer horns at Christmas.

Makes about 48
merveilles

Start an hour ahead
Preparation: 1 hour
Cooking: 30 minutes

1 lb/500g flour
½ teaspoon salt
5 eggs
1 pint/600ml double
    cream (as thick as
    possible)
2 oz/50g melted butter
1 small glass kirsch
    or other *eau-de-vie*
    (optional)

To finish
Either half butter, half
    lard for deep frying
    (traditional) *or* frying
    oil plus a knob of
    butter (modern)
caster *or* icing sugar

Sieve and bowl, whisk
    and bowl, rolling pin
    and deep-fryer

Sieve the flour with the salt.

Beat the eggs until they are pale and fluffy. Stir in the cream, the melted butter and the kirsch.

Using your hand (it adds a necessary warmth), beat the flour gradually into the egg mixture until you have a light spongy dough which no longer sticks to your fingers – you may need more or less flour as eggs vary greatly in size.

Cover the dough and leave it to rest in a cool place for at least an hour.

Cut the dough into 4 pieces. Roll each piece out in a long sausage, and cut the sausage into 12 pieces. Make each piece into a little ball. Flour the table and the rolling pin, and roll out each ball into a disc about the thickness of a penny.

In a deep-fryer heat the fat or oil you have chosen. If you are using oil, add a little piece of butter to it for the flavour.

When a blue haze rises from the pan, slip in the discs one at a time. They should gild and puff up immediately. Remove and put them to drain on kitchen paper. When they are cool, powder them with sugar.

Merveilles will only keep for a day or two. They are delicious with fresh cream cheese or thick yoghurt, or the Moutarde de Benichon on page 45.

10. Breads and Cakes

Yeast Cakes

Europe has a wide range of enriched breads for the storecupboard, the forerunners of our modern rich fruit cakes. Bread doughs worked with butter, eggs and dried fruit have given us our celebration treats for many centuries. The young ladies of Saxon Britain had to bake a bride cake to prove their marriage skills – today's brides come more easily by their wedding cakes.

The educated ladies of Queen Elizabeth I's Renaissance England were the first to taste the feathery delights of cakes raised with beaten eggs. Those who had to beat the eggs by hand without the assistance of such modern gadgets as whisks and electric mixers must have been less enthusiastic about the labour involved. The alternative raising agent, commercially prepared baking powder, did not come to their rescue until Victoria was in her prime. Now it replaces yeast as a more convenient and quicker-acting raising agent, although sometimes the traditional method survives side by side with the innovation: South Wales housewives now make *bara brith* with self-raising flour, but North Wales continues to prefer yeast as the raising agent for this fruit bread.

To convert a yeast-bread recipe, replace 1 oz/25g yeast with 1 teaspoon of baking powder, and use one of the two standard methods of cake-making with the rest of the ingredients: either beat up the sugar and eggs until stiff before incorporating the flour and melted butter, then stir in cold milk until you have a soft dropping consistency; or beat the sugar with the butter until light and fluffy before incorporating the eggs and the flour.

Norwegian Malt Bread
Vøterbrød

The Norwegians, who have a taste for sweet and salt together, like their *vøterbrød* with a slice of dried meat. In Britain malt bread is a popular tea bread, particularly in the north of England – perhaps the Norwegian sailors who traded their berries for cloth in Newcastle during the eighteenth century taught their Geordie lady friends how to cook it. There are to this day strong links between Newcastle and Norway's Vesterland. The *vørter* beer which is used in the making of this bread is strong and dark but non-alcoholic.

QUANTITY
Makes 2 loaves

TIME
Start 3 hours ahead
Preparation: 20-25
  minutes
Cooking: 1 hour 20
  minutes

1½ lb/750g strong white
  flour
1 oz/25g fresh yeast *or*
  ½ oz dried
8 oz/250g rye flour
8 oz/250g molasses
teaspoon salt
1 teaspoon powdered
  aniseed
½ teaspoon powdered
  cloves
½ teaspoon ground
  pepper
4 oz/100g raisins
1 pint/600ml *vørter* beer
  or stout *or* Newcastle
  brown ale

Sift the two flours together with the salt into a warm bowl. Stir in the three spices and the raisins. Make a well in the middle.

Bring the beer to the boil to evaporate the alcohol, then let it cool down to finger temperature. Dissolve the yeast in a little of the warm beer, mix it with the rest of the beer and pour the liquid into the well in the flour. Working with a circular movement of one hand, blend the flour gradually into the liquid. Knead in the molasses. Work the dough well until it is smooth and less sticky – you may need extra flour. The working takes much Scandinavian muscle-power: rye and molasses make for a heavy mixture which is not easily pushed around. Persevere until all is smooth.

Knead the dough into a ball and cover it with a damp cloth. Put it in a warm place to rise for 2 hours – a plastic bag loosely knotted round the bowl provides a warm, damp greenhouse atmosphere in which the yeast cells can develop and multiply. Be sure to give it enough time to rise – dough made with rye is on the heavy side.

When the dough has doubled in bulk, knock it down, knuckling with your fists to distribute the air bubbles. Cut the dough in half and knead it into two loaves, round or oval. If you wish to be Norwegian, put them on a baking tray; tuck them into a pair of small greased bread tins if you would prefer your loaves in the English style (I find they rise better in a tin).

Cover as before and leave them to rise again for at least another hour until doubled in bulk.

Preheat the oven to 375°F/190°C/Gas 5.

To finish

2 tablespoons sugar

2 tablespoons boiling
  water

UTENSILS

A warm bowl, a
  saucepan, an electric
  mixer would be
  helpful, and 2 loaf tins

Put in the loaves and bake them for 20 minutes. Turn the oven down to 350°F/180°C/Gas 4 and leave them to bake for 1 hour. When they are done, the crust will feel firm to the finger, and the base will sound hollow when you tap it. Make a little syrup by dissolving 2 tablespoons of sugar in 2 tablespoons boiling water, and paint the loaves with it to give them a shine.

Malt bread is best after 2-3 days on the shelf, wrapped in a clean cloth.

Nut Bread

Pain de noix

Pain de noix is sold in most markets through France and Switzerland, often with other semi-wild products such as honey and home-pressed apple juice. Both walnuts and wild-gathered cobnuts are considered valuable larder stores throughout Europe. Raisins can be included in the mixture, and a pinch of cinnamon or powdered cloves.

QUANTITY
Makes 1 loaf

TIME
Start 1 hour ahead
Preparation: 25 minutes
Cooking: 1 hour

1 lb/500g strong white
   flour
2 eggs
8 oz/250g powdered
   nuts (hazelnuts and/*or*
   walnuts)
4 oz/100g sugar
½ teaspoon salt
1 oz/25g yeast *or* ½
   oz/12g dried
butter for greasing
¼ pint/150ml warm milk

UTENSILS
A sieve and mixing bowl,
   a small bowl, a clean
   cloth, a loaf tin and
   rack

Dissolve the yeast in a little of the milk. Mix in the rest of the milk and pour it into the well in the flour. Dust the surface with a sprinkle of the flour, and put the bowl aside in a warm place for 10 minutes to allow the sponge to set.

Beat the eggs lightly with the sugar and the salt. Grease a large loaf tin well with butter (butter gives a delicious flavour if used to grease a cake tin, even if there is no butter in the recipe).

Add the egg mixture to the liquid in the flour, and work all well in with your hand. Knead thoroughly (you may need extra milk or flour – it depends on the size of the eggs) until the dough is soft and elastic and no longer sticky. Form the dough into a sausage and lay in the loaf tin. Press it into the corners with your knuckles. Cover with a damp cloth and leave it in a warm place to rise for an hour.

Preheat the oven to 375°F/180°C/Gas 5.

Bake the bread for 50-60 minutes, until well risen and brown. When it is done, the loaf will have shrunk away from the sides of the tin and, when you tip it out, the base will sound hollow when you tap it. Leave it upside down in the turned-off oven for a few minutes to gild the underside.

Wrap the nut bread up in a cloth and leave it in the larder for 3 or 4 days before you cut it.

Provençal Breakfast Bread
Pougno

Pougno is a breakfast bread, to be taken with a generous cup of scalding *café au lait* – made in the French manner with a little very strong black coffee stirred into a cup of hot milk. The countrymen of Provence would add a little shot of brandy to the brew in winter.

QUANTITY
Makes 1 small loaf

TIME
Start 1½ hours ahead
Preparation: 20 minutes
Cooking: 12-15 minutes

1 oz/25g fresh yeast *or*
  ½ oz/12g dried
2 oz/50g butter
1 oz/25g sugar
zest of 1 orange and 1
  lcmon
1 tablespoon milk
2 tablespoons orange
  flower water
8 oz/250g strong white
  flour
2 oz/50g chopped
  crystallized fruit and
  2 oz/50g slivered
  almonds (*optional*)
2 eggs
1 teaspoon salt

UTENSILS
A sieve, a mixing bowl,
  a clean cloth, a baking
  sheet and a rack

Liquidise the yeast with the sugar and milk. Warm the flour in a basin in a low oven. Mix in the eggs, salt, and enough orange flower water to make a soft dough. Knead all together thoroughly, pulling and pushing with the ball of your hand, until the dough is smooth and elastic.

Chop the butter into little pieces and work it in. Work in the orange and lemon zests. Form the dough into a smooth cushion, ends tucked neatly underneath. Put the dough back into the bowl, cover loosely with a damp cloth or cling film, and put it in a warm place to rise for an hour.

Knock the dough down and knuckle it well to distribute the air. Form it into a round flat cushion about 1 in/2cm thick, and dig a hole in the middle with floured fingers. Pull the hole out until you have a round crown of dough – it needs coaxing as it bounces back all the time. Transfer the crown to a buttered baking sheet. Cover it as before and put it back into your chosen warm place to rise once more. This should take about ½ hour – the dough is ready when it has doubled in thickness, and bounces back when you press a finger-tip into its surface.

Preheat the oven to 375°F/190°C/Gas 5.

Nick the crown all round the top with kitchen scissors, dipped in cold water to stop the dough sticking to the blades. Brush the top with milk. Fill the slashes with crystallized fruit and blanched almonds if you are using them.

Bake in the preheated oven for 12-15 minutes, keeping a careful eye on it to see it doesn't burn.

Remove and transfer to a wire rack to cool. The bread is best after a few days in the tin. You can mix the almonds and the crystallized fruit, chopped small, into the dough if you prefer.

Casserole Cake

Gâteau mollet

This *gâteau mollet* is a rich dough cake from the Ardennes in north-western France, by the Belgian border, where the wooded hills yield up plenty of game for the pot. It used to be cooked on the top heat in an earthenware casserole, with coals on the upturned lid – hence the name. This is a celebration bread, like the Austrian *kulgelhopf*. It is the traditional wedding cake of the Ardennes: a silver ring was baked in the dough as a promise of marriage for the young girl in whose portion it was discovered.

QUANTITY
Makes 1 cake

TIME
Start 1½ hours ahead
Preparation: 20 minutes
Cooking: 30-40 minutes

1 lb/500g strong flour
12 oz/350g butter
1 oz/25g fresh yeast *or*
  ½ oz/12g dried
4 eggs
1 oz/25g sugar
3 tablespoons milk

To finish
Your best home-made
  jam

UTENSILS
A sieve and a large bowl, a
  small saucepan, a small
  bowl, a clean cloth and
  a hinged high-sided
  baking tin (an ordinary
  cake tin will do, but
  won't be so dramatic)

Sieve the flour into a large warm bowl and make a well in it. Liquidise the yeast with a little of the sugar and the milk. Pour this mixture into the flour, sprinkle with a little loose flour, and leave it for 10 minutes for the yeast to bubble up.

Melt the butter so that it just oils but does not fry.

Beat the eggs lightly together in a bowl with the rest of the sugar. Work all the liquids, including the melted butter, into the flour until you have a soft dough. Pummel the dough until it is a smooth soft ball. Cover with a clean damp cloth (or tie it into a plastic bag – as a miniature greenhouse), and leave to rise in a warm place for an hour.

Preheat the oven to 350°F/180°C/Gas 5.

Butter a tall cake tin and line the base with paper. Beat down the dough to distribute the air bubbles. Form it into a neat cushion. Settle the dough cake in the tin. Put it to rise again for ½ hour.

Bake in the preheated oven for 30-40 minutes, until well-risen and brown and firm to the finger.

Serve it with your best jam. Not strictly a keeping cake, it nonetheless keeps well wrapped in a cloth in the larder for a few days, and is quite delicious toasted and makes excellent rusks if slices are dried in the oven. Wonderful too with a strong blue cheese, or with *foie gras*, if any should come your way.

Rich Doughnuts

Frivolles

Frivolles are carnival treats popular in the Ardennes. I like them because they are also known by the rather less elegant name of *crottes d'âne* – donkey droppings. I am very fond of donkeys, having had for many years the care and somewhat loose control of one. Bernardo had the measure of the household, accepted passengers with great reluctance, and did very little in the way of earning his corn, apart from keeping the grass of our Andalusian valley neatly mowed.

QUANTITY

Makes about 24
  doughnuts

TIME

Start 1 hour ahead
Preparation: 20 minutes
Cooking: 20 minutes

8 oz/250g flour
2 tablespoons warm milk
½ teaspoon salt
2 tablespoons warm
  water
6 oz/175g butter
3 egg yolks
1 oz/25g fresh yeast *or*
  ½ oz/12g dried
oil for frying
1 oz/25g sugar

UTENSILS

A sieve and a large bowl,
  a clean cloth and a
  deep-fryer

Sieve the flour and salt into a warm bowl. Cut the butter into little pieces and scatter it in.

Cream the yeast with the sugar and beat it up with the milk, water and egg yolks. Pour the mixture into a well in the flour. Knead all together until you have a soft dough – you may need a little more water. Knead the dough into a cushion and put it in a warm place to rise for an hour, covered loosely with a damp cloth or a piece of cling film.

When the dough is well risen, using a sharp knife dipped in flour cut it into diamonds or squares the size of small biscuits.

Put the oil to heat in a deep-frying pan until a faint blue haze rises from the surface. Test the heat by throwing in a small cube of bread: it should fry golden in a moment – if it blackens, the oil is too hot, if the bread stays pale, the oil is too cool.

Fry the *frivolles*, no more than 6 at a time lest the oil cool too much, until they are well risen and golden. Put them to drain on kitchen paper.

They are at their best eaten hot, with a mug of hot chocolate or coffee made with hot milk. Or roll them in sugar and eat them within a day or two.

Keeping Cakes

The modern feeling that cakes are sinful self-indulgence is nothing new: Eliza Acton dubbed them 'sweet poisons'. She included in her *Modern Cookery for Private Families* of 1845 a bare dozen or so recipes for the plainest possible of the tribe, but seemed to approve heartily of the same mixtures when boiled as puddings. She offers a splendidly opulent recipe for *Publisher's Pudding*, which she declares (heaping in the almonds, glacé fruits and vintage brandy with a sidelong glance at her publisher, Longmans) 'can scarcely be made too rich'.

All these cake mixtures can be boiled or steamed in a pudding basin tied up with a cloth. Allow approximately 1 hour for the first pound/ 500g of raw mix, then ½ hour for each subsequent pound/500g. Steaming will take a little longer than boiling.

Bara Brith

This recipe for Welsh speckled bread comes from Mrs Dorothy Thomas, who bakes her own *bara brith*, Welsh cakes and scones for fortunate visitors to her tearooms at the Rosebush Post Office near Clyderwen, South Wales. Rosebush is the highest village in Pembrokeshire and is built of the beautiful blue slate to which it owes its original existence. Mrs Thomas's family recipe uses no butter in the mix, preferring instead to spread it on the finished bread.

QUANTITY
Makes 2 small loaves

TIME
Start a day ahead
Preparation: 20 minutes
Cooking: 1¼ hours

12 oz/350g dried fruit
  (stoned chopped
  apricots, prunes,
  peaches, figs, raisins,
  sultanas, pears,
  peaches)
1 pint/600ml strong hot
  tea
1¼ lb/575g self-raising
  flour
2 eggs
1 lb/500g dark brown
  sugar

UTENSILS
A bowl, a sieve, 2 small
  loaf tins and a rack

Soak the fruit and sugar overnight in hot tea (Mrs Thomas's neighbour uses cold tea) – you can use the dregs from the teapot, which have a good strong colour. The teapot never runs dry in a Welsh household – as soon as one pot runs out another goes on.

When you are ready to bake, sieve in the flour and stir the eggs, lightly beaten, into the fruit.

Preheat the oven to 300°F/150°C/Gas 2.

Line 2 small loaf tins with buttered paper.

Divide the mixture between the tins. Bake the *bara brith* for 1¼ hours. Cool on a rack and store in a tin for 2-3 days, when the bread becomes moist and rich. *Bara brith* keeps for weeks.

Slice the *bara brith* and spread it with butter – the Welsh like their butter well-salted. Excellent for breakfast with a pot of strong tea.

Four-Quarter Cake
Quatre quarts

Quatre quarts is the first cake French children learn to make. For me, it was knowledge hard-earned with an aching twelve-year-old arm in the Alsace farmhouse kitchen of my then-best-friend's family. It was late summer when I went to spend a two-week holiday with them: I remember being taken to gather *cèpes* in the russet-leaved beech woods, and instructed to avoid the ones which were stained blue. The kitchen was my favourite room – warm and sweet-smelling with the fragrance of apples and the rich ripe scent of curing hams. The cook would give me small tasks to perform such as trimming beans or peeling shallots, until one day she decided I was fit for higher things. First she sent me out to fetch the brown-freckled eggs from the boxes in the hen house. The cake had an unpredictable element dictated by the weighing of the eggs which delighted me – 3 bantam's eggs would weigh the same as one mature hen's. Proud of promotion, under her instruction I beat the mixture until my arm could take no more, and the result remains my favourite teatime treat.

QUANTITY
Serves 6-8

TIME
Preparation: 25-30 minutes
Cooking: about 1 hour

6 eggs (1 large egg weighs about 2 oz/50g)
about 12 oz/300g butter
about 12 oz/300g caster sugar
about 12 oz/300g self-raising flour (it works with plain flour, too)
about ¼ pint/150ml milk
1 lemon, grated zest

UTENSILS

Weigh the eggs and then weigh out the butter, sugar and flour to match.

Soften the butter in a warm bowl, and beat in the sugar with a wooden spoon. Beat the mixture until it is pure white and fluffy – a mixer will do the job for you, but this basic mixing is very important and will dictate the lightness of the cake at the end. Beat in the eggs whole, one at a time. After you have incorporated 4-5 of the eggs, the mixture may look a little grainy and you will need to stir in a spoonful of flour (sprinkle it in through a sieve) to soak up the extra moisture. When all the eggs are beaten in, sieve in the flour, a spoonful at a time, and fold it in with a metal spoon. Add enough milk to give you a soft smooth mixture which drops easily from the spoon. Stir in the grated lemon zest.

Preheat the oven to 350°F/180°C/Gas 4.

Butter a 10-in/25-cm square cake tin and line the base with greaseproof paper cut to size. Drop in the cake mixture and push it well into the corners. Smooth down the top.

Bake it in the middle of the oven for 1 hour. By this time the cake should have shrunk from the sides and be well-risen and golden brown – if it feels soft to your finger and is still hissing,

Kitchen scales, a mixing bowl, an electric mixer would be useful, greaseproof paper, a 10-in/25-cm square cake tin and a rack

put it back in for another 10 minutes. Check that it is cooked by running a skewer through the middle – it should come out clean. Leave the cake to settle in the tin for a few minutes, and then tip it out onto a rack to cool. Peel off the paper.

Store when cool. It is best after a day or two, and keeps well. Ice it, if you like, with a thick layer of icing made of sieved icing sugar mixed with lemon juice.

Gingerbread

The Moors, well-entrenched in Spain by the eighth century, made themselves responsible for the culinary emancipation of the spice-deprived cooks of northern Europe. Since then, northern cooks have turned for comfort in cold weather to southern spices. Frozen toes and icy fingers thaw quickly when there is gingerbread and spiced biscuits for tea.

QUANTITY
Makes one sticky cake

TIME
Preparation: 30 minutes
Cooking: 1½ hours

10 oz/275g self-raising flour
8 oz/250g molasses (treacle will do, but the cake will not be so dark and rich)
1 teaspoon ground ginger
1 teaspoon ground cinnamon
4 oz/100g soft brown sugar
1 teaspoon ground nutmeg
1 egg
4 oz/100g butter
½ pint/300ml yoghurt or soured cream

Sieve the flour and spices into a large bowl.

Melt the butter, the molasses and the sugar together until they are quite liquid. Pour the warm mixture into a well in the flour and mix all well together.

Beat in the egg and the yoghurt or soured cream.

Preheat the oven to 325°F/170°C/Gas 3.

Line a small loaf tin with greaseproof paper, and butter it well. Pour in the gingerbread mixture.

Bake in the preheated slow oven for 1½ hours, until the cake is set and firm. Don't worry if it sinks in the middle as it cools – it will be all the more sticky and delicious. Transfer it to a rack to cool. The gingerbread will keep for months in a tin.

UTENSILS

A sieve, a large bowl, a loaf tin about 8in/20cm x 5in/12.5cm, and grease proof paper

Irish Fruit Cake

This is a recipe from County Down. Baked in the roasting tin, it cuts into convenient pieces for the pocket. This is a really excellent cake.

QUANTITY

Makes 1 large cake

TIME

Preparation: 30 minutes
Cooking: 1¼ hours

First cooking

6 oz/175g currants

6 oz/175g raisins

4 oz/100g brown sugar

2 tablespoons water

2 tablespoons vinegar

Second cooking

1 lb/500g self-raising
   flour

2 oz/50g sugar

4 oz/100g butter *or* lard

¾ pint/450ml buttermilk

UTENSILS

A small saucepan, a sieve
   and a mixing bowl, a
   10-in x 12-in/25-cm x
   30-cm roasting tin and
   a rack

Put the ingredients for the first cooking into a small pan and simmer them gently for 10 minutes, stirring occasionally. Take the pan off the heat and let the contents cool.

For the second cooking, sieve the flour into a bowl and mix in the sugar. Rub in the fat until the mixture is like fine breadcrumbs. Stir in the buttermilk and then the fruit mixture from the first cooking.

Preheat the oven to 400°F/200°C/Gas 6.

Pour the mixture into the greased baking tin. Bake in the preheated hot oven for the first ½ hour, then turn the heat down to 325°F/170°C/Gas 3 and bake for a further ¾ hour, until the cake is well-risen and brown – keep an eye on it and cover with greaseproof paper if it burns. Transfer to a wire rack to cool. Store in a tin. It will keep for a month at least.

Yorkshire Parkin

Yorkshire housewives are skilful with oatmeal and have their own version of oatcakes, made as a yeast batter rather than a biscuit dough. This parkin made with their two favourite ingredients, oatmeal and syrup, remains a larder staple. It is a firm textured bread-like cake. Slice it thin and spread with butter. I like it on a picnic, with a slice of Wensleydale cheese.

QUANTITY

Makes 1 large cake

TIME

Start a week ahead
Preparation: 20 minutes
Cooking: 45-50 minutes

8 oz/250g plain flour
1 lb/500g medium
   oatmeal
1 teaspoon baking
   powder
2 lb/1kg golden syrup
½ teaspoon salt
8 oz/250g butter (*or*
   dripping *or* lard)
1 teaspoon powdered
   ginger
6 tablespoons milk
1 teaspoon powdered
   allspice

UTENSILS

A sieve and a bowl, and a
   roasting tin 10 in x 12
   in/25 x 30cm

Heat the oven to 350°F/180°C/Gas 4.

Sieve the flour together with the baking powder, salt and spices in a bowl with the oatmeal. Warm the syrup with the butter or other fat and work it into the dry mixture. Stir in the milk.

Pour the mixture into a greased roasting tin and bake it for 45-50 minutes. It is done when the middle no longer yields to finger pressure. Tip it out onto a cooling rack.

Yorkshire parkin is traditionally stored in a wooden box rather than a tin, so that the air can get at it and soften it. It will be ready in a week.

Rich Fruit Cake

Saxon brides-to-be prepared a bride-cake much like this to prove their marriage skills. The English have baked such cakes to mark special celebrations ever since.

In the eighteenth and nineteenth centuries young girls in domestic service were allowed to bake a Simnel cake to take home to their mothers on Mothering Sunday. The richness of the ingredients was supposed to reassure anxious parents that their little ones were getting adequate nourishment in their new home – one of the earliest mass public relations exercises. The cake was then kept for three weeks to be eaten on Easter Sunday. For an Easter Simnel cake, bake a layer of almond paste in between two layers of the cake. Top with another layer of almond paste after baking, and don't forget to decorate it with the thirteen little marzipan balls which commemorate the Last Supper.

For a Dundee cake, decorate the top with concentric circles of whole almonds.

For a Christmas cake, top with a layer of marzipan and finish with snowy royal icing, made with 8 oz/250g icing sugar mixed with 1 whisked white of egg and a squeeze of lemon juice.

For a Christmas pudding without suet, add 2 grated apples. Turn the mixture into a well-buttered bowl, cover and tie it with a cloth. Boil it for 3 hours in enough water to come two-thirds up the bowl.

QUANTITY
Makes 1 cake

TIME
Start ½ hour ahead
Preparation: 30 minutes
Cooking: 2½-3 hours

2 oz/50g whole almonds
6 oz/175g butter
6 oz/175g prunes
6 oz/175g soft brown
  sugar
8 oz/250g sultanas
1 tablespoon molasses *or*
  dark honey
8 oz/250g raisins
4 eggs
4 oz/100g mixed peel

Chop the almonds roughly. De-stone and chop the prunes. Pick over the fruit, checking for little bits of stalk and pips. Sprinkle in a tablespoonful of flour and toss the fruit in it (this helps prevent the fruit sinking to the bottom of the cake). Beat the butter and sugar together until light and fluffy – the more you beat, the easier it is to incorporate the eggs without the mixture separating. Beat in the molasses, then the eggs one by one – if the mixture does curdle, stir in a spoonful of flour. Sieve the flour with the salt and fold it in. Fold in the ground almonds, fruit, nuts and spices. Stir in enough brandy or whisky to give a soft mixture which drops easily from the spoon.

Preheat the oven to 325°F/170°C/Gas 3.

Line the cake tin with buttered paper and drop in the cake mixture. Level the surface of the cake and decorate with a circular pattern of whole almonds. Leave it to one side for ½ hour so that the fruit can swell.

Bake for 2½ -3 hours in the preheated oven until the cake is well-browned and firm to the touch. If it looks as if it is browning too early, cover with greaseproof paper after 1½ hours.

6 oz/175g self-raising
   flour
4 oz/100g glacé cherries
½ teaspoon salt
2 oz/50g ground
   almonds
1 teaspoon cinnamon
1 teaspoon nutmeg
1 small glass brandy *or*
   whisky

To finish
whole almonds

Allow the cake a few minutes to settle. Turn it out and peel off the paper. Store in an airtight tin when it is quite cool. Rich fruit cake improves famously with the keeping.

UTENSILS

Small bowls, a large mixing bowl and a sieve, greaseproof paper, a deep 8-in/20-cm diameter cake tin and a rack

Date and Walnut Loaf

This was a tea-time treat from my childhood – the picnic cake. We sometimes had it for tea, with custard. It keeps very well and is delicious spread with butter.

QUANTITY
Makes 1 loaf

TIME
Preparation: 20 minutes
Cooking: 1¼ hours

4 oz/100g walnuts
½ teaspoon ground
   cinnamon
1 lb/500g dates
2 oz/50g butter
12 oz/350g self-raising
   flour
2 oz/50g caster sugar
½ teaspoon salt
2 eggs
½ teaspoon ground
   cloves
about ⅓ pint/200ml milk

Heat the oven to 350°F/180°C/Gas 4.
   Grease the loaf tin and line it with buttered paper.
   Chop the nuts roughly. Stone and chop the dates small.
   Sieve the flour with the salt and the spices. Soften the butter and beat it with the sugar to a pale fluffy cream. Beat in one of the eggs. Sift in a tablespoon of flour. Beat in the second egg. Stir in the rest of the flour, the nuts and the dates, roughly chopped. Stir in enough milk to give a soft mixture which drops easily from the spoon.
   Tip the mixture into the loaf tin and smooth it into the corners. Bake in the preheated oven for 1 hour 15 minutes, until well risen and firm to the finger.

UTENSILS

A sieve, a loaf tin, and a mixing bowl

Seed Cake

Bake a caraway seed cake after you have made mayonnaise, as the recipe uses no yolks. This is the classic Edwardian tea-cake and very good too for taking on picnics. Caraway is a digestive – useful after the exertion of carrying the picnic basket.

QUANTITY
Makes 1 cake

TIME
Preparation: 25 minutes
Cooking: 1 hour 10
minutes

8 oz/250g self-raising
flour
4 oz/100g caster sugar
½ teaspoon salt
¼ pint/150ml milk
1 tablespoon caraway
seeds
whites of 3 eggs
4 oz/100g butter,
softened

UTENSILS
A sieve and a mixing
bowl, a 6-in/15-cm
square baking tin,
greaseproof paper and
a rack

Preheat the oven to 350°F/180°C/Gas 4.

Sieve the flour and salt and stir in the caraway seeds. Beat the softened butter to a cream with the sugar. Stir in the milk alternately with spoonfuls of the flour.

Whisk the egg whites to a stiff froth (stop just before you think you should, or the whites will go grainy). Fold the froth into the cake mixture, turning it with a metal spoon.

Tip the mixture into a buttered 6-in/15-cm square baking tin lined with buttered paper. Bake for 1 hour 10 minutes, until well risen and firm. Store in an airtight tin when quite cold.

Olive Oil Cake

Biscocho

Mediterranean housewives have easier access to olive oil than butter, and use it in many of their cake and biscuit recipes – perfect for those who are worried about cholesterol. This Spanish *biscocho* has been a family favourite since we lived for many years in Andalusia. It must be the easiest cake ever invented. As with the French four-quarter cake, all main ingredients should weigh the same as the eggs – large eggs weigh about 2 oz/50g.

QUANTITY
Makes 1 medium cake

TIME
Preparation: 10 minutes
Cooking: 1 hour 10
minutes

3 eggs
½ teaspoon salt
6 oz/175g plain flour
6 oz/175g light olive oil
1 teaspoon baking
powder
6 oz/175g sugar

UTENSILS
A small bowl and whisk,
a large bowl and
wooden spoon, a loaf
tin and greaseproof
paper

Whisk the eggs lightly together in a small bowl.

Sieve the flour, baking powder and salt into a large bowl. With a wooden spoon, beat in all the rest of the ingredients until the mixture is smooth and free of lumps. That's all.

Preheat the oven to 350°F/180°C/Gas 4.

Oil a loaf tin and line the base with paper. Tip in the mixture and spread it into the corners. Bake the cake for 45 minutes, until well risen, firm to the finger and shrunk from the sides. Transfer it to a wire rack to cool.

Nut Cakes

The European storecupboard of native-born nuts includes the walnut, the chestnut, the hazel or cob nut and its close relation the filbert (distinguished by an involucre or leaf-like husk which fully encloses and extends beyond the nut: Kentish cobs are really filberts).

France, Italy and Romania are the walnut specialists of Europe. The chestnut was a most important item of the Mediterranean diet until displaced by maize (after the discovery of the New World's amiable and hardy vegetables) as an all-purpose flour for porridge, soups and feeding the family pig.

The most popular nut in the world, the almond, is a native of the near east, but is now thoroughly naturalized in Europe. Plantations of Jordan almonds were established in south-eastern Spain by the Moors, although the nut was appreciated long before then. Neolithic middens of Crete contain almond husks. The Romans thought highly of almonds, used them ground to thicken soups and sauces, and appreciated the fine clean oil as a luxurious cosmetic.

Nut oil was a popular home-milled every-day cooking medium in areas of southern and central Europe where the olive did not thrive. It was from the residue of pulped nut-meat milled out from the oil that the Swiss, French and Italian repertoire of nut cakes developed. Those countries which used butter or lard as their cooking fat (including Britain) usually ate the nuts whole, and such recipes do not naturally figure in the national repertoire.

Chestnut Slab

Pavé aux marrons

The recipe for this simple but delicious preparation is Swiss, but it appears in various guises wherever chestnuts are grown and harvested. You could add a little vanilla sugar (see page 36) for the delicious perfume of the seed pod of a New World orchid – particularly suitable if you include chocolate, another New World import welcomed with enthusiasm in Switzerland. Swiss mercenaries travelled widely – they guarded the Ottoman Emperor as well as the Pope in the Vatican – and returned to their fertile valleys laden with the imports from the Americas including chocolate and vanilla, as well as the more familiar Eastern spices such as pepper for sausages, and cinnamon and cloves for flavouring biscuits and cakes, and mulled wine.

QUANTITY
Serves 6 – it's very rich

TIME
Start 3-4 hours ahead
Preparation: 10 minutes
Cooking: 45 minutes

1 lb/500g chestnuts
4 oz/100g sugar
½ pint/300ml milk
1 tiny glass of kirsch
    or any *eau-de-vie*
    (*optional*)
4 oz/100g butter
4 oz/100g grated *or*
    powdered chocolate
    (*optional*)

UTENSILS
A large saucepan, a
    baking tin or shallow
    dish, and oiled paper

Put a pan of water on to boil. Prick the chestnuts with the point of a sharp knife on their domed sides. When the water boils, plunge them in. Simmer for 5 minutes, then drain them. Peel them as soon as they are cool enough to handle. Put them back into a saucepan with the milk and simmer for 15-20 minutes until soft. Either drain them, reserving the milk, and push the chestnut flesh through a sieve, then beat the warm milk back into the chestnut flour. Or put the contents of the saucepan into the liquidizer and reduce all, while still warm, to a thick purée.

Meanwhile, melt the butter (with the chocolate if you are using it) until it oils but does not fry. Beat the butter mixture into the chestnut purée, add the (optional) kirsch, and work it well until you have a smooth soft paste.

Line a baking tin with greaseproof paper and oil it lightly (a nut oil, hazelnut perhaps, is good for this – most cooking oils are too strong, butter too sticky). Pour in the chestnut paste and smooth it out into a thick layer. Cover with a sheet of oiled paper, and leave it for a few hours in a cool place or the fridge to set firm. Serve with whipped or soured cream.

Hazelnut Tart
Gâteau aux noix

I first tasted this Swiss *gâteau aux noix* in a little cake shop in the Vaud region, where it was made with the *nillon*, the solid cake-like residue left after the pressing of nuts for oil. *Nillon* can be bought in local markets, sold in little hard cubes, or already grated, ready to be put to swell overnight in milk before being used to make breads and pastries. Cream and *eau-de-vie* remain standard items in a self-sufficient dairy farmer's larder.

If you can get some *nillon* to make your pie, use less cream (the nut paste will need a few hours soaking in milk first), and sprinkle some nut oil over the surface before you bake the tart.

QUANTITY

Serves 6-8 (it's very rich)

TIME

Preparation: 30 minutes
Cooking: 45 minutes

For the pastry

6 oz/175g flour

1 tablespoon sugar

4 oz/100g chilled butter

1 egg yolk

1 tablespoon *eau-de-vie*,
  or brandy (*optional*)

3-4 tablespoons cold
  water

For the filling

8 oz/250g powdered nuts

4 oz/100g sugar

1⅓ pint/200ml thick
  double cream

1 teaspoon powdered
  cinnamon

Sieve the flour into a large mixing bowl and scatter in the sugar. Chop the cold butter, and rub it into the flour with cool finger-tips until you have a mixture like fine breadcrumbs. Beat up the yolk with the *eau-de-vie* or a tablespoon of cold water and work it into the dough. Add the rest of the water gradually, until you have a soft, workable dough – you may need extra water. Roll the dough into a ball, cover it with a damp cloth and leave it in a cool place to rest for 10 minutes.

Preheat the oven to 450°F/230°C/Gas 8.

Mix the nuts with the sugar.

Roll out the pastry to fit a tart tin 8-9 in/20-23cm in diameter. Prick the pastry base well and spread in a layer of the nuts and sugar.

Put the tart to bake in the preheated oven for 15 minutes. Take it out and pour in the cream. Turn the oven down to 400°F/200°C/Gas 6 and put the tart back for another 25-30 minutes to finish cooking. It may need a little less or longer – tart tins and ovens are variable quantities.

The pie will keep for a week.

UTENSILS

A sieve and a large mixing bowl, pastry board and rolling pin, and a tart tin 8-9 in/20-23cm in diameter

Almond Torte

Gâteau Pithiviers

This to my mind is the best of French pastries. The puff pastry in the recipe is according to the great Edouard de Pomiane's method and measurements, and I have never had a failure with it yet. Dr Pomiane not only taught the postwar servantless *bourgeoisie* of France how to cook (through his weekly wireless broadcasts) but he was also a professor of medicine much interested in the chemistry of cooking. The professor's achievements were all the more remarkable since he was, being Polish by birth, a foreigner in France. This gave him an irreverent view of the holy laws governing *haute cuisine* – which extended as far as the making of a *pâte feuilleté*, the crowning glory of the pastry chef's art:

> 'The technique I am about to describe is not the time-honoured technique, yet it has this great advantage: I have always seen it crowned with success, even in the hands of the least experienced beginner.'

QUANTITY
Serves 4

TIME
Preparation: intermittent
    attention, 1 hour
Cooking: 20-30 minutes

For the pastry
9 oz/250g flour
½ teaspoon salt
approximately 2
    tablespoons water
7 oz/200g unsalted
    butter

Make the pastry in a very cool place. See that the butter is firm without being hard.

Take a large bowl and sieve in the flour with the salt. Cut in 3 oz/75g of the butter with a sharp knife until you have a mixture like fine breadcrumbs. Mix in enough water to make a paste which does not stick to the fingers. Knead lightly. Set the dough aside for 20 minutes, with the rest of the butter beside it so that pastry and butter both reach the same temperature.

Roll out the pastry to a thickness of about ¼ in/½cm. Place on it with your fingers small pieces of butter the size of hazelnuts – use for this one-third of the butter left over. Then fold the pastry into three, like a napkin, and again into three, disposing the folds in the opposite direction. Set aside for 20 minutes.

Go through the last process twice more, adding the same amount of butter each time. The butter is then all used up. Set the pastry aside for 20 minutes after each process. Then leave another 20 minutes before using it. These intervals are strictly necessary in order that the pastry may lose some of its elasticity.

Divide the pastry in half, and roll it out into a pair of rounds about 10 in/25cm in diameter, and let it rest for the last time while you make the filling.

$\longrightarrow$

For the filling

4 oz/100g blanched
  almonds

4 bitter almonds (*or 4
  drops almond essence
  – this is made from
  bitter almonds*)

2 egg yolks

3 oz/75g sugar

4 oz/100g softened
  unsalted butter

1 tablespoon kirsch *or*
  orange flower water

To finish

1 small egg, beaten, to
  glaze

UTENSILS

A large bowl and a
  sieve, a pastry board
  and rolling pin, a
  pestle and mortar *or*
  food processor, and a
  baking tray

Pound both kinds of almonds to a paste in a pestle and mortar, adding the egg yolks (and almond essence if you are using it) as you do so. This can be done in the food processor if you prefer. Let the mixture rest for a moment, and then work in the sugar, diced butter and kirsch *or* orange flower water. Work well until you have a smooth paste.

Transfer a round of pastry to a flat baking tray (no need to grease it) and spread the almond paste over, leaving a border round the edge. Dampen the border with warm water and cover with the second round of pastry. Press the edges of the pastry together with a fork. With a sharp knife, mark the top with a lattice pattern, without cutting right through to the filling. Paint the top with a little beaten egg.

Bake the *gâteau Pithiviers* in a moderately hot oven (375°F/190°C/Gas 5) for 25-30 minutes, until the cake is well risen and golden.

The heavenly scent of hot almonds and butter is irresistible, so it never needs long storage.

Almond Cake

Torta di mandorle

Torta di mandorle is a favourite special-occasion sweet throughout Italy. Each family has its own recipe – this one I learned many years ago from Michaela, the cook in the *pensione* in which I stayed when, as a seventeen-year-old student, I spent six months in Florence. Large families such as Michaela's are the norm rather than the exception in Italy. This means that parties are usually family affairs, with everyone invited from great-granny to the youngest baby. Italian home cooks have such a wealth of wonderful fruit with which to finish a meal, that they do not much bother with puddings and sweet dishes. City dwellers can buy delicious sorbets and ice creams made with pure fruit – a tradition which goes back to Roman times.

QUANTITY
Serves 4

TIME
Preparation: 20 minutes
Cooking: 45-50 minutes

8 oz/250g ground
    almonds
1 lemon
4 eggs
1 tablespoon honey
4 oz/100g caster sugar
1 small glass Marsala *or*
    Vin Santo

UTENSILS
A mixing bowl, a whisk
    or electric beater, and
    a cake tin 6-7 in/15-
    18cm in diameter

Line the cake tin with a circle of paper. Butter the tin and the paper thoroughly, and sprinkle with a little of the ground almonds.

Preheat the oven to 375°F/190°C/Gas 5.

Whisk the whole eggs together until frothy. Sprinkle in the sugar, and beat the mixture until it is white and stiff enough for the whisk to leave a trail. This is easiest with an electric beater – it takes twice as long as you expect.

Fold in the ground almonds and grate in the lemon rind (save the fruit itself for later). Don't be afraid to turn the mixture well over to 'tire' it. Tip it into the lined buttered cake tin.

Bake in the pre-heated oven for 45-50 minutes, until the cake is well-browned and firm to the finger. Leave it to settle for 5 minutes and tip it out onto a plate.

Squeeze the lemon juice and warm it with the honey and sweet wine. Soak the hot cake with this liquor. You will find this a deliciously light, sharp and moist finish to any meal, especially good with sliced oranges or peaches.

Use Cointreau and orange instead of the wine and lemon. If the cake is for children, leave out the alcohol.

Honey and Hazelnut Cake

Honey is one of the most useful of stores. When I lived in Spain, my beekeeping neighbour, an old farmer who had turned the family smallholding over to his son, would never sell me the current year's honey – he said that honey which had not over-wintered was poor thin stuff and not worth eating. He bottled his nectar from bees pastured on wild rosemary and thyme, in old wine bottles. I never did work out a satisfactory way of getting the thick matured honey through the narrow necks.

QUANTITY
Makes 1 small rich cake

TIME
Preparation: 30 minutes
Cooking: 1 hour

4 oz/100g shelled
   hazelnuts
8 oz/250g self-raising
   flour
10 oz/275g honey
1 teaspoon ground mixed
   spice
6 eggs
butter for greasing

UTENSILS
A pestle and mortar *or*
   a food processor, a
   mixing bowl, a small
   bowl, a 6-in/15-cm
   cake tin, greaseproof
   paper and a rack

Pound the hazelnuts to a powder – easily done in the food processor. Put the honey in a large bowl. Separate the eggs. Beat the yolks into the honey and reserve the whites.

Line a 6-in/15-cm cake tin with greaseproof paper, and butter the paper and the sides of the tin thoroughly.

Preheat the oven to 350°F/175°C/Gas 3.

Sieve the flour with the spices and fold it with the pounded hazelnuts into the honey and egg yolk mixture. Lastly, whisk the egg whites until stiff and then fold them in with a metal spoon – turn the mixture thoroughly to distribute the air bubbles from the egg whites throughout the cake.

Bake the cake in the preheated gentle oven for 1 hour. It is done when it feels firm to your finger and no longer hisses steam. When you open the oven door, you can hear food going through its cooking process – noises are important in the kitchen.

Store in an airtight tin. This cake keeps well.

11. Sweets and Candy

The earliest sweetmeats known in Europe were confections of honey, nuts and fruit pastes. The Romans made *dulcia domestica* by stuffing dates with almonds and baking them in honey. The technique of crystallizing the sweet juice pressed out of sugar cane was already understood in India by 500 b.c. By the time the Persians settled in the Euphrates valley in the sixth century a.d., they too had picked up the confectioner's skills. From them the news spread throughout Arabia. When the Moors settled in Spain two centuries later, the *halvas* and syrup-soaked sweetmeats, which still delight all Middle Easterners, were fully established in their culinary repertoire. Alicante, last stronghold of the Moors in Spain, still has a thriving industry making marzipans, nougats and *turrón*, a delectable honey-and-almond *halva*.

Europeans were the last to learn of the delights of Arabian candy – the root-word is *khandakah* in the original Sanskrit. The Crusaders on their way to the Holy Land, delayed in the orange groves and cane fields round Acre, brought news of the sweet juice home to their native lands. Even so, honey remained the universal sweetener, and sugar the rich man's pleasure, for many more centuries.

Venice, through her control of the spice trade and her special relationship with the Ottoman Turks, imported most of medieval Europe's sugar and supplied the sumptuous courts of Europe. Queen Elizabeth I was reported by a contemporary to be so fond of sugar that her teeth went quite black in her old age. But it was not until Christopher Columbus carried the first sugar canes for planting to the West Indies that the price came down enough for the luxury to become an addiction for the masses. By the turn of the eighteenth century, cookery books devoted exclusively to confectionery began to appear. Mrs Mary Eales contributed her *Receipts, by the Confectioner to her late Majesty Queen Anne* – herself a lady with a famous passion for sweet things, including chocolate, with a figure to prove it. Mrs Eales was followed, in 1760, by Hannah Glasse's popular *Compleat Confectioner*.

In 1747, the Prussian chemist, Andreas Marggraf, perfected a method of extracting sugar from white beetroot. It took another century and the patronage of Napoleon Bonaparte to provide Europe with her own product and the raw material to feed her growing addiction.

Notes on Candy-Making

When sugar-cooking, a sugar thermometer makes everything much easier.

To make a simple candy, heat 1 lb/500g sugar with ½ pint/300ml water. The following step-by-step account of the various stages will be useful:

As it heats, the sugar will dissolve and the mixture will begin to boil.

As it continues to boil, so the water evaporates. Water boils at **212°F/100°C** (and it cannot exceed this temperature).

As more and more water evaporates, so the mixture can become hotter and hotter.

The more water the sugar contains, the softer the finished product.

At **230°F/110°C** the mixture is syrup (thread)

At **235°F/113°C** it begins to turn into fudge (soft ball)

At **245°F/118°C** it begins to turn into soft toffee (firm ball)

At **250°F/120°C** it begins to turn into nougat (hard ball)

At **270°F/130°C** it begins to turn into hard toffee (soft crack)

At **300°F/150°C** it begins to turn into butterscotch (hard crack)

At **320°F/160°C** there is no more water left. This is the temperature at which undiluted sugar liquefies and begins to caramelize with ferocious rapidity.

At **335°F/170°C** the sugar is dark brown and should be removed from the heat immediately or the kitchen will be filled with black smoke.

The next determining stage is the cooling down of the syrup to **80°F/27°C** (well below boiling point). As it cools the sugar solution is highly volatile and liable to granulate – desirable for fudge and fondant, but no good for clear sweets and candy. Granules seed themselves and form other granules – a wonderful process to watch.

The hotter the temperature at which a mixture granulates, the larger the granules formed. So fudge has to be cooled rapidly and beaten thoroughly and constantly, so that the granules form like fine sand and the mixture finishes smooth and soft.

Clear sugar candy has to be cooled rapidly and undisturbed so that the mixture has no chance to granulate – that is why it is poured onto a chilled surface such as marble, or cooled in cold water.

Butter Fudge

This is often the first thing children learn to cook. Suitably educational it is, too: there is chemistry as well as cookery here, particularly if the process goes a little wrong and the mixture granulates too soon, seeding itself rapidly with starry crystal molecules. Be careful no-one burns their fingers on the boiling sugar.

QUANTITY
Makes about 5 lb/2.5kg
   fudge

TIME
Preparation: 40 minutes

1 pint/600ml whipping
   cream
10 oz/275g unsalted butter
3 lb/1.5kg caster sugar

UTENSILS
A large heavy saucepan,
   a wooden spoon, an
   electric whisk, a sugar
   thermometer and a
   baking tray

Put the cream, the sugar and the butter, chopped into pieces, into the saucepan. Bring all gently to the boil over a really low heat, stirring regularly. Making fudge, you can never stir too much. Boil the mixture until it reaches the 'soft ball' stage – 235°F/113°C. Put the pan in a basin of cold water to cool down to 80°F/27°C.

Now beat it with a wooden spoon until your arm can take no more – an electric whisk would be helpful, but the wooden spoon is safer if you have no sugar thermometer. If the mixture does seize up and granulate, melt it down again – the finished fudge will be delicious, but not so silky in texture.

Stop beating when the fudge loses its shine and turns opaque. Pour it into an oiled baking tray. Mark it in squares as it cools.

Store it when cool. After a day in a tin or stoppered jar, the fudge becomes softer and smoother. Best eaten within a month.

Tablet

Tablet is the Scottish fudge. No nation took so delightedly to the sunshine-substitute from the West Indies as the Scots – with the possible exception, that is, of the Scandinavians, who were soon sugaring everything, including their pickled herrings and black puddings.

Walnuts, chocolate, vanilla, coffee can all be added to the basic mix.

QUANTITY
Makes about 3 lb/1.5kg

TIME
Preparation: 30 minutes

2 lb/1kg brown sugar
1 pint/600ml single
　cream

UTENSILS
A large heavy saucepan, a
　wooden spoon, a sugar
　thermometer and a
　baking tray

Put the ingredients into a saucepan and bring all gently to the boil. Cook for a few minutes until it reaches the 'soft ball' stage (235°F/113°C). Take the pan off the fire (at this point add any extra flavourings).

Rest the pan in a bowl of cold water and beat like fury with a wooden spoon until the mixture begins to fudge around the edges. Keep stirring until the mass is nearly all fudged. Pour it into a buttered tin. You may not get this perfect first time, but it will taste just as delicious.

Walnuts

Butterscotch

The Scots love their sweeties. Highland gatherings, otherwise concerned with serious matters such as the breadth of a cow's horns, the straightness of the ploughed furrow, the skill of the shepherd's collie, always accommodate one or two well-patronized stalls selling four or five dozen varieties of sweets – sold loose by weight straight out of the box.

QUANTITY
Makes about 3 lb/1.5kg

TIME
Preparation: 30 minutes

2 lb/1kg brown sugar
juice of 1 large lemon
8 oz/250g softened
   unsalted butter

UTENSILS
A heavy saucepan, a fork,
   a sugar thermometer
   would be useful, a
   baking tray

Melt the sugar very gently in a heavy pan. When it is melted, beat in the softened butter small pieces at a time.

Cook until it reaches the 'hard crack' stage (300°F/150°C). The mixture should harden when dropped into cold water. With a fork, beat in the lemon juice. Pour the mixture, without further beating, straight into a buttered baking tray in a layer about the thickness of a finger. Break up the butterscotch into bite-sized chunks when it cools, wrap the pieces in wax paper and store in an airtight tin.

Treacle Toffee

Peppermint, vanilla or any other flavourings (try powdered ginger with a little ground pepper) which take your fancy can be added to the basic toffee mixture. Molasses gives a stronger basic flavour.

QUANTITY
Makes about 2 lb/1kg

TIME
Cooking: 30 minutes

4 oz/100g butter
1 lb/500g molasses *or*
    golden syrup
2 tablespoons vinegar
1 lb/500g moist brown
    sugar

UTENSILS
A heavy saucepan, a
    wooden spoon, a sugar
    thermometer, and a
    baking tray

Melt the butter in a saucepan with the vinegar.

When the butter is liquefied, add the molasses or syrup and the sugar. Heat gently, stirring with a wooden spoon, until the mixture boils. Stop stirring and let it boil steadily for 20 minutes.

By then the mixture should have reached 270°F/130°C (soft crack – test by dropping a blob into cold water). If not, continue boiling until it reaches the required stage. Pour it quickly into an oiled tray and mark into squares when it is nearly set.

Apricot Pastilles

This is one of our most traditional sweetmeats. Both Mary Eales and Hannah Glasse have similar recipes. Make it with fresh apricots or with any other acid-flavoured meaty fruit such as damsons or quinces – you will not need the overnight soaking, of course, and the paste may take a little longer cooking. It is delicious, too, with a few chopped walnuts or almonds stirred in at the end.

QUANTITY
Makes about 2 lb/1kg

TIME
Start a day ahead
Preparation: 30 minutes
Cooking: 1 hour

1 lb/500g dried, stoned
    apricots
1 pint/600ml water
2¼ lb/1kg granulated
    sugar

To finish
icing sugar

UTENSILS
A bowl, a mincer *or* food
    processor, a large heavy
    saucepan, a baking tray

Put the apricots to soak overnight in the water in a bowl.

The next day, drain the fruit thoroughly and put it through the mincer or process it. Weigh the pulp – it should be 2 lb/1kg. If the weight is less, use proportionately less sugar. Put the minced apricots into the saucepan with the sugar and bring all to the boil slowly, stirring with a wooden spoon. Boil very gently for 1 hour, stirring regularly, until the paste is thick.

Pour into a lightly oiled baking tray to cool thoroughly. The paste should cut cleanly with a knife dipped in icing sugar. Cut it into lozenges, roll them in icing sugar, and store.

Coconut Ice

This is the simplest of fondant preparations. For the familiar pink-and-white sweetshop treat of childhood, colour half the mixture pink and pour it in the tray in two layers.

. . . .

QUANTITY
Makes about 4 lb/2kg

TIME
Cooking: 30 minutes

2 lb/1kg caster sugar
¼ teaspoon cream of
    tartar
½ pint/150ml water
10 oz/300g desiccated
    coconut

UTENSILS
A heavy saucepan, a
    sugar thermometer, a
    baking tray

Put the sugar, milk and cream of tartar (this impedes crystallization of the sugar) into the pan, and bring all gently to the boil stirring constantly. Cook for 10 minutes, until the mixture is at the 'soft ball' stage, 235°F/113°C. Take it off the heat and stir in the coconut.

Rinse the baking tray round with cold water. Pour in the mixture and leave it to set. It will firm up as it cools.

Acid Drops

These are plain boiled sweets. Add any flavouring or colouring you please. If you use peppermint, replace the lemon juice with the same volume of water.

QUANTITY
2 lb/1kg

TIME
Cooking: 30 minutes

1½ lb/750g sugar
¼ pint/150ml water
¼ pint/150ml lemon
  juice
½ teaspoon cream of
  tartar

To finish
icing sugar

UTENSILS
A heavy saucepan, a
  sugar thermometer, a
  marble slab *or* similar
  cold surface, and a pair
  of scissors

Put all the ingredients into the saucepan. Bring to the boil very gently, stirring with a wooden spoon. As soon as the mixture boils, stop stirring. Let it boil for about 20 minutes, until it reaches 'soft crack' stage – 270°F/130°C. With a wooden spoon, stir in any additional flavouring or colouring – strawberry with red, lemon with yellow, lime with green and so on.

Tip the mixture out onto the cold slab. As soon as it is cool enough to handle, form it into thin ropes. Snip the ropes into short lengths with the scissors. Roll in icing sugar and store in a tin.

Marchpanes

These, along with the fruit pastilles on page 279, are Europe's most ancient sweetmeat. Marchpane or marzipan confections were known and admired in fourteenth-century renaissance Italy, when the busy merchants of Venice and Florence imported and emulated the luxuries of their sybaritic trading partners of the East.

Marzipan in the hands of a talented pastry chef with a good paintbox of edible colours can become a cornucopia of beautiful fruits to light up a confectioner's winter window. Around Christmas there appear, particularly in northern France, little decorative baskets of scarlet-cheeked marzipan strawberries, cherries, grapes, little oranges and lemons. These small nutty biscuits are a delicious Christmas treat – the fruits of autumn squirrelled away for the hard times. Hazelnuts or pistachios can replace the almonds.

QUANTITY
Makes 2 lb/1kg

TIME
Preparation: 30 minutes
Cooking: 10 minutes

1 lb/500g shelled
   almonds (*or* 14
   oz/400g ground
   almonds)
3-4 tablespoons orange
   flower *or* rose water
   (from the chemist)
1 lb/500g icing sugar

To finish
icing sugar
orange flower or rose
   water

Put the shelled nuts into a bowl and cover them with boiling water to loosen the skins. Peel the nuts, and throw them into a bowl of cold water. When all are done, drain them and dry them well in a clean cloth.

Pound them to a fine paste with the orange flower or rose water, either with a pestle in a mortar, or in the food processor. The flower water is important because it will stop the pounded nuts oiling – use more if you need it. Sieve the icing sugar and work it in to the nuts until you have a smooth paste.

Cook the paste gently over a low heat, turning it over and over so that it does not burn but roasts very lightly. When it gives off that delicious scent and flavour of roasted nut, it is ready. Remove it from the heat and transfer the paste to a cool china plate well dusted with icing sugar.

When the paste is just warm, roll it into a long thin sausage the diameter of a 10p piece, and cut the sausage into disks about ¼ in/0.5 cm thick.

Arrange the marchpanes on a baking tray lightly oiled with nut or seed oil and put them to bake in a moderate oven 350°F/180°C/Gas 4, for 10 minutes or so, until the little biscuits are the colour of autumn leaves.

UTENSILS

A bowl, a cloth, pestle
and mortar *or* a food
processor, a heavy
saucepan, a sieve,
a large plate, and a
baking tray

To finish, make a little icing with 4 tablespoons of icing sugar, mixed to a consistency of pouring cream with the flower water. Ice the hot marchpanes and return them to the oven for a few moments to glaze the icing – it will rise a little and then it is done.

Transfer them to a wire rack. Store them only when they are quite cool, in an airtight tin.

Stuffed Figs
Figues fourrées

A similar little treat was enjoyed by the Romans – Apicius gives instruction for the stuffing of dates with almonds in Book Seven of *De Re Coquinaria*. *Figues fourrées* are one of the twelve desserts of the Provençal Christmas. The beautiful plump figs of Smyrna are best for stuffing.

QUANTITY
Makes 1 dozen

TIME
Preparation: 15 minutes

12 dried figs *or* dates
1 tablespoon ground
  almonds
2 oz/50g butter
12 shelled hazelnuts *or*
  almonds
2 oz/50g grated
  chocolate

UTENSILS
A bowl, wooden spoon
  and a teaspoon

Nip off the hard little stalk on each fig (or stone each date) and widen the opening to the width of a hazelnut.

Mash the butter, chocolate and ground almonds together into a paste. Stuff each fig or date with a little nugget of paste and close the opening with a hazelnut or almond. That's all. Eat them freshly made.

Crystallized Chestnuts

Marrons Glacés

The chestnut plantations of the Ardèche are reckoned to produce particularly fine nuts. Commercially prepared *marrons glacés* are now very expensive indeed, and the manufacturing process is rather more complicated than the home-prepared version. Home-made ones never look so professional – but the ingredients are cheap, the results delicious, and any inelegant results can be sieved into a delicious purée to form the basis of a variety of *soufflés* and sweets.

QUANTITY
Makes about 2 lb/1kg

TIME
Start ½ hour ahead
Preparation: 40 minutes
Cooking: 20 minutes

40 fresh chestnuts
 (chestnuts fall easy
 prey to mould and are
 best straight from the
 tree)
1 lb/500g preserving
 sugar
¾ pint/350ml water

Slit the skin of each chestnut without digging into the flesh, and arrange the nuts on a baking tray. Put them to bake in a moderate oven (375°F/190°C/Gas 5) for 20-30 minutes, until the skins have burst and the nut meat has softened but has not taken colour.

Meanwhile put the sugar in a roomy saucepan and pour in the water. Heat gently until the sugar melts to form a syrup – 230°F/110°C.

As soon as the chestnuts are cool enough, peel them carefully, taking care to remove all the bitter pith as well as the outer skin. Pierce each chestnut with a toothpick or skewer (put any broken or imperfect nuts aside).

Bring the sugar syrup to a lively boil. Skim and continue to boil and skim until no further froth rises – if you don't do this, the sugar will crystallize. A tablespoon of glucose for every 1 lb/500g of sugar will also stop the sugar crystallizing. The water you have used is only just enough to dissolve the sugar, and

A baking tray, a
saucepan, a skewer, a
sugar thermometer,
40 toothpicks *or* little
wooden skewers, and a
shallow dish

it will have all evaporated by the time the surface is covered in little close bubbles. Once the water is gone, the sugar heats up very rapidly.

The sugar must be cooked to nearly 'hard crack' point, or 290°F/145°C on your sugar thermometer – if you do not have a thermometer, dip the handle of a wooden spoon into the boiling syrup and then straight into a cup of cold water: the correct stage has been reached when the lump which forms on the end of the wooden handle does not stick to your teeth when you bite it.

When the sugar is ready, take the pan off the heat immediately. Leave the syrup to cool for a moment or two. Then dip in each chestnut one by one, holding it by the stick and turning it in the syrup until it is thoroughly impregnated. Remove and prop each one on its stick to drain in a shallow dish. Remove the sticks when the *marrons* are quite cold. Wrap each in a twist of waxed paper and store in a lidded jar in the refrigerator (they do not last long in today's central heating).

Put any broken bits in the syrup when you have finished with the whole nuts. Save the bits to use in a cake filling or to make a *Mont Blanc*, that most delectable arrangement of candied chestnut, meringue and whipped cream.

White Nougat

'Nougat' comes from the Latin for nut-cake – the Romans were here first, and this is certainly one of the earliest of sweetmeats. It also figures among the thirteen desserts served for the Provençal Christmas Eve supper. These nougats were always made in-house, with honey from the household's beehives and almonds from the tree in the yard. It was famous as a jaw-breaker – particularly the dark version, so don't pour it out in too thick a layer.

QUANTITY
Makes 2 lb/1kg nougat

TIME
Preparation and
  cooking:
  40 minutes

1 lb/500g runny honey
1 lb/500g blanched
  toasted almonds
1 lb/500g sugar
2 sheets rice paper
2 egg whites

UTENSILS
A roomy saucepan, a
  sugar thermometer, a
  whisk and a bowl, and
  a baking tray

Bring the honey to the boil with the sugar in a roomy saucepan stirring until the granules dissolve. Boil for 3 minutes, and remove from the heat.

Whisk the egg whites until they hold their shape (don't overbeat or they will go grainy). Fold the whisked whites into the hot mixture. Return the pan to the heat and reheat the mixture gently, stirring vigorously, until it is hot but not quite boiling.

Stir in the nuts and reheat the mixture, still beating with enthusiasm.

When it is good and hot, remove from the heat and pour it into the rice paper-lined baking tray. Cover with the other sheet of rice paper and press it gently into a layer about ½ in/1cm thick.

Leave the nougat to cool and then store it, broken into large pieces if more convenient, in an airtight tin.

Dark Nougat

This is second of the thirteen desserts, and a Christmas treat all round the Mediterranean. These honey-based nougats have a wonderful flavour – much superior to the commercial mixtures.

QUANTITY
Makes 2 lb/1kg nougat

TIME
Preparation: 20 minutes
Cooking: 20 minutes

1 lb/500g almonds *or*
  hazelnuts, *or* a mixture
  of both
1 lb/500g sugar
2 sheets rice paper
1 lb/500g runny honey

UTENSILS
A bowl, a heavy iron pan,
  a baking tray, and a
  heavy saucepan

Blanch the almonds if this has not been done: cover the shelled nuts with boiling water and then slip the white kernels out of their brown skins (this is a lovely job for an autumn evening by the fire).

Dry-fry the nuts over a gentle heat in a heavy iron pan until they are toasted golden brown, or spread them out on a baking sheet and roast them in a moderate oven, 375°F/190°C/Gas 5, for 10-15 minutes.

Line a baking tray with one of the sheets of rice paper.

Put the honey and sugar into a roomy pan and heat it to boiling point, stirring with a wooden spoon. Boil it for 3 minutes. Stir in the nuts and bring the mixture back to the boil. Cook it until it reaches the 'hard crack' stage – that is when the sugar thermometer registers 300°F/150°C. If you have no thermometer, this is when a drop of the syrup deposited in a saucerful of cold water sets firm (the stage before this is 'hard toffee'). Take the mixture off the heat immediately – it reaches the next stage, one away from caramel, very fast.

Pour the molasses-brown mixture into the rice paper-lined baking tray. Smooth the mixture out into an even layer with a wooden spoon dipped in hot water or lemon juice. Lay the other sheet of rice paper over the top.

Break into large pieces when cool, and store in an airtight tin.

Sugared Almonds
Almendras garrapiñadas

Along with almond nougats, *almendras garrapiñadas* are the great treat of the *ferias* of Spain. Even the smallest village fair accommodates several stalls and carts laden with these little treats for the children.

Small girls submerged in the frills and flounces of polka-dot flamenco dresses teeter on strap-fastened dancing shoes, their dark hair pulled into bright plastic combs, casta-nets clicking under tiny painted fingernails. In the alleys of stalls, the traditional toasted sunflower and melon seeds, fresh coconuts split open and cut in wedges, walnuts, hazel and pine nuts, compete with the modern delights of chewing gum, gobstoppers and liq-uorice bootlaces.

Sugared almonds are often prepared in the fairground by the vendor himself over a little charcoal-heated brazier. The scent of warm caramel and toasting nuts curls around the big dipper and the dodgems, and is its own advertisement.

. . . .

QUANTITY
Makes about 2 lb/1kg

TIME
Preparation and
  Cooking: 20-30
  minutes

1 lb/500g whole
  unskinned almonds
2 tablespoons water
½ lb/250g sugar
a little nut *or* sunflower
  oil
4 oz/100g runny honey

UTENSILS
A baking tray, a
  heavy pan, a sugar
  thermometer, and a
  marble slab *or* similar
  cold surface

Spread the almonds on the baking tray and toast them lightly at 300°F/150°C/Gas 2 for 20 minutes, until the nuts are a warm gold under their crisp skins.

Warm the sugar and honey with the water. Bring gently to the boil to dissolve the sugar. Stir over the heat until the sugar no longer feels gritty. Let the mixture caramelize to a rich chestnut – 320°F/160°C. Remove from the heat immediately and fold in the almonds. Tip the mixture onto an oiled (use nut or sunflower oil) board – a marble slab is perfect.

Keep moving the nuts to make sure that the sugar sticks to them. Almonds are oily, so this is a hit-and-miss business. Separate the nuts as they cool – which will be a rapid process.

Store them when they are cool in a glass-stoppered jar.

Sugared almonds are delicious to nibble with coffee at the end of a meal, or as a treat for children instead of all-sugar sweets. Put a handful in the blender and pulverize them for a moment if you need a *praline* to top a cake or flavour a cream.

Spanish Soft Nougat
Turrón

Jijona, a small unprepossessing little town folded into the rolling hills above Alicante on the east coast of Spain, has been known for its almond-and-honey *turrón* since the fifteenth century. The modern nougat factories operate seasonally, from May to December, round the clock in three shifts. All their product is consumed over the twelve days of Christmas – an interesting Christian conversion of a recipe acquired from the infidel Moors, whose last stronghold in Spain was at nearby Valencia. Over seven centuries of occupation, the Moors planted almond groves so that they could be supplied with *halva*, made with fine Jordan almonds and the beautiful wildflower honey from bees pastured on the fertile mountainside of their adopted home.

The oldest form of *turrón* is the Jijona, made to a recipe indistinguishable from that of good quality almond-and-honey Middle Eastern *halvas*. Marzipan and nougat – called *turrón de Alicante*, and made of the Jijona mixture before it is crushed and recooked – were added later to the range, and by a process of tracking the recipe back to its roots, rather than by carrying it a stage further.

Some of the utensils still in use are of ancient origin: *boixets*, the baskets in which the almonds are kept before toasting, are made of hand-stripped and plaited esparto grass from the rocky slopes surrounding the town. In the old days, the almonds were crushed with stone rolling pins, on stone tables curled like Mexican chocolate-crushing anvils – the *mortero* and the *puncha* – then cooked in a *perola*, a copper boiling pan. Mechanical versions of these now do the job with rather less physical labour.

The last job of the season is the making of *Turrón a la piedra* for the employees of the factories. Prepared to the most ancient recipe of all, it was made in the old days with all honey, and hazelnuts were sometimes included. What follows is the housewife's *turrón*. Notice the dusting of cinnamon – eastern spicing is still much used in stews and savoury dishes in this part of Moorish Spain.

Makes about 3 lb/1.5kg

Preparation: 1 hour

1 lb/500g skinned
   hazelnuts
8 egg whites
1 lb/500g blanched
   almonds
grated rind of 1 lemon
1 lb/500g sugar
1 teaspoon powdered
   cinnamon
1 lb/500g clear honey

A baking tray, heavy
   saucepan, a food
   processor, a marble
   slab *or* similar cold
   surface, and wooden
   forms

Pick over the almonds, spread them on a baking sheet and toast them in a gentle oven until they are pale brown and squeaky when you bite into them. Pulverize the almonds in the processor. Whisk the egg whites.

Bring the sugar and the honey gently to the boil in a heavy saucepan, stirring constantly. Stir in the crushed almonds and the egg whites. Cook for 10 minutes, still stirring. Stir in the grated lemon rind.

Spread the mixture out onto an oiled marble slab.

When it is cool enough, process again until the mixture sticks and forms lumps. Press it into a form – wooden honeycomb frames are good, a soup plate will do fine.

Sprinkle on powdered cinnamon to finish.

12. Syrups, Cordials and Liquors

The syrup experts of Europe are the Scandinavians, who make delicious cordials from the berries which carpet their uplands in summer. Before sugar was widely available these were prepared with only the natural sweetness gathered by the fruit itself in the twenty-four-hour sunlight of the Arctic summers. All northerners love sweet things – perhaps to compensate for the lack of natural sugar in their home-grown vegetables and fruits.

The English, Europe's most enthusiastic amateur naturalists, had a wide repertoire of cottage wines made with wild flowers and hedgerow fruits. Hawthorn blossom, broom, birch-sap, heather, cowslips, primroses, rose-hips, rowan, crab-apples, haws, coltsfoot, elder, dandelions and daisies have all gone into the brewer's vat – but they are a subject for a specialist wine maker. Flavoured vinegars and cordials such as elderflower make refreshing summer drinks. The Mediterranean adds some unusual nut milks and herb-flavoured syrups to its storecupboard.

Your own homemade cordials will cost you less and should please you more than shop-bought potions – and you will know exactly what has gone into them. Here are a few general guidelines:

Fruits (and flowers and leaves) used in these preparations should be ripe, fresh and unblemished.

Use glass, china or pottery jars for maceration and storage. Plastic containers are no good – they are not resistant enough.

On the stove, stick to enamelled or special preserving pans.

A paper coffee-filter is excellent for straining syrups. If you use a cloth, let it be clean and loosely woven. Don't press the pulp or the juice will be cloudy. A cheesecloth nappy or old stocking both perform well.

Sterilize your well-rinsed bottles either in boiling water or in a low oven for 10 minutes.

If, in spite of your best efforts, your cordials grow a friendly little crop of blue and green fungi, all is not lost. Strain the liquid carefully, boil it up and pour it, warm, back into its re-sterilized containers.

Mint Syrup

Syrop menthe

Syrop menthe is a favourite thirst quencher in the bars of southern France – particularly among schoolchildren and old ladies. Lovely on a hot day, after a long dusty walk through the lavender-scented sage-brush of a hot Mediterranean hillside. Add a few drops of green colouring if you prefer. You can make any herb syrup in the same way – try thyme for a hot winter cordial, or fennel for the digestion.

QUANTITY
Makes 2 pints/1.2 litres
    syrup

TIME
Start a day ahead
Preparation: 15 minutes

2 handfuls fresh green
    mint
2 lb/1kg sugar
2 pints/1.2 litres boiling
    water

UTENSILS
A bowl, a cloth, a
    saucepan, and
    sterilized bottles

Rinse and dry the mint leaves if you cannot speak for their provenance. Put the leaves in a bowl, pour in the boiling water and stir to dissolve the sugar. Cover loosely with a cloth and leave to infuse overnight.

Strain the liquid. Bring it to the boil with the sugar. Turn down the heat and simmer very gently, loosely covered, for an hour. Skim and bottle when cold. It is ready to drink immediately.

mint

Elderflower Cordial

English country housewives who put up their own larder stores all have their own particular recipes for this simple infusion. I make it every year in early June, sometimes with fresh lemons; sometimes with citric acid – 1 oz/25g to 1 pint/600ml liquid; sometimes with cider vinegar – which I expect is the original English recipe, lemons having been as difficult to come by as chemicals in pre-twentieth-century rural kitchens. I prefer the flavour of the lemon, although it does not seem to keep as well. However, if the syrup grows little green fungi, I strain them out – and have never yet come to any harm. If the liquid goes fizzy, it has started to ferment. Boil it up and re-bottle.

QUANTITY
Makes 2 pints/1.2 litres cordial

TIME
Start a day ahead
Preparation: 15 minutes

20 elderflower heads
2 lemons
2 lb/1kg sugar
2 pints/1.2 litres boiling water

UTENSILS
A large bowl, a clean cloth, and sterilized bottles

Pick the elderflower heads in full blossom on a dry day, from a dust-free hedgerow not too near a busy road. Don't remove the stalks or wash the flowers.

Put the heads into a large bowl with the sugar and the lemons, sliced.

Pour the boiling water over all. Stir, cover with a clean cloth and leave to infuse for 24 hours, giving an occasional stir.

Strain and bottle in small sterilized bottles – empty screw-top tonic or soft drink bottles are perfect.

Ready immediately, the cordial should be kept in a cool larder or in the fridge. It should remain good, unopened, all winter.

To serve, dilute with water as for any cordial. The syrup is delicious as a short cocktail, poured undiluted over ice, with the same volume of gin – the perfume of the flowers marries beautifully with the juniper. I use it too to add bouquet to a fruit salad. Undiluted but mixed with extra lemon juice and a whisked egg white, it makes a very delicate sorbet.

Blueberry Vinegar

This is an old-fashioned English vinegar cordial. It needs a little time on the shelf to loose its fierceness, but then makes a deliciously refreshing summer drink diluted with fizzy or plain water. Make it in the same way with raspberries or blackcurrants.

QUANTITY
Makes about 4 pints/2.5
   litres cordial

TIME
Start 4 days ahead
Preparation: 30 minutes

3 lb/1.5kg blueberries
about 3 lb/1.5kg sugar
3 pints/2 litres vinegar

UTENSILS
A large bowl, a large
   preserving pan, and
   sterilized bottles

Pick over the berries and put them in the bowl. Pour the vinegar over the berries, and cover loosely. Leave to stand for 4 days.

Strain the juice into the preserving pan, but do not squeeze the berries or the cordial will be cloudy. Add 1 lb/500g sugar for each pint of juice. Bring to the boil, and simmer for 15 minutes. Bottle when cool. It will be ready in a month. Dilute as for any cordial.

Strawberry Cordial

This is not only good diluted as a long drink, it is also delicious warmed as a sauce for ice cream, or with white wine as a *vin blanc fraise*. Make raspberry or blackcurrant syrup in the same way. These syrups are a favourite mixer in Berlin, where the beer is drunk in summer *'mit schuss'*, with a dash of strawberry or raspberry syrup – refreshing on a hot day.

QUANTITY

Makes about 2 pints/1.2 litres cordial

TIME

Start 3 days ahead
Preparation: 20 minutes
Cooking: 30 minutes

2 lb/1kg strawberries
2 lb/1kg sugar

UTENSILS

A large bowl, sterilized bottles, and a thermometer would be useful

Wash and hull the berries carefully. Put them into a bowl alternating with layers of sugar. Cover with a clean cloth and put in a cold larder for 3 days to macerate and ferment lightly.

Tip the mixture into a sieve lined with a cloth and press gently to extract all the juice.

Bottle and sterilize in a bain marie for half an hour at 70°C. The cordial is ready immediately.

Orange Syrup

Syrop à l'orange

This French *syrop* is a great improvement on commercial orangeade and is very easy to prepare. Make it when you are putting up marmalade. It can be made with lemons or grapefruit as well.

QUANTITY
Makes about 3 pints/2
  litres syrup

TIME
Preparation: 20 minutes
Cooking: about 40
  minutes

12 juicy oranges
1¼ pints/750ml water
2 lb/1kg sugar

UTENSILS
A large bowl, a sieve,
  a saucepan, a scrap
  of clean cloth, and
  sterilized bottles

Pare the rind off the oranges and put it in a sieve placed over a large bowl. Squeeze the juice and pour it over the orange zest into the bowl.

Put the sugar and water into a saucepan and bring all to the boil. Stir and simmer for 5 minutes uncovered so that the syrup thickens. Pour the hot syrup over the zests and into the orange juice. Return the liquids to the pan. Tie the zests into a scrap of cloth and put them in with the liquids. Bring all back to the boil and cook uncovered for 5 minutes. Remove the scum and the bag of zests.

Bottle when cool, and store in a cool larder or the fridge. Ready immediately, dilute the orange syrup with water for a delicious long drink, or with hot water in the winter.

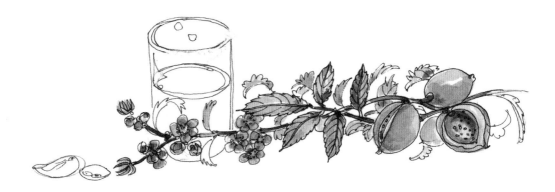

Almond Milk Syrup

Soumada

Soumada is the traditional Greek wedding-breakfast drink. These nut milks were popular in Britain in earlier days: medieval English cookery books have recipes for them. The Greek *soumada* and the Spanish *horchata*, a similar infusion of crushed tiger nuts (an African native plant), seem to be Arab in inspiration – both Ottoman Turks and Moors were fond of them.

QUANTITY
Makes about 2 pints/1.2
    litres

TIME
Preparation: 15 minutes
Cooking: about 45
    minutes

8 oz/250g blanched
    almonds
few drops almond
    essence *or* 3 bitter
    almonds
1½ lb/750g granulated
    sugar
1¾ pints/1 litre water

UTENSILS
A food processor *or*
    pestle and mortar,
    large saucepan, a
    sieve and bowl, and
    sterilized bottles

Roughly chop the almonds (with the optional bitter almonds), and put them with half the sugar and a third of the water into the food processor.

Process all well together until you have a thick milky paste. If you have no processor, you will have to pound the almonds by hand.

Bring the rest of the sugar and the water to the boil in a large saucepan. Boil for 15 minutes, and skim off any impurities.

Stir in the almond paste and return all to the boil. Boil for another 15 minutes, stirring regularly and watching that the syrup does not boil over. Add the almond essence if you have not used bitter almonds. Strain and pour the milky syrup into warm sterilized bottles.

Best stored in a very cool larder or the refrigerator, this syrup should be used within a month.

Stir a tablespoon or two of the almond syrup into a glass of cold water for a refreshing summer drink.

Make a praline with the leftover almond pulp. Spread it on a baking tray and put it to dry in a cool oven. Turn up the oven when the crushed nuts are quite dry and let them toast to a golden-brown. Store the praline in a well-stoppered jar. It will keep for months. Use it to sprinkle on cakes or as the basis for a praline ice. It is quite delectable as a topping for ice cream.

Liquors

Southern Europe was fortunate in that its vineyards provided plenty of good material for the home distillers. These days, even in France very few are permitted this privilege: the right to distil your own liquor may only pass from father to son as long there is no change of abode. After two World Wars, changing economic circumstances, and the machinations of the Code Napoleon, such rights are rapidly vanishing. Rural Eastern Europe still makes, with or without the tolerance of the authorities, its own triple-strength belly-burning brandies with plum or apricot, apple or grape.

Mile Louise Morell, born at the turn of the last century in Buis-les-Baronnies in Haute Provence, clearly remembers the travelling distiller. He toured, she explained to me in 1985, the surrounding villages on market day. He would set up his still in a corner of the market, for the time necessary to attend to local requirements. Those who had their own vines would bring him the fermented juice from the pips and skins of their own grapes. The distiller's apparatus did its work. Then the *eau-de-vie* could be prepared and scented with walnut leaves, or cranberries from the hill, or whatever, said Mile Morell, you desired.

French grocers sell unflavoured *eau-de-vie* and *marc* so that housewives can put up their flavoured brandies and aperitifs to the old family recipes. For the rest, Customs and Excise has found factory-brewed liquor far too profitable and easily gathered a source of revenue ever to let the art of distilling out of its control again.

Unflavoured *eau-de-vie* of 40 to 55 degrees is the recommended base for most of these infusions. The longer the intended period of maceration, the stronger the alcohol should be. A clear, unflavoured spirit such as plain vodka, unflavoured aquavit or white rum can replace the *eau-de-vie*.

Cherry Brandy

This is the classic British sportsman's tipple, to be carried in a hip flask on a cold day out in the butts or on the hunting field.

QUANTITY
Makes about 5 pints/3
   litres

TIME
Start 3 months ahead
Preparation: 20 minutes

2 lb/1kg dark red
   Morello cherries
3¼ pints/2 litres brandy
6 oz/175g caster sugar

UTENSILS
A bowl and wide-necked
   bottles

Wipe the cherries and trim the stalks to ½ in/1cm. Pack the cherries in the bottles up to just over halfway, layering them with the sugar. Fill up the bottles with brandy. Cork tightly and store for 3 months before using.

Sloe Gin

Wait until the sloes have had a frost before you gather them. If you cannot wait, give them a night in the freezer. The freezing weakens the skins and makes the subsequent infusing more complete. Damsons can substitute for wild-gathered sloes.

QUANTITY
Makes about 2 ½
   pints/1.5 litres

TIME
Start 3-12 months ahead
Preparation: 20 minutes

1 lb/500g sloes
1¾ pints/1 litre gin
caster sugar

UTENSILS
A needle, a plate, and 2
   wide-necked bottles

Prick the sloes all over with the needle. Roll the sloes thoroughly in a plateful of sugar, then pack them into the bottles. Pour in the gin and cork tightly. That's all. Ready in 3 months, sloe gin is best in a year.

Summer Fruit Brandy

Eau-de-vie de fruits

I first tasted this *eau-de-vie de fruits* in the depths of one of the coldest winters France has ever had to bear. Even the sap had frozen in the roots of the olive trees of Provence. This wonderful aromatic brandy was the house speciality of a bar in the little town of Florac at the head of the Gorges du Tarn. The red-roofed houses shelter under the lee of a steep ravine – a harsh cradle to rock the fertile valley which annually supplies the rest of France with its *primeurs*, the first sweet young vegetables of spring. Even in that year, by the end of February, the fruit trees which fringe the valley's floor were already in blossom. This delicious liquor has all the fragrance of summer fruit – the best and ripest the valley can offer.

QUANTITY

At least 4 pints/2.5 litres, if using 8 oz/250g of each fruit

TIME

Preparation: minimal (the jar is filled gradually)

granulated *or* preserving sugar

apricots, stoned (add the kernels from the stones)

eau-de-vie (fruit brandy)

strawberries

cherries

redcurrants

peaches, peeled and stoned (add the kernels from the stones)

ripe pears, peeled and cored

raspberries

white grapes

Starting with strawberries (you will finish with grapes), pack the jar with an equal weight of soft fruit and granulated or preserving sugar, plus enough fruit brandy, or your chosen spirit, to cover. Cover tightly and keep in a cool place.

Add your choice of the fruits in sequence as they come into season, taking care that the weight of prepared fruit and sugar is always equal, and topping up with enough brandy or white spirit to keep the fruit submerged. Re-cover tightly each time.

The scents of summer will be ready for release by Christmas.

UTENSILS

Choose a large stoneware jar with a well-fitting lid *or* a large kilner jar, and scald it with boiling water to sterilize

Quince Brandy

Bocau de coing

Northern France makes its favourite after-coffee *digestif, bocau de coing*, using apple brandy – in its more elegant form, Calvados. Any flavourless white alcohol, including vodka, will do fine. Those who have inherited the right to distil their own firewater still do so, and remain untrammelled by commercial limitations of alcohol percentage. A little glass of the home-brewed is usually pretty strong stuff.

. . . .

QUANTITY
Makes 4 pints/2.5 litres

TIME
Start 6 months ahead

10 fresh green walnuts
scrap of mace
3¼ pints/2 litres
    eau-de-vie 65°
    or vodka
2 cloves
2 sticks of cinnamon
1 lb/500g caster sugar
zest of 2 lemons

UTENSILS
A liquidizer *or* pestle and
    mortar, storage bottles
    and a strainer

Peel the quinces, leaving them whole, and put them into a large bowl with the sugar. Turn them thoroughly.

Cover and leave them overnight to make a syrup. The next day, slice the quinces into ½-in/1-cm thick segments. Pack them into jars with their syrup.

Leave them overnight and the next day pour in the white alcohol to cover. Seal the jars down. The brandy is ready in six months, and your patience will be well rewarded.

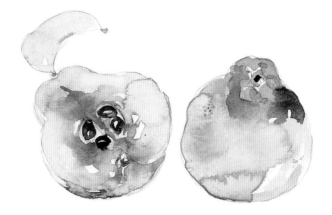

Walnut Brandy

Broux de noix

My neighbour in the Languedoc, M. Guilhermat, refilled his cellar every year without recourse to the wine merchant. In common with all the prosperous peasantry of France, M. Guilhermat made sure of the quality of all his larder stores by growing his own. A well-favoured strip of ground at the bottom of his vegetable garden was given over to the cultivation of his vines, harvested for wine. The walnuts he gathered from the tree in his courtyard on St John's day. He had the further good fortune, having inherited his farm from his father, to have the right to distil his own *digestif*. A shot of homemade *broux de noix* was his favourite 'stiffener' on a cold winter morning.

QUANTITY
Makes 4 pints/2.5 litres

TIME
Start 6 months ahead

10 fresh green walnuts
scrap of mace
3¼ pints/2 litres *eau-de-vie* 65°   *or* vodka
2 cloves
2 sticks of cinnamon
1 lb/500g caster sugar
zest of 2 lemons

UTENSILS
A liquidizer *or* pestle and mortar, storage bottles and a strainer

Pick the walnuts when they are tender and can still be pierced by a needle – no later than mid-July. Cut them in half and remove the outer husks. Pulverize the nut meat – in a liquidizer if you have one.

Put the resulting paste in a large jar. Pour in the *eau-de-vie* or vodka and add the cinnamon sticks. Seal carefully and leave the jar in a warm place for the nuts to infuse for a couple of months. M. Guilhermat put his among the geraniums in a sunny corner of the courtyard.

At the beginning of September, strain the liquor through a scalded cloth. Add the lemon zest, the mace, the cloves and the sugar – allowing 1 lb/500g sugar per 2 pints/1.2 litres of liquid. Stopper again and leave to infuse for a month. At the end of that time, strain and bottle the liquor. It will be ready when the really cold weather comes in around Christmas.

Broux is delicious on its own in winter. In summer mix an Edwardian *Floster*: Blend well together in a jug 1 wine-glass sherry, 1 wine-glass *broux*, 1 sugar lump. Serve with soda water in a long glass with a slice of lemon and a straw.

Orange Wine
Vin d'orange

This aromatic aperitif is prepared every year in the autumn by the housewives of the Rhône valley – including my landlady in the little village of Villes-sur-Auzon in the foothills of Mont Ventoux. Madame Traverse brought the bottle of *vin d'orange* out of the cupboard to celebrate our family's arrival. With it we had a tapenade of green olives chopped with anchovies and capers, mixed with lemon juice and a few drops of *marc*, perfumed with a pinch of fresh thyme from her garden. When we left Villes she gave us the recipe for her special tipple. It is, says Madame Traverse, a tonic and restorative, good as an aperitif or as a dessert wine.

QUANTITY
Makes 6 bottles

TIME
Start 2 months ahead
Preparation: 30 minutes

1¾ pints/1 litre *eau-de-vie*
2 cloves *or* a short length
  vanilla pod
10-12 strips orange peel
6 pints/4 litres (5
  ordinary bottles)
  light red wine such as
  Côtes-du-Ventoux
3 strips lemon peel
1-in/2.5-cm piece
  cinnamon bark
1 small tumbler brown
  sugar

UTENSILS
Clean bottles and a
  strainer

Uncork the bottle of *eau-de-vie* and pop in the orange and lemon peel, the cinnamon and cloves (or vanilla). Re-cork and leave to infuse for a month.

At the end of the month, strain the liquid carefully – two or three times if necessary – until it is quite clear and clean. Mix the *eau-de-vie* with the wine and sweeten the liquor with the brown sugar (less or more as you please). Bottle and cork tightly.

Store it in a cool dark cupboard. It will be delicious after a month, if you have the patience to wait that long.

Blackcurrant Wine

Vin de Cassis

This blackcurrant wine is also one of Madame Traverse's specialities. Try it with well-iced white wine, as a *vin blanc cassis* – or, my own special favourite, with champagne as a *kir royale*.

QUANTITY
Makes 4 pints/2.5 litres

TIME
Start 3 days ahead
Preparation: 10 minutes
Cooking: 20 minutes

2 lb/1 kg blackcurrants
2 lb/1 kg sugar
2 pints/1.2 litres red wine

UTENSILS
A bowl and a cloth, and
   sterilized bottles

Rinse and drain the blackcurrants (don't bother to remove the stalks). In a large bowl, mash the fruit thoroughly. Pour in the wine. Cover with a cloth and leave to infuse for 3 days.

Strain the liquid into a saucepan and stir in the sugar. Bring to the boil and cook it for 10 minutes. Pour into sterilized bottles and seal. It is ready when you are.

Grapes in Anis

Uvas en aguardiente

Uvas en aguardiente were always prepared by my farming neighbours in the remote valley in southern Spain where I lived with my family for many years. They were a Christmas treat – at New Year the adults in the household would be required to eat one (pips, liquor and all) on each stroke of midnight. Failure brought a year of bad luck – success a year of plenty and good harvests. They certainly contributed to the collective hangover.

QUANTITY
Makes 4 pints/2.5 litres

TIME
Start 1-3 months ahead
Preparation: 20 minutes

3 lb/1.5kg small sweet
   grapes
1 teaspoon aniseed
¼ pint/150ml water
2 pints/1.2 litres aniseed
   liquor *or eau-de-vie*, or
   vodka
4 oz/100g sugar

UTENSILS
A needle and wide-
   mouthed jars or bottles

De-stalk, rinse and dry the grapes. Prick them with a needle – they must be able to drink the liquor – and pack them into sterilized jars or bottles.

Make a syrup by boiling the water and the sugar. Stir in the aniseed. Let the syrup cool and then mix it with the alcohol. Cover the grapes with the liquor. Seal and store in a cool dark place. Ready in a month, it will be better in three.

13. Infusions

The two great stimulant infusions, coffee and tea, did not trickle into Europe until well into the second millennium a.d. Until then, Europeans made do with a variety of lesser brews of herbs and leaves to comfort and inspire. The difference, in the case of tea and coffee, was that the nature of the raw material was radically altered by prior preparation before infusion – so they were not something which could be stumbled on by accident. Coffee berries were used in Africa as a food and for the making of wine long before the delights of the roasted, ground and infused beans were discovered.

By the middle of the nineteenth century the two infusions had become so popular that nutritionists were worrying over their effect on the diet of their populations. In Scandinavia, coffee was increasingly drunk in preference to the nutritious soured milk and whey which had balanced the northerners' traditional diet of fish, oatmeal and berries. In Britain, tea began to replace beer as the working man's staple thirst-quencher, thus removing up to one third of his daily food intake.

Thomas Baines, in his handbook for nineteenth-century explorers, *Shifts and Expedients of Camp Life*, makes the point clearly. Here are his admirable instructions for the making of billy-can tea – his method can apply to any infusion including coffee:

> Tea is one of the most valuable and important stores carried by the explorer or traveller, and an ample supply should always be taken. We prefer the Australian method of tea-making to any other; and, whether with our brass pot or tin quart mug and pint cup, proceed in the same manner to brew it. We first pour as much water as we think requisite in the pot, put it on the fire, and raise it to the boiling point; then take it off and add tea in proportion to the number to be brewed for, covering down the vessel with an inverted tea bowl until the tea has drawn; it is then fit for use.

CHAMOMILE TEA____This makes an excellent post-prandial infusion very popular in Mediterranean countries. It acts as a calmative and mild sleeping potion. Brew it as for ordinary tea, one teaspoon of flowers to each ½ pint/300ml freshly boiled water. Let it infuse for 5 minutes. Sweeten it, as you please, with a spoonful of honey. Modern French homeopaths recommend this infusion against hardening of the arteries.

LIME BLOSSOM TEA____*Tilleul* is the favourite infusion of France. It is taken much as the British take a cup of Indian or China tea – at any time during the day, and at the conclusion of a meal. Make an infusion with 6 of the dried bracts and flowers per ½ pint/300ml boiling water. Sweeten it with a little sugar or, best of all, lime-blossom honey. *Tilleul* is the herb dedicated to Venus and a favourite in the old days of sorcerers for love potions. Medieval doctors used it as a cure for epilepsy and as an anti-plague treatment.

MINT TEA____The national beverage of Morocco. In the Andalúz valley where I lived for many years, the infusion was one of the few Moorish habits which had survived the Inquisition. In common with my neighbours, I grew a few small tea-plants and a large mint patch for the making of mint tea. On a clear day we could sip our infusion looking across the narrow straits which divide Europe from the blue-hazed mountains of Africa.

To make Moroccan mint tea: cram a handful of fresh mint into a long glass. Pour in as much freshly made green tea or plain boiling water as will cover the mint. Leave to infuse for 2-3 minutes. Add enough sugar to sweeten to your taste. I like a squeeze of lemon juice in it too.

CHINA AND INDIAN TEA____A century after the first consignments of the addictive leaves were imported from China to Europe in the middle of the sixteenth century by the merchants of Venice, the beverage found its most enthusiastic imbibers in the British. There was at first some misunderstanding as to the preparation of the infusion. Bewildered country cousins threw away the liquid and spooned up the solids as if it were porridge. Even the sophisticates of London were not entirely sure how the brew should be taken. Still now not everyone can master the trick. A female friend of the late Bertrand Russell reported that the eminent philosopher and mathematician had not discovered, by his ninetieth year, how to make a pot for four o'clock tea. Obliged to be out at the time, she left instructions for him in chalk on the slate table in her Welsh kitchen: 'Lift up the bolster of the cooker; move kettle on to hot-plate; wait for it to boil; pour water from the kettle into tea-pot. . . .'

Further instructions were offered in 1664 by Sir Kenelm Digby, founder member of the Royal Society and author of a fine posthumously published recipe book, *The Closet Open'd*. Sir Kenelm had the information, he said, from a Jesuit lately returned from China. Digby learned that *cha*, as his friend informed him the preparation was known in its country of origin, was ill-prepared in England: 'In these parts, he sayth, we let the hot water remain too long soaking upon the tea, which makes it extract into itself the earthy parts of the herb. The water is to remain on it no longer than whiles you can say the Miserere Psalm very leisurely.'

The British were responsible for the tea plantations in India and Ceylon. Thomas Sullivan, a merchant of New York City, can take the blame for the ubiquitous teabag. In 1904 Mr Sullivan's teabags were made of light unbleached silk – product of a now-vanished industry which provided many a peasant farmer's wife with her corner-of-the-apron money.

There are three main methods of manufacturing the raw leaves for infusion. *Black tea*, (most to the British taste) is made from leaves that are dried and rolled, then allowed a kind of fermentation (a matter of hours) to develop the tannins which give the tea its strength and vigour. For *green tea*, the leaves are dried and rolled but not fermented: the resulting brew is much milder. *Oolong* is made with leaves which are dried, rolled and very briefly fermented, so gives a tea of medium strength.

A warmed china or pottery teapot brews better than a metal one. Empty the kettle and start with fresh water – re-boiled water is not properly aerated and will not make a good infusion. Make the tea – approximately 1 heaped teaspoon for each ½ pint/300ml cup – as soon as the water boils. Infuse it for 3-4 minutes before pouring it out.

CHOCOLATE____Thomas Gage, Catholic monk turned anti-Papist Minister under Lord Protector Cromwell, was, in his early years, the first Englishman to travel to New Hispania with the Spanish Dons. Whatever his morals (and even his biographer calls him a scoundrel), Thomas had a most discerning and curious palate. In his account of his sixteen years as a Dominican friar, *The English-American*, he gives a detailed description of the preparation of a new and wonderful beverage:

> This chocolate is an Indian name, and is compounded from the *atle* which in the Mexican language signified 'water', and from the sound which the water, wherein is put the chocolate, makes, as *choco choco choco*, when it is stirred in a

cup by an instrument called a *molinet*, or *molinillo*, until it bubble and rise into a froth. The chief ingredient, without which it cannot be made, is called cacao, a kind of nut or kernel bigger than a great almond which grows upon a tree called the tree of cacao, and ripens in a great husk. . . .

Brother Thomas set sail from the port of Sanlúcar de Barrameda at the mouth of the great Guadalquivir river. The drink he loved is still prepared in Sanlúcar to much the same recipe to this day.

You will need, for four: 4 oz/100g plain chocolate, ¾ pint/450ml water, ¾ pint/450ml milk, 1 small stick cinnamon, 1 teaspoon cornflour slaked in a little water. The chocolate will probably be sweet enough for there to be no need of extra sugar. Mix the milk and water in a saucepan and break in the chocolate. Put in the cinnamon stick. Heat, whisking throughout, until the chocolate dissolves and the mixture is just on the boil. Whisk in the cornflour and simmer until the mixture is as thick as double cream.

COFFEE___ In Vienna, the spiritual home of coffee in Europe, the Viennese say that good coffee should be 'hot as hell, black as the devil, pure as an angel, sweet as love'. Rosl Philpot, Vienna-born author of *Viennese Cookery* (Hodder, 1965), offers these instructions for the preparation of her countrymen's favourite beverage:

> The best coffee I ever drank was made by my landlady in Vienna. . . . she bought good coffee, freshly roasted and in small quantities, from a reliable coffee merchant. She put the china coffee-pot, with its china filter on top, in a pan of gently-boiling water to get it really hot. She ground the coffee in a hand-operated coffee-grinder. Using freshly-drawn water the moment it came to the boil, she poured it into the filter, not all at once. As soon as enough water had worked its way through the ground coffee to fill the coffee-pot, she lifted off the filter, put a lid on the pot and brought me my breakfast.

The Viennese had their coffee, and added cream to it, from the Ottoman Turks. The Turks had theirs from the Syrians. The Syrians came upon it, they say, through the good offices of a Mullah, who was much tormented by his inability to keep awake at his devotions. The Prophet took pity on him and arranged that the holy man's path should cross with that of a goatherd. The goatherd was in his turn troubled by the hyper-activity of his flock of goats, who appeared to keep themselves fighting-fit on a diet of little berries from a grey-barked shrub. Guided from on high, the Mullah gathered and roasted the berries, pounded them and brewed up a powerful stimulant infusion. News of the beverage spread like wildfire, and soon every dervish in Islam was lively as a cricket.

Turkish coffee is brewed in a *briki* – a special long-handled pot, made of tinned brass or bronze, in sizes to make from 2 to 8 cups. The pot is tapered at the top so that froth can form swiftly. You will need 2 teaspoons fine-ground (really powdered) light-roast coffee to 1 coffee-cupful of cold fresh water per person. And the required amount of sugar (1, 2, or 3 teaspoons per cup). The sugar cannot be added later, because the coffee, being full of grounds, cannot be stirred. Bring the coffee to the boil in the *briki*. As soon as the froth rises, take the coffee off. Skim off equal amounts of the froth into each little cup. Pour the coffee into the cups.

Do not stir the coffee. Sip it as hot as possible, from the top. Be careful not to burn your tongue. Do not drink right to the bottom of the cup or you will get a mouthful of grounds. The coffee should be fragrant, strong and of an exact sweetness to the taste of its consumer. To appreciate its perfection, take it with a glass of cold water.

If you want your coffee at its best, buy it green (unroasted) and store it in a tin or well-stoppered jar, away from damp. In more leisured days, unroasted coffee beans were reckoned to improve with the keeping, and seven-year-old Government Java was the Chateau d' Yquem of the crop. Good coffee merchants will be glad to sell you green coffee. Find a reliable merchant and talk to him about the different beans he can supply: Brazilian,

Colombian, little peaberry from Kenya, Jamaican Blue Mountain (the most expensive of all), Mocha from Ethiopia, Mysore from India, coffees from Java, Angola, China, Honduras, Tanzania, Nicaragua, New Guinea, Haiti, Mexico, the Yemen, Sumatra. The higher the coffee is grown the better the flavour of the bean.

Roast the beans as you need them, in a sturdy lidded pan over a gentle heat. You can buy a coffee-roasting instrument – a pan with a stirring device in the lid, so that beans can be constantly turned while they roast, but I do not find such tricks are really necessary.

I get perfectly good results by roasting the beans like popcorn in an ordinary good-quality saucepan with a lid. Cover the base of the pan with a layer of coffee, let beans and pan heat up gently undisturbed for 4-5 minutes, then shake the pan as the coffee roasts to the degree of darkness you prefer. The beans pop a little as they cook, and slough off a light skin which can be blown away like chaff. I like a light roast for breakfast, a dark one for the evening. Turn-of-the-century French instructions suggest that a cobnut of butter and a dessertspoonful of sugar should be mixed in with each 3 lb/1.5kg coffee to be roasted – this gives a slightly caramelised, dark roast with a powerful flavour.

The whole process takes about 15 minutes. The bonus is that your kitchen will smell delicious, like a café on the corner of a Turkish souk, particularly when you grind the beans and release the true rich aroma – it has absolutely nothing in common with the scent of instant coffee powder.

A small electric coffee grinder is quicker than a hand-turned one for large quantities. For small amounts, there is not much in it.

14. First Aid

By our cures shall we be known. Throughout Europe household remedies reflect national habit. Hangover and cold cures are the main preoccupation in northern Europe: onions, garlic, paprika, mustard and plain solid food are the solution. Aching livers and indigestion seem to be the ills of the south: black coffee and a shot of aniseed-flavoured liquor are the morning remedies, with egg froths and herbal infusions as the next line of defence.

The French have maintained their enthusiasm for the old herbal remedies – and not just in the form of prepacked pills in the homeopathic chemist, either. It is ancient markets such as those of the herb gatherers of Provence that have kept the traditional knowledge of herbal remedies alive. The herb sellers, who buy direct from the gatherers, can all explain the use of their wares. They travel from market place to market place, laying out their jars of sweet-scented leaves and flowers for brewing infusions; tiny bottles of herb-scented oils and flower essences. Stacked up against the trestle tables, sacks of dried herbs (sometimes with a dried viper from the lavender fields buried in them to scare the tourists) – lemon balm for the nerves, gentian to calm a stomach, borage. The herb seller will blend special mixtures for the housewives, who pay their *sous* for a little sugar-paper twist of an infusion of fennel seeds to cure the baby's colic, a chamomile tea to soothe the insomniac. Often, too, they can sell the honey to suit the infusion – rosemary honey for a stimulant tea, lime-blossom honey for the *tilleul*.

During my travels with my own young family, we have sampled more than a few of other people's home remedies. Our neighbouring farmer's wife in France recommended onion soup made with twice the usual quantity of onions – in real emergencies, she said, a whole head of garlic should join the onion. In Spain, warts were rubbed with a live snail, and the mollusc was then put in a matchbox and buried. It seemed to work fine. The magical creature also reappears in my own favourite remedy – a stew of little snails as prepared all over Andalusia in *feria*-time. The active ingredient is the cooking broth, a clear dark brew flavoured with pennyroyal, black peppercorns and coriander. Anything which was not covered by the snail (unrequited love, winter gloom, early mornings), could be cured with a raw egg yolk, beaten up with a small glass of sherry and a spoonful of olive oil.

Spanish Egg Nog
Ponche

This is the favourite Spanish pick-me-up. Like *zabaglione* in Italy, *ponche* is a cure-all for colds and other maladies, particularly for old people's ailments and children's sniffles. It is now sold ready-made in bottles as a liquor.

QUANTITY
Makes about 1¾ pints/1 litre

TIME
Preparation: 25 minutes

1 pint/600ml single cream
4 egg yolks
3 oz/75g ground almonds
¼ pint/150ml brandy
2 oz/50g sugar

UTENSILS
A medium saucepan, a whisk, and sterilized bottles

Mix the milk, ground almonds and sugar in a saucepan and bring it just up to the boil.

Meanwhile, beat the egg yolks until light and fluffy. Pour the hot milk and brandy in a thin stream into the yolks, whisking as you do so.

Serve the *ponche* warm to your invalid, with a little dry biscuit. Or offer it after a meal, with a bunch of sweet grapes and some sugared almonds (see page 288), as a delicious little dessert for non-invalids.

It will keep, bottled and sealed, in the fridge for two weeks at least. Shake it up before you pour it out.

SUGGESTIONS

Ponche makes a delicious ice cream if you freeze it (add a little more sugar and a little vanilla – iced flavours need to be stronger). Or use it as a light custard sauce with a pie or stewed fruit.

Lemon Barley Water

The barley water is to be taken hot or cold throughout the day and night until the patient improves. Although this is the classic Victorian sickroom special, it is made throughout Europe. In Spain, barley water is highly recommended by the shepherding communities of the high inland plateaux.

QUANTITY
Makes 2 pints/1.2 litres

TIME
Preparation: 10 minutes
Cooking: 1 hour

1 oz/25g pearl barley
rind and juice of 2
    lemons
2 pints/1.2 litres cold
    water
4 oz/100g sugar

UTENSILS
A saucepan, sieve, jug,
    and storage bottles

Put the barley, water and lemon rind into a saucepan and bring all to the boil. Turn the heat down to simmer and leave to cook gently for an hour.

Strain the liquid through a sieve into a jug (the barley and lemon peel can be discarded), and add the sugar and lemon juice. Stir thoroughly. Bottle and store, tightly corked.

Sometimes my grandmother would add a drop of whisky to the brew when she made it hot for me last thing at night.

Gripe Water

This is the solution for babies with wind. A teaspoon of the cold liquid brings the bubble up like a pistol cracking. I believe it works on the same principle as throwing cold water into coffee – the heavy stuff sinks to the bottom. It's pretty good for adults too.

QUANTITY
Makes 1 pint/600ml

TIME
Start a day ahead
Preparation: 10 minutes

1 teaspoon caraway *or*
   dill seeds
1 pint/600ml boiled
   water

UTENSILS
A pestle and mortar, a
   sterilized bottle and a
   strainer

Bruise the seeds. Put them into a clean bottle with the water. Shake thoroughly and leave overnight to infuse. Strain, re-bottle and cork tightly. Ready for use immediately. Quite apart from its properties as a digestive, caraway was an important active ingredient in love potions. Perhaps the two uses are not so unconnected: indigestion has never been a good aphrodisiac.

Cherry and Honey Cough Syrup

This is one of the nicest ways to comfort a cold. Children love this – but remember it is also a mild laxative, so don't let them have too much. If you use rosemary or lavender honey, it will add the herb's special disinfectant properties to the syrup.

QUANTITY
Makes about 1
   pint/600ml

TIME
Preparation: 20 minutes
Cooking: 10-15 minutes

Wash and de-stalk the cherries and put them in a saucepan with just enough water to stop them sticking. Lid and simmer them for 10-15 minutes, until they are quite soft. Strain them through a linen cloth, wringing it to squeeze out all the juice. Stir in the honey and lemon juice and mix well. The mixture should be quite thick – add more honey if it is too thin. Rinse out the storage jars with a little whisky or brandy before bottling the syrup. Cork tightly and use as required.

4 lb/2kg ripe black
   cherries
1 lb/500g honey
½ pint/300ml water
juice of 1 lemon

UTENSILS

A medium saucepan, a
   clean cloth and storage
   bottles

Nettle Syrup

This is an old-fashioned tonic for the convalescent. Only the top four leaves of the young nettles must be used. Be careful when you pick them – they are only young, but they sting just the same.

QUANTITY

Makes 4 pints/2.5 litres

TIME

Preparation: 10 minutes
Cooking: 1¼ hours

2 lb/1kg nettle tops
approximately 2 lb/1kg
   sugar
4 pints/2.5 litres water

UTENSILS

A large saucepan, a
   strainer, and storage
   bottles

Put the nettle tops and the water in a roomy pan. Boil for 40 minutes, and then strain. Measure the liquid, which will have much reduced, and add 1 lb/500g sugar for every pint/600ml of liquid. Boil for another 30 minutes. Leave to cool. Rinse the storage bottles out with brandy or whisky before filling them. Cork and store. Nettle syrup is ready to use immediately. Dilute with cold or hot water for your convalescent.

In the summer, nettle syrup makes a refreshing long drink, with soda water, ice and a slice of lemon.

Parsley Honey

This is a fine old-fashioned remedy: a tonic for the nerves. Nervous people can take it incognito – it can masquerade as jam, or as a sauce for cold meats.

QUANTITY
Makes about 1½ lb/750g

TIME
Preparation: 10 minutes
Cooking: 30 minutes

1 breakfastcup picked
   parsley
½ pint/300ml water
2 lemons
1 lb/500g sugar

UTENSILS
A small saucepan and
   sterilized jars

Put the parsley in a small saucepan. Pare off the rind of one of the lemons and squeeze the juice of both. Add the water, rind and lemon juice to the pan. Bring all to the boil and cook for ½ hour uncovered, until the mixture thickens like runny honey. Pot and seal while still warm.

Italian Cream Cheese
Tira Mi Su

Tira mi su started life as an Italian pick-me-up, although these days it is more often served as a delicious dessert. To make it for more people, increase the quantities in proportion and spread it in a large shallow dish. Grate on a little dark chocolate to finish.

QUANTITY
Serves 1

TIME
Start a few hours ahead
Preparation: 10 minutes

2 sponge fingers
2-3 tablespoons strong
  coffee
1 teaspoon brandy *or*
  marsala or sweet sherry
1 whole egg
1 tablespoon caster sugar
2 tablespoons
  Mascarpone cream
  cheese *or fromage frais*,
  or Quark

UTENSILS
A tall glass

Break the sponge fingers roughly and put them in the base of a long glass (a sundae glass if you have one). Soak the biscuits with the coffee and your chosen liquor.

Separate the egg. Beat the yolk and the sugar into the Mascarpone. Whip the white until stiff and fold it in.

Spoon the mixture over the soaked sponge fingers. Refrigerate for half an hour before serving. Absolutely delicious, and even better the next day.

Invalid Champ

This is the Irish solution for the poorly. I had a schoolfriend who came from County Mayo and her mother used to make this as the household cure-all. My friend said it almost made the sneezes worthwhile.

QUANTITY
1-2 servings: Enough to build up the invalid's strength

TIME
Preparation: 15 minutes
Cooking: 20 minutes

1 lb/500g potatoes
2 oz/50g butter
1 fine fat leek *or* 1 small bunch spring onions
1 egg
salt and pepper
3 tablespoons milk

UTENSILS
A saucepan, a colander and a small bowl

Rinse the potatoes but do not peel them, and put them to boil in salted water until soft.

Wash and slice the leek into fine rings, including as much of the green as possible. Put them in a colander.

Drain the cooked potatoes through the same colander – the boiling water will blanch the leeks, leaving them bright green and with their vitamins intact. Peel the potatoes and mash them with the milk, the leeks and half the butter. Reheat gently. Beat in the raw egg. Taste and add salt and pepper. Put the champ into a bowl, make a hollow in the hot potato and put in the rest of the butter to melt. Eat with a spoon. Buttermilk is the traditional Irish accompaniment.

Paprika Broth

Paprika is the Hungarian solution to most of winter's ills, from colds to hangovers. This quantity of broth is enough for one sick person. One sick person at a time is quite enough for a Hungarian household – the Slavs do not take these matters lightly.

QUANTITY
Serves 1

TIME
Preparation: 5 minutes
Cooking: 5 minutes

1 level tablespoon flour
½ teaspoon salt
1 tablespoon lard *or*
   vegetable oil
1 heaped tablespoon
   paprika
1 teaspoon caraway seeds
¾ pint/450ml cold water

UTENSILS
A saucepan

Put the flour to fry gently in the lard or vegetable oil until the mixture is sandy and golden. Sprinkle in the caraway seeds and the salt. Stir in the paprika, quickly followed by the water (don't let the paprika fry – it burns easily). Bring the broth to the boil, simmer for 5 minutes, and serve.

Lettuce Soup

Beatrix Potter's Peter Rabbit fell asleep after eating lettuces in Mr McGregor's garden. They are indeed soporific. Take a bowl last thing at night.

QUANTITY
Serves 2

TIME
Preparation: 10 minutes
Cooking: 20 minutes

1 lettuce
1 pint/600ml fresh water
1 fat leek *or* 1 medium
    onion
1 oz/25kg butter
1 stick celery
salt and pepper
2-3 sprigs parsley
1 level tablespoon
    cornflour
1 teaspoon chopped
    fresh savory *or* lovage
    (*optional*)
1 glass cold milk

UTENSILS
A saucepan and a small
    bowl

Wash and shred the lettuce. Rinse the leek (or peel the onion) and chop into fine rings. Chop up the celery and parsley. Put the vegetables and herbs with the water and the butter in a saucepan. Add salt and pepper. Bring all to the boil, turn down the heat and simmer for 20 minutes. Stir in the cornflour mixed to a cream with a little of the milk. Bring back to the boil and mash the vegetables a little to thicken the soup. Remove from the heat and add the cold milk. Serve without reheating.

Double Onion Soup

Onions were for centuries the handiest of homegrown cure-alls. The onion and its cousin the garlic were a useful preventative medicine as well: many a labourer in the fields did a full hard day's work on a midday meal of a hunk of bread and an onion. The raw materials came in handy as first aid: a piece of cut onion is the country salve for a wasp sting. Some old recipe books recommend infusions of onion in unflavoured spirits, *eau-de-vie* or gin, as powerful medicine for everything from the common cold to dropsy. This soup is a rather more palatable way of taking the potion.

QUANTITY
Serves 2

TIME
Preparation: 15 minutes
Cooking: 20 minutes

3 large onions
salt and pepper
2 tablespoons olive oil *or* (best) goose fat
1 heaped tablespoon chopped parsley
1 pint/600ml water *or* homemade chicken stock
1 egg yolk
2 spring onions *or* 1 small onion

UTENSILS
A saucepan, a bowl and whisk

Peel and slice the onions finely. Warm the oil or goose fat in a saucepan. Add the sliced onions and fry them golden. Pour in the water or stock. Add salt and pepper. Bring all to the boil. Turn the heat down and simmer for 15 minutes. Remove from the heat. Stir in the parsley. Whisk a ladleful of the hot broth into the egg yolk and pour it back into the soup. Stir in the spring onions, chopped finely.

Olive Oil

Homer's Greeks rubbed their bodies with olive oil for winter warmth – a kind of Classical thermal underwear. The ladies found this a particularly valuable property: life in the slave-owning democracy of Greece was leisurely but lacking in central heating.

Olive oil has further uses unconnected with the dressing of salads. If, for example, your ringlets are out of sorts, rub a little warm oil into your hair, wrap your head in a towel, and shampoo the oil out after half an hour. Mix a tablespoon of oil with a few drops of lemon juice and use it 2-3 times a week as an anti-wrinkle cream. The same mix makes a delicious suntan oil – although its devotees do tend to smell like a crisply-fried Greek chip.

For a smile as pearly-white as a soap-opera star, rub a little olive oil into your gums each morning. (Furthermore, a bowl of strawberries eaten after a meal will, say the old wives, clean your teeth of tartar.)

A tablespoon of olive oil taken before breakfast achieves as much as a bowl of muesli with none of the roughage. Swallow a tablespoon of oil as a preventative measure before a night on the town – devotees swear the alcohol then slides gently through the liver with scarcely a twinge.

Scented Oils

Make your own scented oils for the bath and as a massage rub. Rosemary oil is particularly good for massage, lavender for scenting the bath – make up your own balance of scents. Put your chosen herbs to macerate in oil, straining out and putting in new herbs until you have the strength of perfume you need. Olive oil is the best medium, but use grapeseed oil if you prefer its lighter scent.

To make lavender oil, useful not only cosmetically and for its lovely scent but also as a salve for burns and eczema, put 20 fresh flower heads in 1¾ pints/1 litre oil in a kilner jar. Leave to infuse for 3 hours in a very low oven. Strain, add another handful of lavender flowers, and infuse for a further three hours. If you live in the warm sun of Provence, 3 days on the windowsill will have the same effect as the low oven. Strain the oil into bottles and cork it tightly. Ready to use immediately.

Make other perfumed oils in the same way. The five great sisters of Provence, rosemary, thyme, savory, sage and basil, are all members of the same fragrant family, the *labiatiae*. All five make beautiful scented infusions.

Carefully dried herbs will retain the strength of the fresh leaves and can be used interchangeably – remember that fresh herbs will weigh somewhat heavier, depending on the natural fleshiness of the plant – although thyme, being a naturally dry woody little plant, weighs very nearly the same dried or fresh.

Mustard Bath

Here is the advice of the excellent Mary Thorne Quelch in her *Herbs for Daily Use* (Faber, 1941). Wartime concentrates the mind on practical and available remedies for minor ills, and Mrs Quelch, a devotee of the great seventeenth-century herbalist Nicholas Culpeper, has much sound advice on the English way with medicinal plants:

> A mustard bath cannot be too highly recommended to those suffering from chill or suppression. As a makeshift, a foot bath will work wonders, but it is better to have a complete bath, which should be very hot with sufficient 'made' mustard added to change the water to a pale straw colour. Such a bath followed by a hot drink taken when in bed, will drive away almost any cold.

Selected Bibliography

Acton, Eliza, *Modern Cookery for Private Families* (London, 1845)

Apicius, The Roman Cookery of, translated and adapted by John Edwards (Hartley & Marks, Washington, 1984)

Aubert, Claude, *Les Aliments Fermentes Traditionnels* (Terre Vivante, Paris, 1985)

Baines, T. & Lond, W. B., *Shifts and Expedients of Camp Life* (London, 1871)

Beeton, Isabella, *Household Management* (facsimile first edition, and 1912 edition, Ward Lock, London)

Belaiche, Paul, *Guide Familial de la Médécine par les Plantes* (Hachette, Paris, 1982)

Bennett, H. S., *Life on the English Manor, a Study of Peasant Conditions 1150-1400* (Cambridge, England, 1948)

Blum, Jerome, *The End of the Old Order in Rural Europe* (Princeton, 1978)

Blum, Jerome (ed), *Our Forgotten Past* (Thames & Hudson, London, 1982)

Boisvert, Clotilde, *La Cuisine des Plantes Sauvages* (Dargaud, Paris, 1984)

Bontemps, Michel and Roseline, *Mes Secrets de Sante* (Editions Generique, Paris, 1983)

Calera, Ana Maria, *Cocina Valenciana* (Everest, Leon, 1983)

Chaillu, Paul du, *The Land of the Midnight Sun* (London, 1881)

Chamoux, Simone, *Les Olives dans la Cuisine* (Lys, France, 1985)

Chantiles, Vilma Liacouras, *The Food of Greece* (Avenel, New York, 1979)

Chapman, Charlotte Gower, *Milocca: A Sicilian Village* (Allen and Unwin, London, 1973)

Clair, Colin, *Of Herbs and Spices* (Abelard Schuman, London, 1961)

Cobbett, William, *Rural Rides* (London, 1830)

Dabitesse, M. L., *Revolution Silencieuse* (Paris, 1931)

David, Elizabeth, *French Provincial Cooking* (Michael Joseph, London, 1960) *Italian Food* (Macdonald, London, 1954)

Delaveau, Pierre, *Les Epices, Histoire, Description et Usage* (Albin Michel, Paris,1987)

Digby, Kenelm, *The Closet of Sir Kenelm Digby, Knight, Opened* (London, 1669)

Drummond, J. C. and Wilbraham, A., *The Englishman's Food* (Cape, London, 1959)

Dumas, Alexandre, *Grande Dictionnaire de Cuisine* (Paris, 1873)

Eales, Mrs Mary, *Receipts* (facsimile of 1718 edition, Prospect Books, 1985)

Evelyn, John, *Acetaria* (London, 1699)

Fisher, M. F. K., *The Art of Eating* (Faber, London, 1963)

Franklin, S. H., *The European Peasantry* (London, 1969)

Gage, Thomas, *The English-American. Travels in the New World* (1648) (ed. J. E. S.Thompson, Oklahoma Press, 1958)

Glasse, Hannah, *The Compleat Confectioner* (London, 1760) *Gloucestershire Housewives, Gleanings from* (London, 1948)

Grigson, Jane, *Charcuterie and French Pork Cookery* (Michael Joseph, London, 1967)

Hall, D. J., *Roumanian Furrow* (London, 1939)

Hartley, Dorothy, *Food in England* (MacDonald, London, 1934)

Heaton, Eliza Puttnam, *By-Paths in Sicily* (Dutton, USA, 1920)

Hellman, Lillian and Feibleman, Peter, *Eating Together* (Little Brown, Boston, 1984)

Henderson, T. F., *Old World Scotland* (Edinburgh, 1893)

Hoskins, W. G., *The Midlands Peasant* (London, 1957)

Hough, P. H., *Dutch Life in Town and Country* (London, 1901)

Howitt, William, *Rural Life of Germany* (London, 1842)

Johnston, Isobel Christian, *The Cook and Housewife's Manual of Mrs Margaret Dods* (Edinburgh, 1826)

Leyel, Hilda, *Herbal Delights* (Faber, London 1937), *Elixirs of Life* (Faber, London, 1948)

Luard, Nicholas, *The Last Wilderness, a journey across the Great Kalahari Desert* (Hamish Hamilton, London 1981)

Luke, Sir Harry, *The Tenth Muse* (Putnam, New York, 1954)

McGee, Harold, *On Food and Cooking* (Scribner, New York, 1985)

McNeill, F. Marian, *The Scots Kitchen* (Blackie, Edinburgh, 1929)

Médécin, Jacques, *Cuisine Niçoise* (Trans. Peter Graham) (Penguin, London, 1983)

Mennell, Stephen, *All Manners of Food* (Blackwell, London, 1986)

Montagne, Prosper, *Larousse Gastronomique* (Larousse, Paris, 1938)

The Oxford Book of Food Plants (OUP, 1969)

Oxford Symposium Notes (Prospect Books, 1981,1983,1985)

Pagnol, Koscher and Mattern, *Les Recettes de la Table Provençale* (Strasbourg, 1982)

Palaiseul, Jean, *Nos Grand-mères savaient* (Robert Lafont, Paris, 1972)

Philpot, Rosl, *Viennese Cookery* (Hodder & Stoughton, London, 1965)

Pohren, D. E., *Adventures in Taste: The Wines and Folk Food of Spain* (Seville, 1972)

Pomiane, Edouard de, *Conserves Familiales et Microbie Alimentaire* (Albin Michel, Paris, 1943)

Poulsen, Frederik, *Travels and Sketches* (London, 1923)

Quelch, Mary Thorne, *Herbs for Daily Use* (Faber, London, 1941)

Reboul, J.-B., *La Cuisinière Provençale* (Marseilles, 1895)

Redgrove, H. S., *Spices and Condiments* (Pitman, London, 1933)

Rohde, Eleanour Sinclair, *Culinary and Salad Herbs* (CountryLife, London, 1940)

Root, Waverly, Food (Simon and Schuster, New York, 1980)

Rothschild, Miriam, *Animals and Man* (Clarendon Press, Oxford, 1986)

Rousseau, Jean-Jacques, *Entile*, Trans. Barbara Foxley (Everyman, London, 1911)

Russell, Bertrand, *Dear Bertrand Russell* (Allen & Unwin, London, 1969)

Shand, P. Morton, *A Book of Food* (Cape, London, 1927)

Stratilesco, Tereza, *From Carpathian to Pindus: Pictures of Roumanian Country Life* (London, 1906)

Vidoudez, Michel and Grangier, Jacqueline, *A la Mode de Chez* (Lausanne, 1976)

Viski, Karoly, *Hungarian Peasant Customs* (Budapest, 1932)

Ward, Harold, *Herbal Manual* (C. W. Daniel, London, 1936)

Warriner, D., *The Economics of Peasant Farming* (London, 1964)

Wheaton, Barbara Ketcham, *Savoring the Past* (Philadelphia, 1983)

White, Florence, *Good Things in England* (Cape, London, 1932)

Wilson, C. Anne, *Food and Drink in Britain* (Constable, London, 1973)

Index